HOW I DROPPED IN ON VLADIMIR PUTIN

Как я зашел к Владимиру Путину

(and other stories)

The Drills, Spills and Thrills,

Japes, Scrapes and Escapes

of a

Royal Navy Russian Interpreter

**By Lieutenant Commander Alan Pearce,
Royal Navy (Rtd)**

A life story)
(mine, not his)

ISBN: 97987874243635

With great thanks to Ian and Genevra, who helped enormously with the formatting.

DEDICATION

To those who fell, when I didn't

INTRODUCTION

This is my story, the story of a family man, Naval Officer and Russian Interpreter. I hope it will interest you, enlighten you, and amuse you. I slightly apologise that this tome will seem to be all about me. There are three reasons for this. Firstly, it is an autobiography. Secondly if I were to write a biography summarised as "Young man goes to work, falls in love and marries; they have three lovely children and live happily ever after" then it would be no different from thousands of other life stories and no-one would want to read it. Thirdly, I was asked to record all the amazing things I have been involved in, before I die, and I am complying with that request. I didn't keep a diary - I wish I had. I may have mixed things up but I have chronicled things to the best of my memory and ability - but time blurs and I am getting old.

If you are hoping for official facts herein, for formal statements, authoritative pronouncements or executive analysis, you will be disappointed as there is nothing in here that is not already public knowledge somewhere or another and I have merely drawn the strings of the stories together. Any opinions are solely my own. This is more of a romp through memorable personal occasions and jolly events to human blunders and mishaps - as if from the sublime to the ridiculous. I must confess to having used artistic licence herein, but if you'd like to know what really wasn't in the sous chef's succulent meat pies, why the vicar's wedding cake was bright green, how to make time go backwards, how to make stars go backwards, what happened on the butcher's slab, where the Little Sisters of Goodness and Mercy went quite a bit adrift, how to shoot a pig, why the young Russian woman had 16 children, the secret of dwile flonking in Denmark, when to freshen the nip and whether the Mounties ever got their man or not, then this is the tome for you. Please read and enjoy!

The author, by Russian artist, 1992

EXECUTIVE SUMMARY

Speakin' in general, I 'ave tried 'em all -
The 'appy roads that take you o'er the world.
Speakin' in general, I 'ave found them good
For such as cannot use one bed too long,
But must get 'ence, the same as I 'ave done,
An' go observin' matters till they die.

What do it matter where or 'ow we die,
So long as we've our 'ealth to watch it all -
The different ways that different things are done,
An' men an' women lovin' in this world;
Takin' our chances as they come along,
An' when they ain't, pretending they are good?

In cash or credit - no, it aren't no good;
You 'ave to 'ave the 'abit or you'd die,
Unless you lived your life but one day long,
Nor didn't prophesy nor fret at all,
But drew your tucker some'ow from the world,
An' never bothered what you might ha' done

But, Gawd, what things are they I 'aven't done?
I've turned my 'and to most, an' turned it good,
In various situations round the world -
For 'im that doth not work must surely die;

But that's no reason man should labour all
'Is life on one same shift - life's none so long.

Therefore, from job to job I've moved along.
Pay couldn't 'old me when my time was done,
For something in my 'ead upset it all.
Till I 'ad dropped whatever t'was for good,
An' out at sea, be'eld the dock-lights die,
An' met my mate - the wind that tramps the world.

It's like a book I think, this bloomin' world,
Which you can read and care for just so long
But presently you feel that you will die
Unless you get the page you're readin' done,
An' turn another - likely not so good;
But what you're after is to turn 'em all.

Gawd bless this world! Whatever she 'ath done -
Excep' when awful long - I've found it good.
So write, before I die, "'E liked it all!"

'Sestina of the Tramp-Royal' by Rudyard Kipling

CHAPTER 1
Joining the Royal Navy

During the 1940's and 1950's I had been with my father round all the coasts and inlets and shipyards and boatyards and docks and weirs on the Clyde and elsewhere and become quite besotted with thinking of all the exotic and exciting places these ships and boats had been to. So it was almost inevitable that I had decided to join the Navy - and my father had decided in his heart that it should be the Royal Navy. Thus I (we) applied and when I was twelve years old I set off on my own by train to Liverpool to attend the preliminary, weeding out, interview at HMS EAGLET, the Royal Navy Reserve Centre. HMS EAGLET was an old, very old, warship moored alongside in the port of that city and was used to train Reservists against the possibility of running out of trained personnel for the next war. I remember absolutely nothing about the interview: the only thing I can recall - and quite vividly - is that I was bought a new suit to attend the interview (my first long trousers!) and it was made of very coarse material which rubbed away the skin of my inner thighs right from when or even before I got on the train that morning; it was exceedingly uncomfortable, painful even, and I must have been walking like a bow legged sailor by the time I got to the interview room. Perhaps they thought I was a "natural", but whatever, they accepted me and put me forward for the next interview stage at the AIB.

The Admiralty Interview Board must be one of the greatest successes in the HR industry: it costs a lot to run, but the wheels grind so finely that the end success result was astonishingly good, and wastage rates low. Rather than describe it I will describe my passage through it, for it makes interesting and edifying reading.

It is a two-day event, and at the evening dinner you suspect that you are being closely watched to ensure that aspirants are socially acceptable and clean about the house (because, of course, being a Royal Naval Officer entails not only fighting wars and "showing the Flag" around the world, but also carrying out diplomatic functions in potentially sensitive situations). I must have done satisfactorily, thanks to good table manners and a mother who made me touch the brim of my cap when meeting her adult friends.

First there was the gymnasium exercise: In teams of six or eight the task was to get a large object across a "river" marked on the gym floor using the ropes spars and beams provided. Each team had a leader, taking it in turns to use the ropes which were just a bit short and the beams ditto and the rather short spars. Actually, the inquisitors were not particularly looking for success in crossing the "river", they were looking for leadership qualities in the person temporarily in charge - the assessment of the situation, the culling of advice, the judgement of the chances of each option succeeding, the instructions given and the degree to which the others followed the instructions.

Second was an interview with a Headmaster - a carefully chosen headmaster, who, being familiar with boys, could winkle out a lot of information and derive conclusions from that information; boys (remember we were thirteen year-olds) were a bit in awe of headmasters, but headmasters were used to that, knew how to cope with it and use it to advantage and were rarely wrong on the subject of "potential". Certainly they could divine "character".

Then there were group discussions on chosen subjects. The penultimate interview was with a psychologist. This one was strange - as the psychologist intended it to be. I was ushered into a room with black painted walls and no natural light. He sat at a huge desk with an angle lamp on it pointing at the applicant's chair - just as you see in detective or spy films. The chair had one leg sawn off a bit, so that it wobbled - most disconcerting for those liable to be disconcerted. I sat. There was a long silence - a very long silence; I think I was being watched to see if I fidgeted - I guessed this, so tried very hard not to fidget. After a continuation of the silence the psychologist suddenly leaned forward and said in a very loud voice "Do you love your father and mother?" and without thinking I said "Yes". He said "Why?" I said "I don't know" and that was the end of that little exchange. He must have asked me other questions which after over fifty years I can't remember, but the final flurry I do remember. He said "how many guns have the new County Class cruisers got?" and I remember thinking, quite deliberately, "I haven't got a clue, but I'll bet he hasn't either" so I looked him straight in the face and said "Four". He said "Sure?" and I said "Yes". He seemed satisfied, and dismissed me.

The last interview was a classic example of a formal interview, with a panel of interviewers and one interviewee. It must have gone all right, because not long afterwards my parents received a letter saying that I had been given a place at Royal Naval College Dartmouth in the September after I had attained the necessary "A-Levels". It (the letter) then went on to create two large problems, one immediate, one long-lasting. It said I had to achieve "Two Advanced Level GCE's including either Mathematics or a Science subject". Now, you have to remember that in those days A-Levels were really something; very few people had any at all, and even the most brilliant brains in the whole country only had three, maximum. So it was about the equivalent of a moderate sort of Bachelors' degree entry today. But "two A-Levels" it was, and that was that. They foolishly didn't say what grades.

And so from the age of thirteen to seventeen I really enjoyed myself. To the detriment of my school work. I was a Boy Scout and I roamed the country, camping, making fires, living off the land, breathing fresh air and making whoopee, scree walking in the Lake District (before it was banned), kayaking on Ullswater, cycling all round the Lake District and North Wales and later across the Pennines to Scarborough (where one of my Aunts lived), shooting, building boats and canoes, making model aircraft and trying to make radio control for them, playing sport as often as I could, cycling with two friends around the Netherlands (literally: we started at Amsterdam and ended at Rotterdam, having many adventures on the way), relating with girlfriends in the evenings and generally enjoying myself. Then, one day, about January 1963, someone said "Alan, you've got to get two A-Levels" and so I swotted like hell for three or four months and got two quite disgracefully poor (but successful) exam results - A Levels they were, and I was in, which was all I wanted. But I do not recommend this course of action to other young people, because while I had only one target in mind, they have probably not and have to go further academically.

The second problem, which I won't dwell on, was this: because my birthday is 25th April and A-Level and results are over by June/July each year, I joined Dartmouth at the (technically underage) age of seventeen - in law, a child.

My school friend Kerry Morecroft and I spent the period after A-Levels fishing in boats off the coast of Norway, and then joined Britannia Royal Naval College Dartmouth together in September 1963. It was the beginning of a huge, stupendously enjoyable life adventure (most of the time).

CHAPTER 2
Early Training

The Britannia Royal Naval College Dartmouth was built in 1903 in extensive grounds on a steep hillside overlooking the River Dart in Devon, and has a broad access to the river, where docks and boatyards and sheds and piers had been erected. Seen from the air, the vast main building had the look of a large anchor whose flukes had been flattened out so that it had a vertical spine going North to South, and two arms on each side going East and West. Across the bottom of the building was a wide, flat boulevard and to the South of that the parade ground, rectangular East to West but with rounded ends so that in effect the parade ground was an extended oval shape. It had an oval "ramp" round it - a road wide enough to take road traffic easily (when permitted, such as when HM visited).The vertical spine held the nerve centre of the establishment: Captain and Second-in-Command's offices overlooking the parade ground, other administrative offices, meeting rooms, the library, and the entrance porch with Sergeants' and Guards' offices on each side of the large entrance door. And in the centre of the spine, the Quarterdeck. Now, on a seagoing ship, the Quarterdeck is the aftmost deck which is the area from which the stern wires are operated during berthing or other manoeuvres involving wires or cables (c.f. the Fo'c's'le, where the for'rard wires are worked). However, at BRNC Dartmouth the Quarterdeck is the centre-spine congregation hall - a large, beautiful, wooden-decked, highly polished and much statued area big enough for about a thousand people to fall in and be counted, ("mustered", in naval terms) with a wide balcony the whole way round it at the second high-storey level. It was used for parades on rainy days, and for any other large gatherings, for dances and balls, for exhibitions and for major cocktail parties. And just as on a warship, it had to be saluted - by all naval personnel - on being entered.

The top - Northernmost - side arms held dormitories and other accommodation, together with classrooms. The "anchor fluke" side arms held laboratories and other study areas and a music room. At the Westernmost end of this fluke is the Wardroom and Sub Lieutenants' Mess, and at the Easternmost end, the Chapel and the Captain's House (Commanding Officers of naval shore establishments were expected to live on the premises, with their families). An aside: most importantly, for new Cadets each year, between the centre spine and the music room was The Hairdressers Shop. It was the first stop for all Cadets. "But I had my hair cut yesterday, specially" didn't cut any ice. I have to be fair, and say it wasn't as bad as the American servicemen receive, and it wasn't actually dreadfully short, but a haircut it was, and you had to have it.

So, well over a hundred of us had caught the train, changed at Newton Abbot and descended on Kingswear station on that portentous day in September 1963. Kingswear is across the river Dart from Dartmouth, so we had to cross, a package of late sixth-formers, now Cadets and therefore of a much lower status, group by group on the ferry across the river with our suitcases. At the other end we were met by a cohort of naval Senior Ratings, mostly of the parade ground variety, and told to "Get fell in". Somehow, we all realised that this was not the time for us to correct Authority's grammar, for Authority this clearly was. (And talking of "authority" it is surprising to some people that at no stage had we ever signed anything to say that we were willing to serve in the Royal Navy, nor had anyone given us any contract or any job description - and never at any stage, then or later, did we ever swear any oath of allegiance. Neither did we have an official number. It wasn't necessary. In those days, if you put on a Royal Naval Officer's uniform, you were "in". That was it. A bit like the press gangs who put a coin in the bottom of a pub tankard (the King's shilling) and if you drank the contents, you were "in" - which is why so many tankards in those days had glass bottoms!

Anyway, as we were to find out as Cadets, all Officers were "Sir" and all Ratings were "chief", whoever or whatever they were. "Lift suitcases, quick march!" came the order. We hadn't a clue, but we did. All the way up to hill to the RNC. We "Got fell in" again in our groups, or "Divisions" as they are called in the RN, were allocated our Messes (dormitories, as we had always known them) and stood by our beds (bunks) as we were deprived of our suitcases and other belongings and issued with our kit. Our "kit" was everything we needed. It was not only uniform trousers and jackets, and shirts, socks, underpants, shoes and boots, braces (two pairs), caps, coats (rain) and coats (cold weather) but also silk pyjamas (two pairs), slippers (one pair) razor (one) and blades (five), sewing kit and a toothbrush. Nowadays it might be seen as demoralising and demeaning; in those days it was seen as "character building", and I am in no doubt, observing which society is more decent, caring, useful and productive, was more fair. This is a debatable subject; how can I say that all the privations we went through were "more fair"? And the answer is that you knew exactly where you stood, and you knew that nobody was going to go out of line, that you were going to be treated honestly, if harshly - and that other people expected you to do the same. I now know that this built enormous trust among ships' companies - it didn't matter whether you were an Admiral or an Ordinary Seaman: you were expected to know your job and to be reliable. Because, of course, if the ship sank it didn't matter whether you were the former senior person or the latter junior person - you were both swimming in the water together, hoping to be picked up.

This was the theme throughout Dartmouth days. "We are going to teach you your job. We are going to make sure that anything that happens to you when you are in the Fleet, other than being physically injured or laying down your life, will be less demanding than what we put you through here. And if you can't make it, you must go"

Having tumbled into bed ("Bunk, lad, bunk") having been fed, we slept, wondering what strange thing had happened to us. Just time for a dream or two and then all hell was let loose. The Army call it "reveille", the Navy call it "Call the Hands" but whichever there was no doubt what it meant. I looked at my (issued) alarm clock. There must have been some mistake. It was 05.30. The Sub Lieutenant who burst into the dormitory (mess) soon disabused us of this. Amazingly, it was down to the river, quarter of a mile down a steep hill, to jump into a cutter - a rowing cutter. We were soon informed that it wasn't "rowing" - "that's what the nancies at public schools do" - it was "pulling", and "pulling" it has remained. No-one had a clue what they were doing, and at first we were a severe navigational hazard until 06.30 when we were sent to "clean and fall in for breakfast". Fortunately breakfast was substantial. All meals were substantial. It was acknowledged that we needed the calories. The Cadets' dining arrangements were overseen by Ma Bulla, a formidable lady who had some catering experience as a wartime Wren. We ate. We then Got Fell In again for some general training before we went on to do the day's naval training: sometimes it was PT, sometimes it was swimming, sometimes etiquette, or letter writing, or history, or music or one of other arts; this was called "ABR" (After Breakfast Routine). Everything, but everything, had an acronym: what we had completed before breakfast was "EMA" - Early Morning Activity. All this early morning stuff really did not appeal to me, although I was sanguine enough to know that it was necessary. Just not at that time of the day, I thought. So when I heard that you could join the choir and that choir practice started at 06.30 on Tuesdays and Thursdays (the Choirmaster wasn't getting up at 05.30, that's for sure) I suddenly became quite religious and joined the choir. Bliss! An extra hour in bed, twice a week! Then another discovery: the Powers That Be suddenly thought that the more people in the RN who could speak Russian the better had directed that BRNC should encourage young officers to learn the language, and there were to be "extra lessons". Now the Dartmouth day was already overflowing, so it had to be at some bizarre time, and what better that 06.30 (the Russian teacher wasn't going to get up at 05.30, either). I immediately volunteered to join the Russian class, and I did rather well, because although I had failed O-Level, I had a head start on all the others. It was on a Wednesday, so that was three days out of five that I was spared the 05.30 torture.

With ABR went other useful practices, some of which today might have other connotations. One day a week, we did "flashing". We were taught to flash and to recognise flashing. This, however, was nothing to do with raincoats - it was a flashing light up a flagstaff and it flashed in Morse, which we had to learn. Other days, we did "Shouting". We had to stand at one side of a rugby pitch and shout an order to a fellow Cadet on the other side - in competition with several other members of the Shouters Class, shouting at the same time. This was presumably so that one could shout orders audibly on a ship in a gale. Quite a good idea, actually. Then there was Swimming, very useful for naval officers, I'm sure, although I swore never to end up in the water, which was a much better idea. Another was Flag Recognition: flags were hoisted on a flagpole and they had to be recognised and understood. Yet another was how to write "Thank You" letters to a hostess after hospitality. Failure on any day in any of these events resulted in one being placed in the "retake" class. So one became a "Backward Flasher" or a "Backward Shouter" or, the one which amused me most, a "Backward Swimmer". Or of course one could also become a "Backward Letter Writer". We certainly learned to live on our wits: we each had an identical locker and each item of our kit had to be in the locker in exactly the same place, neatly folded, spick and span, ready for inspection. It was really hard work to use things, launder them and replace them in exactly the right order and at the right time. We learned that extra kit was quite cheap to buy (it had to be - we earned just ten shillings and sixpence a day (55p). So we went along to the "shop" and bought duplicates of everything we could. And left our lockers completely alone as far as possible. You will ask where we kept this stuff, if we were so regimented. Easy: in one's laundry basket. No-one ever looked in laundry baskets, particularly not inspecting officers. So sports rig and gym clothes (and everything else which didn't technically have to be ironed, like socks) were in the basket and the pristine locker shelves didn't have to be disturbed.

Cadet Alan Pearce, 1963

We spent hours and hours on the parade ground, which included so many hackneyed experiences that I won't chronicle them. The rest of our working days were nearly all classroom stuff: Navigation, including Decca, Rule of the Road (highway code on the water by day and night, in which the final exam passmark was 98%), Seamanship, radio communications, Relative Velocity calculations, more maths, LLSSA (Limiting Lines of Submerged Submarine Approach), metacentric heights, weights, measures, stability and so on. Then EA (Evening Activities) - which were much the same as ABR and EMA - and supper and then a lecture and then two and a half minutes free time before turning in on one's bunk.

Just when those who remained had learned how to survive, it was then that I first met a new young officer who was to become a lifelong friend - Bill Frisken. To be fair, we didn't have a lot to do with each other at BRNC because we were on different courses, but we were to meet up later in our careers and cement a friendship which has lasted to this day.

The real minus was the Padre.

Just to get the Padre's part in this out of the way, and as an indicator for what is to follow, it was much later and I think before I was thrown out of the choir - which I didn't much mind because there were only a few days left before we went off to sea - my other great friend Jim Brown was being confirmed in the Scottish Revangist or Church of Jockland or something, just before I had been persuaded to become confirmed in the Church of England. (RN vicars of whatever sect got double points for confirming people - first from the navy and second from their own church, and they put a lot of pressure on). So I got confirmed and I attended his and because I had been instructed that taking holy communion was a good idea and in total support of this poor Scottish chap doing so, I threw myself into it. There is a Network, however, and this got back to the CofE padre, one Reverend "Titus" Oates. He sent for me. I got a severe rollicking for taking communion in an heathen church (he didn't of course use the word "heathen" even though that's what he meant). Nonetheless, I was given to understand that my chances of going to heaven had been much diminished. My private reluctance to accept this stuff led, less than ten years later and after a great deal of study, to my move to a more natural, non-man-made or human influenced, non-inquisition-enforced, non-judgemental religious position, of which more later. So much for the Padre. He's bloody lucky I didn't just become an atheist. I suppose I was more lucky not to be labelled a "Backward Prayer" though.

As another aside, Jim had become a great friend not just because he was a jolly good chap but because one knew that one could trust him. Back to trust and fairness, then. This incident illustrates both. Jim was the Divisional Cadet River Rep. which meant that he had to allocate Cadets to boats for the compulsory afternoon River Training. Now, at that time, Dartmouth was the naval training establishment not just for RN officers but also for naval officers from around the world. In the 1963 intake we had young officers from Australia, New Zealand, Malaysia, Thailand, Nigeria, Ghana and Iraq, plus quite a large contingent from Iran. The Iranians all seemed to be nobles of some rank or another, and one of them was in our Division. One cold and wintry day Jim had worked out the boat roster and published it and a certain Iranian noble who had been allocated a rowing or sailing boat (which entailed cold, hard work) wanted a boat with an engine and offered Jim £10 to change the roster. In those days, we earned that ten shillings and six pence per day, so ten pounds represented several days' pay. Jim told him to go and get knotted. The Iranian learned a lot that day. So did I; Jim and his family are still close friends of ours.

This Iranian came another cropper, too. Another of the "character building" things we did was to be dropped off by lorry at an unknown place on Dartmoor in December or January with no money and no possessions and told to get to another place on the other side of Dartmoor by 10.00 the following day. The only ray of hope we were given was that the Royal Navy owned a building at the half-way mark, where we could sleep overnight if we had the time to do so. It was called Ditsworthy Warren House, and sounded rather grand. So off we went, trudging through Dartmoor bog and beset by Dartmoor winds and then rained upon and generally demoralised. The Iranian in our team had to be helped a lot - after all, he came from a hot country and was unused to all this. But we got through. It was a bit tough - we were wet, cold and exhausted, and darkness had now fallen, but we kept going with the thought that Ditsworthy Warren House was now within reach. Then we came over the crest of a small hill and saw the said Ditsworthy Warren house: it was a shell of a building - no doors, no windows, and worst of all, no roof. And the rain was still falling. In the dark, we gathered together bits of old corrugated iron and broken brick and made ourselves a tunnel each, crawled in, sometimes two to a tunnel, and went to sleep. Passed out, more probably. We didn't sleep much, as you might imagine, soaked to the underwear, so by common consent we got up in the dark and prepared to continue our trek or "Yomp" as it has been called since the Falkland Islands War. Except for the Iranian who wasn't interested in common consent and declared that he just wanted to stay where he was and die, or hope that the Embassy would send someone to get him. We persuaded him that he couldn't and they wouldn't, and so off we set for our target destination. It must have been a couple of hours later that the sun came up. I suddenly came to understand why the ancients worshipped the sun; it rose, and warmed our spirits. Then it rose further, and started to warm our bodies, and eventually to dry our sodden clothes. It was the most wonderful feeling, almost ecstatic, and at that moment I felt very close to those ancients and to respect their thought processes. We made it to the rendezvous, and on time - 10 a.m. (or "ten hundred" as we had learned to call it). It took an hour for the bus to get us back to Dartmouth college and what we thought was going to be a nice warm shower and a bit of a rest. We were right about the warm shower - but it was not next to our dormitory, it was next to the college swimming pool, where we had to wash all the muck off before being stood at the side of the pool to be briefed about how many lengths we had to do. The Iranian noble with whom I started this paragraph declared to the Petty Officer Swimming Instructor that he did not feel like swimming, and the Petty Officer Swimming Instructor declared that he did not feel like being told his bloody job by a frigging Cadet - and gave him a huge shove into the cold pool. He had learned two good lessons in three days.

Incidentally, none of these "foreign" officers was any trouble at all, except for the Australians, one of whom, one year, a huge fellow, kept breaking oars on the river; and these were spars, not fragile bits of aluminium. He fell in love with and married a Devon girl (as I did, later) and invited us all to the wedding and the reception but not, of course, to the marital hotel. Unfortunately the other Australians found out where the marital hotel was, and invited themselves, but for later after the nuptial departure. The "hotel" was, in fact, an ancient Devon thatched inn with thick walls and substantial floors. It had a bar downstairs and just two rooms upstairs, one of which was over the bar. This was the room that the newlyweds were to spend their first night in. The Australians, mischievous chaps, paid the inn owner a goodly sum of money to be allowed to drill a small hole through the bar ceiling into the marital bedroom and they attached a small chain to the bedsprings above the hole, and a little bell to the end of the chain which dangled in the bar. This accoutrement to the normal decorations of the bar was then hidden for the time being. They kept out of the way until the bride and groom had gone to their room. Then they started drinking the wonderful Devon ale and cider, having moved the bell and chain from its hiding place so that it hung above the bar. Not very long afterwards the chain trembled and the bell began to tinkle. A huge Australian cheer went up, and the tinkling stopped. Then it started again and another huge cheer went up. The third time there was a pause then an enormous crash as the bar door was thrown open and the completely naked figure of a highly incensed tumescent Australian filled the doorframe. He took one look at his cronies, picked one of them up and threw him out of the window. Which was closed at the time. A fight ensued. The Australians had to pay for all the damage, which they did. They were used to paying for damage they had caused. Revelled in it, in fact.

Back to the Cadet's year. It was divided into three terms because Dartmouth had until quite recently been a public school and much evidence remained, particularly in the anachronous retention of the schoolmasters, who had suddenly become "lecturers". We all did the first term together. Subsequently half the cadets went to sea in the sea training squadron in either the second or the third term - the Easter Term lot to the Caribbean and the Summer Term lot to the Baltic, each for three months or so. It was exceptionally formative in many different ways.

Cadets effectively had no rank at all. We shared messdecks with sailors and in my ship, HMS TORQUAY, we slept in hammocks. This sounds awfully mediaeval but in fact with a hammock slung fore and aft from the deckhead (ceiling to landlubbers) no matter how rough the sea and no matter how the ship rolled, the hammock stayed steady, up and down. I spent some of my soundest nights' sleep in a hammock. We learned to keep our kit clean. We learned to keep ourselves clean - we even had a half hour lecture from a Chief Petty officer on "crabs" and "dhobi rash", (neither of which I had ever heard of before but which apparently were a great threat to the groin area). There is hardly enough space to record all the things we learned, but I'll put down just a few of them. We learned not to interrupt ABs coming back on board after a "run ashore" when they wanted to get to their "mick". I still have a scar on my right hand from a late night encounter with one of them. We learned that Heads (toilets) have to be kept scrupulously clean or danger ensues. We learned how to shower using just a litre or so of water, soap and a flannel. Most valuable of all, perhaps, we learned how to make mistakes. For example, my fellow Cadet John Mellor was told to get his overalls cleaned and advised by an AB with a sense of humour that the easiest way to do it was to tie a rope round them and tow them in the ship's wake for half an hour. He quickly learned that you cannot pull something back in if it's wet and heavy and being towed at fifteen knots, and he never saw his overalls again. We learned, and especially Cadet Israel Onwubiko (Nigerian Navy) did, that if you are parading on the Quarterdeck in summer under a canvas awning with No. 4 rifles and bayonets fixed and the VIP arrives you should order "Present Arms" rather than "Slope Arms". The latter ensures that twenty-four bayonets go through the canvas awning all at once and results in an awful lot of sewing for the next few weeks. (I liked Izzy immensely; he had stood next to me on the parade ground at Dartmouth in that freezing winter of 1963 and responded to my illegally whispered "Izzy, my feet are like ice!" with "And my feet are like choc. ice!"). We learned that a "Lifebuoy Ghost" is a very important man, albeit a very junior person: he sits alone, day and night in watches, above the Quarterdeck watching astern in case anybody has gone over the side. Or for anything else the bridge may be interested in, such as an attack from the stern. He is your last port in a storm. As I said, we all had rank, but in one way we were also equal. He relied on us, we relied on him. We also learned that however much technology you have got, the only incontrovertible evidence is provided by the "Mark 1 Eyeball", not radar or other electronic aids, which are just that - aids . And we learned about skulduggery during - or rather at the end of - the inter-ship evolutions.

Why? Well, there were three frigates in the Squadron, TORQUAY, TENBY and WIZARD and we sailed together in formation. "Evolutions" are exercises carried out to test people, systems, equipment and initiative. And Boy! Did HMS WIZARD have initiative! We were in the Baltic and it was flat calm. As calm as I've ever seen it, before or since. The ships stopped, near each other. The orders were this: "Lower your two (rowed) seaboats. Put them in the water side by side and lash planks between them. Lower an anchor on to the planks and detach it. Row the anchor round your ship, reattach it and haul it up. First home wins". HMS WIZARD won every time. Then one day a supertanker went past and when its wash reached us we all bobbed up and down. So much so that WIZARD's anchor fell off its planks into the sea. And floated! The rapscallions had build a lightweight anchor from wood and painted it grey - no wonder they could handle it so quickly and row it so quickly and win the competition every time.

A typical messdeck - "micks" slung, suspended table ready for supper.

I learned punctuality. For a breach of such I was given six hours of what would now be called "community service" and the following day when we were alongside in a remote Norwegian harbour I was over the side on a Bosn's Chair repainting the ship's identity number. A passing Norwegian fisherman hailed me from his large open fishing boat. "Do you want to come fishing?" he said. In English. All Norwegians speak English. "I can't," I said "I'm required to stay on board for a while." "Tomorrow at 1 o'clock?" he said. "OK" said I, and at 13.00 the following day, Saturday, having expiated my sins, his boat chugged alongside and I got in. (I say "chugged" because Norwegian fishing boats mostly have a single cylinder diesel engine which is started by playing a blowlamp on the cylinder head, then putting a peg in the flywheel and spinning it with the compression off, and then closing the compression so that the internal temperature and pressure would allow the engine to fire. They then go "Thump, thump,

thump" at an astonishingly low rate of revs and with a noise and reassuring beat that no-one who has been to the Norwegian fjords will ever forget. Rather in the same way that the tick tock of an old grandfather clock tells people that all is well with the world and there is no reason to worry.

The author (fishing in Norway 1964)

I'd done a bit of fishing (on the Clyde) and had no fear of disgracing myself. We crossed the fjord and stopped. There was no question of dropping an anchor because the fjord was extremely deep, but there was no wind and no tidal stream, so we hovered in the area that the kind Norwegian fisherman had chosen. Now, when I say "I've done a bit of fishing" what that actually means, as it does in nearly all the coastal waters of the British coast, at least from the middle to the South, is that I have dangled baits and feathers into the waters and trailed lures behind boats for hours on end and occasionally caught something.

Here, we were fishing with a triple paternoster (for non fisherpeople this is a weighted line with three hooks dangling on wires held out at right angles from the line so that they would not tangle) and I baited my three hooks with aplomb sufficient for Jens to recognise that I knew what I was doing. But I was extremely surprised by the result; feeling my first distinct bite after just a second or two I reeled in and found that I had three haddock, all of about one and a half pounds in weight - each hook had caught a fish. I rebaited and went down again. Literally within sixty seconds - same thing. This was repeated and repeated. It wasn't "fishing", it was "catching fish" - and believe it or not, fishermen friends in the UK - it actually got boring after about an hour of this catching cycle. But after two hours we must have had more than a couple of hundred or even more haddock in the boat.

We went back to HMS TORQUAY and tied the boat alongside. Word got round very quickly and the Catering Petty Officer was down on the after deck like a shot, ecstatic, mustering his hands, getting the fish to the galley, where all chefs had been mustered with knives to gut and/or fillet them, and generally chortling to himself that his budgetary worries had ended. My Norwegian friend was invited to the Chief Petty Officers' mess for a libation or two (there was still a rum ration in those days) and I had gone from "under punishment" to "young hero" in just twenty-four hours.

It is necessary here to point out that in the Training Squadron just as at the College one was required to be "under punishment" at some time or another, just so that one would know what it was like and know how recalcitrant sailors feel when they are ditto. Indeed, in those days a list was kept and if you hadn't been under punishment by three weeks before the end of the first year you were put under punishment anyway (presumably for the crime of temerity not to have been under punishment). So I wasn't in fact a bad person; you might almost say I was "a regular guy". By definition, I was.

The Baltic cruise was amazing: educative, challenging, testing, interesting, tiring, sometimes gruelling, but absorbing of all things naval in a very short time. In Bergen, we went to Trollhaugen, Grieg's home, and heard his music being played in the chalet in which he wrote it. It was captivating, an unique experience never forgotten. Enchanting. How can one not weep at a beautifully rendered version of his piano concerto's second movement? (Or, incidentally, if you understand European history, Chopin's first?) In Copenhagen we visited the Little Mermaid and the local historic "kro's" (bistro/restaurant/inns). And I played my pipes at an outdoor festival, which was very popular.

(Later in this book you will learn that my family and I moved to Denmark for a very happy two years, having arrived just after the head of the Little Mermaid was cut off by two vandals, and just before they were caught and sentenced. The Danish people were outraged, of course, as if this were an attack on their very homes and beings, so they were delighted at the Judge's verdict: "You like sawing metal," he said "so I will not send you to jail for a determined period of time; you will go to jail until you have each cut up 100 metres of 1 centimetre square steel bar into 1 centimetre cubes. They you may return to the community.")

In Finland we went to Turku, which was reached by threading our way through hundreds of the most beautiful little islands, each occupied, each beautifully tended and with a little boat bobbing at a small pier, and each with its own Finnish flag flying. People standing on the shores, waving, a blue sky and deep blue sparkling water, little island after little island - this remains, fifty years later, one of the most beautiful sights I have ever seen. After that, we were to have come back through the Kiel canal but something, I know not what, went wrong and we came back through the Kattegat and Skagerrak direct to Plymouth.

Before I close my first year, I have to record, very sadly, what became of two of the above mentioned: one of the Iranian princes was shot in the back of the head on a Paris street after the Ayatollah came to power, and poor Izzy was not heard of again after the Biafra uprising in Nigeria.

CHAPTER 3
Sea Training as a Midshipman

The orders for each of us came through: "proceed on Summer Leave from Dartmouth and then report to HMS........ at ....". Someone, somewhere, had worked out how one hundred Cadets soon to be Midshipmen should be allocated among the seagoing ships of the Fleet. Actually, it was probably easier then than now because two could be sent to each frigate and the remainder divided among the seven aircraft carriers which we then had - and they could absorb just about any number. So during the summer hols (or summer leave as we had now learned to call it) I packed all my kit - blue naval uniform, all my white uniform (for the tropics), day uniform, evening demi-official and evening fully formal, stiff collars, stiff shirts, the lot - and joined the aircraft carrier HMS EAGLE in Devonport. You may imagine the trepidation with which we little squirts trudged our way with all our kit up the huge gangway on to the hallowed Quarterdeck, and how we saluted it in complete awe. Led to our six or seven berth cabins, we were given ten minutes to "clean and shave" and then we "got fell in" again. We were given our instructions. They were clear and unequivocal and bore the overriding message "Thou shalt do what thou art told at all times". OK, Fair Enough. The instructions were, in fact, a timetable not unlike a school timetable, and our training for the next few months was clearly and accurately promulgated.

We were shown round the ship, in great detail which we were all expected to remember, by experts from each department. One of the most startling things was called "ADA" - Automated Data something (I can't be expected to remember everything). Because missiles were coming in to replace guns the speed at which things happened was increasing exponentially, and a difference of a fraction of a second between data being compared could be the difference between a missile hitting and a missile missing. We were taken to a vast cavern of a compartment deep in the bowels of the ship where the vibrations from a crystal of quartz were measured so accurately that time itself could be measured to a millionth of a second. We were in awe. It was not many years later that we were all wearing such a timepiece on out wrists.

HMS EAGLE at flying speed 1964

For a few weeks all went well as we sailed for Gibraltar. Something went not well at Gibraltar and it wasn't our fault (unlike most other things, which were). As part of the programme of showing Spain that Gibraltar was British, we had a huge ceremony on the flight deck, where the Royal Marine band marched up and down under huge floodlights in front of politicians and dignitaries as the sun began to set, and played the Evening Hymn and Last Post before ending up on the aircraft lift (which brings aircraft up and down from and to the hangars below) and disappearing with great ceremony and reverence into the bowels of the ship, leaving a great deal of sentimental reminiscence behind them. Unfortunately, only half of them managed to get onto the lift before the button was pressed, and half the band disappeared into the inside of the ship and the other half were left on the edge of a very deep hole - not knowing what to do because the Bandmaster at the front had gone down the lift with the front half of the band. It was resolved by playing spotlights on the clouds while the rear half of the RM band slunk away.

Still not entirely used to naval discipline and certainly having no cognisance of the import of the word "Desertion" my nearest Midshipman friend and I contrived to tell the Training Officer of one ship's department that we were working temporarily with another department, and vice versa. We then caught a bus to Malaga, then Torremolinos, and from there made our way up into the Sierra Nevada, where we witnessed a bull-run-through-a-village at first hand and were lavishly treated and entertained because I had taken my bagpipes with me and delighted all the locals accordingly. The whole week's holiday was one long party and cost precisely nothing, because of the bagpipes. How on earth we got away with it I do not know. Bit of a jape, bit of an escape, that.

The next lark we did not get away with - none of us. A technical word or two of explanation is necessary. It involved navigation by the stars, which was still an important requirement for Naval Officers. For those who do not know, the procedure is this: at dawn and dusk, when the sun is low, you look for and find a selected star and point your sextant at it. The swinging arm of the sextant moves a mirror, so that if you align the mirror and the star you can then swing the arm down, bringing the reflection of the star with it, until the star "hits" the horizon; you then know its altitude. From this, using a very complicated system of formulae, and knowing the time to the nearest second, you can put a mark on your chart. Get another star, get another mark. Get a third star and you've got a triangle and you know for (reasonably) sure you're in that triangle somewhere. There are two drawbacks. The first is that you need to be able to see both the stars and the horizon so if it's either cloudy or misty you can't do it. And secondly dawn is usually at some God-awful time of the day, such as four or five o'clock in the morning, and if you're an eighteen-year-old Midshipman wanting to stay in your bunk for as long as possible then 04.00 or 05.00 is horrendissimo. But we all had brains and we had Maths Physics and/or Something (those of us who had managed to pass sufficiently in each) and we were all averse to turning out at 04 dubs or 05 dubs and so we used a bit of dog cunning (which has always, by the way, been the key to surviving at sea). Just one of us would actually do a morning starsight. Each evening, one of us in turn (so as not to arouse suspicion) would sneak up to the bridge, look at the chart and find out when we would be at dawn the following morning. And then, using a reverse calculation of the complicated "star reduction equation" we could work out the altitude at which each selected star should have been. This made it possible for us to fill in our starsight books backwards in advance, as if we had really taken the starsights, showing that we were so good at doing these calculations that we always got the right answer - and having the correct amount of sleep which we felt we were entitled to at the same time.

Three things went wrong - at the same time. Half way across the Mediterranean, unbeknown to us, in the middle of the night (we were all worshipping our bunks) the bridge received an SOS and diverted well off course to go and help. Fortunately, the problem was resolved, no-one was hurt, and we were able to resume our course - but one hundred miles from where we should have been. The second was that the real starsight taker slept in. The third was revealed after breakfast the next morning when we were all - all twenty-four of us - mustered on the Quarterdeck by our Training officer for "a talk". "Who did the starsights this morning?" he bellowed. The duty starsight takers duly raised their hands and said that they had done it. "And did you not perhaps notice," he bellowed, "That the sky was completely covered by cloud and that there was so much morning mist that you couldn't see either the stars or the horizon even if you were Gypsy Petulengro with a Hubble telescope?" "Aha" we thought, "We are doomed". And doomed we were.

All twenty-four of us were required to stand on the bridge roof taking horizontal bearings of every lighthouse, buoy, prominent building, scarp edge, camel, dhow, everything, throughout the whole transit of the Suez Canal. We had water, plenty of it, but no food, and the only exception, for hygiene reasons, were lavatorial breaks.

By the end of it, we knew a great deal about the Suez Canal, and most of us remember it to this day. We also knew a little more about naval discipline, and naval justice, which are quite different things as you will see again in a later chapter.

(Earlier on, in Plymouth, we had already had a demonstration of this difference. A sailor had prepared to go on a "run ashore" and found that his packet of "blue liners" (rationed duty free cigarettes) had only one cigarette in it - so he put another packet in his pocket as well. He was stopped at the gate by the MoD police who found twenty one cigarettes when the ration to take ashore was twenty, arrested and cautioned: "You are not obliged to say anything but anything you do say will be recorded and may be used in a subsequent trial" etc. The sailor thought for a moment, and then said "You'll never take me alive, copper." At his subsequent trial on board he pleaded "Not Guilty" so the MoD policeman had to be called personally to give evidence in this case of the heinous smuggling of one cigarette. In front of some thirty or so attendees when asked if the accused had said anything he was constrained to reply "Yes. He said: "You'll never take me alive, copper"". The whole court dissolved in laughter, the MoD policeman slunk away with a red face and the Captain - who really had to find him guilty - fined the sailor £5.)

HMS EAGLE was large and impersonal, but there were several positive things about her which could not be ignored. The first thing is that until her refit and return to the Fleet in 1963 the statistics showed that in aircraft carriers the death rate for aviators (pilots and navigators) was, on average, one death per flying day. It is a very hairy business projecting several tons of metal and either one or two people into the sky off the front of a ship. Until then aircraft at full speed over the bow could only just conquer gravity, systems were not sophisticated, and peoples' mistakes were invariably found out. But EAGLE was state of the art, and life expectancy improved enormously. We had not one death in the six months I was on board - there were no Wakes. Explanation of naval "Wakes": when a naval aircraft "spears in" you rarely got a body back. This was meat and gravy for insurance companies, Hell for widows and loadsamoney for lawyers. But before all

The aircraft carrier HMS EAGLE transits the Suez Canal (Buccaneer aircraft on deck) (photograph taken from enforced imprisonment of bridge roof) 1964

this started, on board there was deep gloom among the aviators. Now, drinking to excess is not only frowned on in the Senior Service (on board, that is) but it is actually severely illegal. The Wake was the only exception; after a death, pilots and navigators and aircrew would shut themselves away in the aircrew recreation space and get completely plastered - the doors were locked and everyone from the Captain down knew that it was not a good idea to try and get in. So they were left alone. They all flew again, of course, when they had sufficiently recovered and de-tox'd. Until the next time.

Back to HMS EAGLE's itinerary. She cleared the Suez Canal and sailed down the Red Sea with us Midshipmen on board all learning avidly. The only thing I can report of any interest was that we saw mirages for the first time - not astrological mumbo-jumbo events but the real effect of severe heat on optical sight lines - ships upside down on the horizon, ships doubled one above the other, and multiple reflections on the sea and in the sky. It seemed that every single seagoing experience was a completely new experience, outwith our previous belief. One of them was certainly outwith mine. It was incredibly hot in the Red Sea, and we had little air conditioning. One day I didn't feel too well, so I went to the sick bay, where they turned me in, that is put me in a bunk. I slept. When I awoke, I felt quite refreshed and somewhat hungry. To my astonishment, this turned out to be unsurprising because it was three days later! But as so often happens in the Services it was a case of "Report to the MO, get diagnosed, get treated, get better (or otherwise), get discharged" and never find out what was wrong in the first place. (Anyone finding this difficult to believe should turn to the page which covers my stay at the BMH (British Medical Hospital) Singapore for enlightenment and confirmation). We called at Aden which was hot, rocky and dangerous and where I bought my first pipe - a Kiko meerschaum-lined briar which lasted me well into the 1990's.

Then on to Mombasa, the main port of Kenya. It was up a wide river, and I got my first glimpse of jungle, on either side. As we were coming in to the berth we watched the little boats handling our wires, and the wide jetty, and what looked like a large floating rusty shed moored at the far end. Unbeknown to me at the time this was to be my next ship - HMS MESSINA.

HMS MESSINA was a tank landing ship, built to go across the English Channel, just once, in 1945. Not a tank landing craft, which held just two tanks, MESSINA had a huge hold capable of holding twelve tanks and able to put them ashore on any reasonably flat beach. Added to that, she had davits which held eight LCVPs (Landing Craft, Vehicle, Personnel) each of which could carry a vehicle and ten soldiers or twenty-four or so fully armed and equipped soldiers. So twelve tanks and some two hundred men was a considerable load of fire power to put ashore. There were three drawbacks in the 1960's. First was that she could only do eight knots, nine with a following gale. Second was that she had no real means of defence at all – anything larger than a rifle would inconvenience her. And thirdly she had become so rusty that by 1964 when I joined the most common reason for sailors to visit the sick bay was not the usual STDs, it was in fact laceration of the calf where their legs had gone clean through the rusty decks.

There were just six officers on board, plus us - two Midshipmen, Mike Buckland-Smith and me. There were cabins for twenty-two officers, because fourteen was the number of officers expected to be required to command the tanks and troops we could put ashore. There was also lots of accommodation for the soldiers or Royal Marines that we might carry.

Being a Midshipman is the second most important rank if what you really want is to have no responsibility at all. It is a contrived rank: you have no stripes but you are technically an officer. And having no stripes means that you have no stripes to take away and so Midshipmen can get away with the most appalling blunders, the most terrible hashes, the most embarrassing contrivances without its damaging their further careers - even if it means temporary stoppage of leave or verbal censure or loss of this or that privilege. Midshipmen can give orders to naval ratings; but naval ratings can quite reasonably tell them whether it is not a sensible thing to do, and the sensible Midshipman listens. We learned, we learned by both our successes and our failures, which was wonderful.

HMS MESSINA and four of her small landing craft 1965

We left Mombasa on a balmy morning and sailed out into the Indian Ocean. We two Midshipmen were allocated watches, which required us to be on the open bridge, out in the fresh air and the sun or the stars for hours on end. We watched the dock lights die, and then we were on our own, making a slow passage via Aden towards the Straits of Hormuz and Bahrein, which was to be our base, the base of the Amphibious Warfare Squadron, which consisted of an old frigate, two Landing Ships and four Landing Craft.

MESSINA and the AW Squadron had two main tasks: the first was to be ready to put the Army ashore and the second was the suppression of the slave trade which was rife in the area. Slavers would take slaves from Pakistan and sell them in Arabia - a very lucrative business. They were shipped in "slave dhows" which looked like ordinary dhows but had enormous engines, and so our chief problem was that they could easily outrun us. But on the passage to Bahrein we did manage to stop such a dhow - it had engine problems and was quite slow. We put a boat across with a boarding party led by a Royal Marine Corporal. In full view of all of us they rounded up the slavers and opened the hatches. The smell from below was awful, even from fifty yards away. The slaves were existing in appalling, insanitary, cruel conditions, in chains. Then two of the slavers moved to draw weapons from belts. The RM Corporal didn't hesitate - he pressed and held the trigger of his machine gun and shot all of them within three seconds. They fell over the side, and we couldn't see the point of recovering the bodies, even if we could have. We towed the dhow to safety and handed it over to civilian authorities, having done what we could for the slaves. It was a dreadful experience.

Interestingly, however, our peripatetic dentist, one Surgeon Lieutenant David Rugg Gunn or Gunn Rugg had requested permission to make his own way overland to Bahrein, just as simply as one might have asked to drive back from Germany rather than flying. But between Aden and Bahrein is a region of desert so inhospitable and dreadful that has its own name - it is called "the Empty Quarter", and there is quite simply nothing there but sand and trouble. In short, it's about a thousand miles of nothing. And no water. I don't know why he wanted to do it, and nor, I learned, did anybody else, but that's what happened. It wouldn't happen nowadays. 'Elf and Safety. But when we got to Bahrein, he was there to greet us. Goodness knows how he had done it. It must have involved camels, because nothing else could have achieved it. Neither do I know why he wasn't murdered en route. What a man!

Bahrein was our shore support base and I can really only remember two things about it: first that it was often quite dangerous to go outside the naval base because at some times of the year the Sunnis and the Shi'ites were knocking hell out of each other and you didn't want a stray bullet or hand grenade. Secondly, that if you go to the club swimming pool and they are draining off the water you really shouldn't dive in off the diving board as did our Engineer Officer, David Abinett, whose broken nose was restored by a young newly recruited medical officer who sewed two fly buttons on each side and told him to take them off in six weeks' time. Needless to say, an officer with fly buttons sewed on to his nose became the butt of many a joke on board - but he survived.

Very shortly we sailed for an exercise - a trial to see if we could achieve what we were supposed to achieve. We took on board a whole host of tanks, ARVs (Armoured Recovery Vehicles), BARVs (Beach Armoured Recovery Vehicles) and towed a huge floating pier for the troops to land without getting their poor little feet wet. The soldiers were billeted on the tank deck floor, or wherever else they could lie down without tripping up some poor army officer or another. The officers themselves were distributed among our cabins.

Mike B-S and I shared a Midshipmens' cabin which was L-shaped and had two double bunks, one above the other. I don't mean that we shared double bunks, as in "double beds", I mean that there were two bunks, each of which folded upward to provide an additional bunk. In "peacetime" - i.e. when we were not at war or having a military exercise - Mike had one lower bunk and I had the other. With troops with their officers on board we put up the top bunks and made room for two other army officers in the bunk spaces provided. Four to the cabin instead of two.

Amphibious assault from HMS MESSINA 1965

We sailed for an invasion of "Quibitra'n", a fictional state which was threatening British interests. We sailors simply had our normal routines, but the guest troops prepared for "war" by cleaning their tanks and guns and other equipment. After dinner on the first night at sea, with three days to go before reaching "Quibitra'n" we all turned in quite early. Mike B-S had quit his bunk and moved to another for the passage and a rather charming young Captain of the Royal Inniskilling Dragoon Guards had occupied his old bunk. A young Lieutenant (RIDG) occupied the fourth bunk. At a quarter to midnight (23.45) the Bosn's Mate was sent from the bridge to waken (or "shake", as it is called in the RN) my colleague Mike to do his midnight to 4 a.m. watch on the bridge. He went to where he knew Mike always slept, aroused the incumbent and said "23.45, Sir" and left. The Royal "Skin" Guard sat up in his bunk and saluted, as army officers do when given a report. And went back to sleep. By five minutes to midnight the officer of the watch was mightily hacked off by the non-appearance of Mike to relieve him on watch and sent down the Bosn's mate again. Mike hastened to get dressed and took the watch, and order was restored. At breakfast next morning, the two week exercise having not yet started, the young Guards Officer announced: "Deshed strange thing happened to me in the middle of the night. Fellow came down from the bridge just to tell me that it was a quarter to midnight". The First Lieutenant, at the head of the table, said without batting an eyelid: "An old naval tradition. Officers are always woken and told that it is a quarter to midnight. Don't forget to salute." We all kept straight faces. The Guards officer accepted this as naval tradition - and was duly awoken every night thereafter at 23.45, just to preserve the tradition, of course. Poor chap. But they were good at assaulting beaches, which was their job - as long as the Sergeant Major and his NCO's were actually running things, of course.

HMS MESSINA was a rustbucket, of that there was no doubt. But she was a lovely and lovable rustbucket. If (when) she went aground in the shifting sands of the Middle East all we had to do was send a boat astern with our kedge anchor on it, drop it over the side and then winch ourselves off backwards. The Captain was called Peter Parfitt and he did not like this ignominy at all but, like the rest of us, he had to put up with it or we would have been on the sands forever. And there is no court martial for going aground on shifting sands if they have shifted since the last chart was made. And MESSINA had a flat bottom, a completely flat bottom. So she was able to sit on sand for as long as the Captain deemed fit. The tides in the Persian Gulf are minimal. Like all old rustbuckets, she had rats. They were amiable rats, and kept out of everybody's way until they came out mostly at night to scavenge any leftover food. The only one to draw attention to itself was the Wardroom rat called "Alfred", which was quite shy, did no harm and was generally ignored. Except that he took to scratching over the deckhead of the Royal Marine Lieutenant's bunk, which disturbed his important sleep (Royal Marines, when they aren't killing people or being killed or ashore taking the afternoon off, do really like to sleep peacefully). So this rat had had it, and our Royal Marine officer Lieutenant Jeff Robinson waited until after tea one day when Alfred was coming down from the overhead fittings and across the room's air conditioning unit and then he shot him. Unfortunately he also shot this, the only air conditioning unit we had, and life became a bit uncomfortable after that, until we got to Bombay for our refit. The temperature in the Persian Gulf was almost unbearable at the best of times, but on board a floating tin box in the full glare of the sun it was excruciating - especially if someone has shot the only air conditioning unit. I remember doing midnight rounds (checks that all is well throughout the ship) in Bahrein in a temperature of forty degrees (one hundred and four in old money). It was awful.

After our combined exercise and the recovery of this fictional Middle Eastern State it was time for us to have a refit. "Refit" in naval terms is very important: it is a period in dockyard hands where all deficient items are repaired and all outdated items are upgraded and the ship's "fighting capability" is restored and enhanced. The little LCTs went to Karachi for their refits and the LSTs went to Bombay, which was further, but bigger. We went into City Dock after a short passage, entering the port with a little bit of colonial pomp and ceremony and tying up alongside with some relief. On arrival, two things happened almost simultaneously. To appreciate the first it is important to understand what the arrival of a warship (even a rustbucket) in a foreign port is all about. It is an expression of mutual diplomatic acceptance. It is a display of friendship between nations. It confirms good relations if they already exist and it signals a thaw in difficult relations if they don't. So when a foreign warship comes in, it is necessary that the local senior military Commander be there to greet it, the local Naval Commander ditto, the Captain of the Port concerned, and the Mayor or equivalent civil dignitary too. There is a pecking order for them all to come on board and welcome the visiting ship's Captain. If this seems stilted behaviour, I can assure you that it has ensured stability throughout the civilised (and sometimes uncivilised) world for centuries; it is a well tried and tested procedure. The only time I have ever seen this procedure violated was our arrival in Bombay.

At this stage you have to understand that even after Independence just twenty years previously there was still the rump of the British Raj, and much respected it was and much power it had, albeit for not much longer. Bombay, Calcutta and all the major subcontinent cities still had economies which were effectively run by British companies. This is what British expat menfolk were doing all day long - keeping the economy going and helping it thrive. They were at work all day long, and so had little to do with what was going on at home and probably didn't know or care much about it as long as they got their Chota Peg or two at the end of the day. No, the real power at that time still lay with the BWI, the British Womens' Institute. Pronounced "Bee Wee", in much the same way that UK was pronounced "Yew Kay", this was the real social power of Bombay in the sense that nothing minor happened without the Bee Wee knowing about it and nothing major happened without the BWI either sanctioning it or organising it. And so it was that on HMS MESSINA's arrival in Bombay neither the Military Commander nor the Civil Dignitaries managed to get up the gangway first when it was put over the side - they were elbowed aside by the Chairwoman of the BWI, who took immediate control of our poor Captain (I'd never thought of him as a "poor Captain" before - we knew him as a rather hard taskmaster, almost a slavedriver) and said imperiously and without fear of interruption or correction "I have had a list of your officers from the Embassy. Now, you'll want to know where you are staying when you are in Bombay" (we hadn't thought about it - we thought we were staying on board the ship, but Madam Chairperson had different ideas, and actually good ideas they turned out to be, because it was so damned hot). "The Captain will stay with the Joneses, the First Lieutenant will stay with Mr and Mrs Smith, the Engineer Officer will stay with Mr and Mrs McDonald, the Royal Marine Officer will stay with ...." and it went on until she got to us two Midshipmen: "Mike will stay with Mr and Mrs Craddock, and Alan will stay at the Normans' residence." Now I'm sure you will have noticed that all these hosts are in the marital doubleton plural except for the family with whom I was to reside for the next six weeks. It was indeed the residence of Mr and Mrs Norman - but Mr Norman was never mentioned, never seen, and the residence seemed to be occupied only by Mrs Norman (of a certain age) and the staff - a Head Boy, two Boys, a Chauffeur, a Guard, two Waiters, and two Maids.

The second thing that happened on our arrival was that three Indian dockyard workers came on board (after the dignitaries had dispersed) and said they were taking our radar set away for repair and refurbishment. It was a stand-alone metal box of a thing which just about worked, and they took it away - and we never saw it again! Nobody could tell us who they were or why they had taken our radar set, but there were many apologies for the lax security - but no radar set. We had to wait to get back to Bahrein before another one could be shipped out from UK. Good job we knew something about starsights - and could, if really necessary, do them forwards as well as backwards.

The next six weeks were absolute magic for a young officer. Bombay was not then a tourist venue, and it was unsullied by tourist excrescences. We wandered around here, there and everywhere looking at things, visiting markets with wonderful previously unseen things in them, soaking up the local knowledge and gaining a sense of history, eating out - dining, that is, not wining and dining because Maharashtra was a completely dry state in 1965. As testament to this, on our arrival the Government gave us all - every single member of the ship's company - a certificate to say that we were allowed to purchase, from one of several regulated sources, an amount of alcohol up to a certain amount. The amount was so high that it didn't perturb even our professional-drinker Able Seamen. The interesting thing, though, was that in order not to alienate Western businessmen and other senior Western expats the Maharashtra Government had said that if someone was declared an alcoholic they, too, could have an "alcohol certificate" for a certain amount of home-consumption alcohol. And it didn't say who in the family had to declare it. But this also did mean that their driving license was taken off them; so all the expat couples in the whole of Maharashtra had to decide which one of them was going to declare themselves an alcoholic and lose their driving licence but gain the right to purchase alcohol, and which was one going to abstain - at least in public.

No doubt some Indian Al Capone lookalike made a fortune out of this situation, but I don't know. In any event, I was offered alcohol several times by accostation on the street, but since it was made by fermenting cabbage leaves and other undesirable discarded vegetable matter and then distilled by passing the alcohol vapour through tubes which were cooled by passing them through holes in the city's sewage system, it was easy to decline. As was the offer of the use of someone's sister for some purpose or another. Life was sometimes dark and dank and disgusting, but as far as I could see it wasn't violent - at least not to a Westerner. Or perhaps I was just lucky.

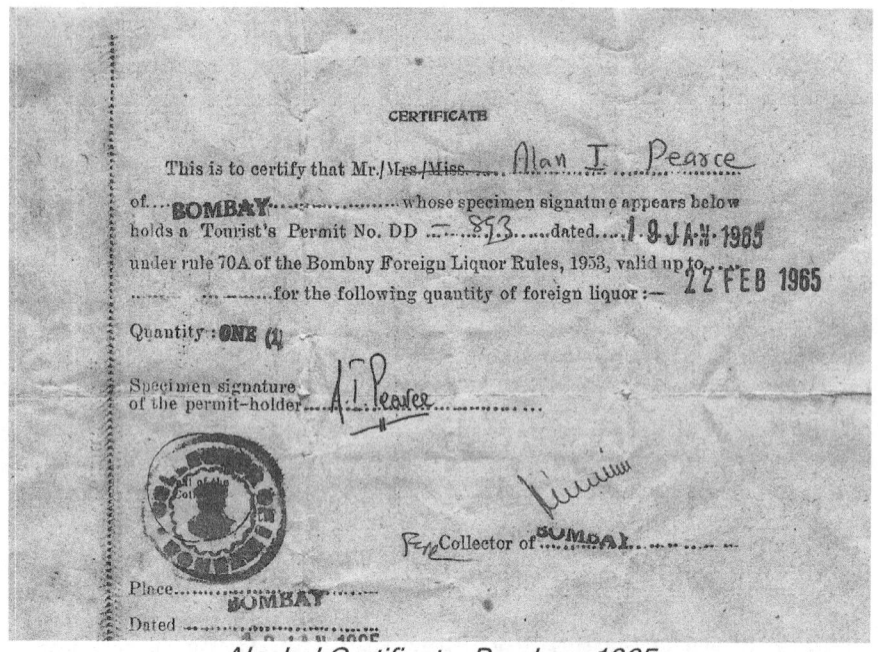

Alcohol Certificate, Bombay, 1965

Far more on my mind was where I was going to kip for the next six weeks. I didn't seem to have much option - the BWI had already decided where I was going to reside. The ship (in dry dock) had neither air conditioning nor fresh water nor sewage facilities and the choice was "take it or leave it" without an alternative to the "leave it" option. So the Normans' residence it was. Not that one could really complain. It was what in

England would have been the equivalent of a small palace, with its own live-in servants. It didn't have aircon but it did have punkahs and punkah wallahs to operate them; and it had overhead fans for when the punkah wallahs were off duty. There was a car to take me down to the ship each day to carry out my duties, and it would always arrive on the dot to take me back to the residence again. The food and accommodation were free. My spare time was (nearly) my own. What more could an eighteen-year-old bachelor gay blade alone in an exotic country want? And it really was "exotic". Every single thing I came across was different from what I had already experienced in my life - but even at that young age I was thoughtful enough to say to myself "This is not England - this is different. When in Rome, do as the Romans do". So I lapped it all up without demur, and certainly without judgement as to whether it was right or wrong. "That's just the way they do it here," I said to myself. What more could I do or want?

I was to find out. It dawned quite slowly. On the first day, a Saturday, I was given a beautiful light lunch, consisting of just four small courses each served on the most delicate china, eaten with silver cutlery, and with drinks in distinctive Royal Stewart cut glass (Royal Stewart and cut glass were "in" at that time). I was informed that we were going out to dinner with the Hargreaves' that evening, so it was necessary to get one's head down for a couple of hours in the afternoon and then dress in black tie rig to go out. This we did. Then off we went to the Hargreaves' in the vehicle, alighted when the chauffeur had opened the doors and then entered, Mrs Norman on my arm as consort protocol required, and went into the Reception. It was delightful to circulate and talk to so many interesting people - there must have been twenty or twenty-four of us - and it became really interesting when we sat down at the table, in correct order, of course. The Really Interesting bit was that I thought I recognised some of the china, the silver cutlery and the cut glass and remarked to Mrs Norman that it was similar to hers. She replied "It's not just similar to mine - it is mine, probably, some of it, anyway. None of us has sufficient for a dinner party of twenty or more and so one's staff bring it round to their staff before the meal, and here it is. Don't worry - it will be back home again before we are". We dined luxuriously, a seamless blend of Indian and English cuisine with just a touch of French thrown in. After the ladies had retired and the gentlemen had smoked and finished their port everyone had had a goodnighter. The vehicle arrived out of nowhere, and we were taken home. There was a cup of tea before we finally retired. As Mrs Norman went out to supervise the delivery of the tea I took a look inside the cavernous sideboard. There was all the crockery and glassware, and cutlery in the cutlery drawer and I really hadn't a clue if it had been there all the time or, as suggested, removed to the Hargreaves' and then returned. I never found out. It mattered not a jot, certainly not to Mrs Norman. And she certainly wouldn't have lifted a finger to count it; only Staff counted crockery and cutlery. Actually Mrs Norman probably couldn't have made the tea, either - she had never in her life had to do so.

The next day was a Sunday, and we went for a drive. Out across the Bombay plain, then south to some charming little coastal villages where we lunched, had a sail (i.e. were sailed), walked a bit and then returned at about tea time. It was a lovely, quiet and restful way to spend the whole day - or so it was at that time, just after tea. Then things changed.

"We will dine at eight" said Mrs Norman. "You will wish to dress, but first please feel free to have a nice cool shower. Meera will help you." Meera was one of the maids. Why I should need her help to shower? I could not imagine, but this was India, not England, and things are different. I assumed she would lay out my dinner jacket and shirt, or something, or take my towel to the laundry afterwards. Perhaps polish my shoes. I went to my room, stripped off, wrapped a towel round myself and set off for the shower, which was a huge, tiled room which would nowadays be called a "wetroom", with multiple showers and a drain in the centre. I had just taken off my towel and gone to the taps on the wall when I became aware of Meera standing by the side of the shower cubicle with a bar of soap in one hand and a large natural Indian Ocean sponge in the other; she was wearing a bright red and gold sari, and beckoning me. I covered myself up quickly and moved sideways into the shower. "Sahib," she said, "there is no need to be embarrassed. I am here to help you. It is what I do when we have guests. Please turn the shower on". So I did, and Meera reached forward with the sponge. I instinctively turned my back, and she instinctively ran her soapy sponge up and down it. "What the Hell do I do next?" I thought, but the decision was taken away from me. "Sahib, my sari is getting wet. So I will take it off and then I will be able to soap you more closely." So she did. My mind, as you may imagine, was in a turmoil. I hadn't a clue whether this was just traditional expat hospitality or whether I was being treated specially or whether this always happened - this was India, and things were done differently.

Meera stepped into the shower and expertly soaped my neck and shoulders. It felt really good. Then she made me hold my arms up and ran the sponge under them. I was trying hard to think of England, or count sheep, or any damn thing, but the sponge ran down my back as far as it could go, and then a little bit further, where it lingered for a while. Then "Turn round, please," she said, and since by now I was on auto, I did so. The sponge was re-soaped, and then slowly circled my chest, then my midriff, then my abdomen. And then she started washing me where only my mother has ever washed me before, (and that was seventeen years previously, prior to putting my nappy back on). But Meera was very assiduous - up and down, round and round. And then up and down again. Until it was all over.

When she had finished and had showered everything off with fresh water I felt the need to sit down on the wetroom bench. I could hardly stand, my legs were so wobbly. She sat next to me, with a big fluffy towel. "Meera," I said, "What was that all about?"

"Sahib," she said, "You are a young man and very strong and

very vigorous. The Mem'sa'ab has instructed me to ensure that there are certain things that she wishes you to accomplish without undue precipitation. And now she would like you to have a little nightcap with her, in her quarters. You may eat later." I didn't have any option, really. They do things differently in the colonies. We didn't eat later.

This magical dream went on in a quite different way just the following morning. Back on board the ship, trying to ensure that the bits we wanted painted actually got painted, I was minding my own business when a large Sikh chap was led into the Wardroom mess. I knew he was a Sikh because he had a turban on; otherwise he was dressed from top to toe in the tropical white uniform of an RN senior rating - a Chief Petty Officer (Gunnery Instructor) to be exact. The only difference was that his cap badge was on his turban, not on a cap. Tall, erect, heavily bearded and very formal, he was a magnificent sight. "On behalf of the Indian Navy," he said, "I would like to invite a group of you to come hunting with me at my hunting area near Poona."

"Excellent thing for the Midshipmen to do!" declared the Captain. But Mike was a pacifist or a vegetarian or something, and declined. I was thus "volunteered". It was decided that an experienced Petty Officer and a Royal Marine Corporal should also go, and a Leading Seaman, too, and a sailor, "for the experience". So it was that the following morning this strange party got together on the concourse of the Bombay Railway Station and entrained, together with the Indian Navy CPO and his bag of shotguns - one for each of us. The huge steam train chugged its way South Eastwards across the vast plain until it reached the hills which heralded the arrival in the Poona region. There, there was a huge scarp. So steep that the train could only get up it if it was completely empty, and only then with another engine shackled on at the back. So we all had to get off. Alongside the track as it rose steeply into the hills was a huge flight of steps cut into the rocks, and it was up these steps that we, carrying our own bags and chattels, had to ascend, on foot, just about keeping level with the snorting, steaming engine and train as it just about made it up the incline. We got on again at the top and carried on our journey. We disembarked at Poona railway station and headed for the "village" of Lonavla and INS SHIVAJI, the Indian Navy's marine engineering training establishment. It was a long, hot bus ride, during which we opened the bag of shotguns and took one each. We also had a mixed box of cartridges each, small shot for birds, and BB (ball bearing) for large animals. We disembarked and marched into the Indian Base. The guard checked our ID, and we set off across the campus for our billet. We had got about a couple of hundred yards before we were stopped by armed guards. "The Commander wishes to see you," they said. We were ushered into his presence. "You cannot wander about my establishment carrying guns," he said. "Which of you is in command?" Now, there was a gnarled old Petty Officer, a battle-scarred Royal Marine Corporal, a Leading Seaman, and a sailor, and they had more than fifty years' service between them, but I was technically an officer and I was to learn what "responsibility" was all about; they all pointed to me - with my six months' experience as a dogsbody - and said, almost in unison "He is." The Commander turned to me and said, quite kindly: "Unless you leave I will have to put you in the jolly clink." I immediately made an officer-like decision that we did not want to be put in the jolly clink so I thanked him on behalf of the Royal Navy and Her Britannic Majesty's Government for his forbearance and said we would leave immediately and by the most direct route. Standing outside the Main Gate we had another decision to make - or, it now rather looked like, I myself had another decision to make. Poona was miles away and we already knew that the last bus had gone. There was a local "village". But I put inverted commas round the word "village" because it was actually a camp-followers tented settlement where the off-duty Indian sailors went to relieve themselves on their nights off.

We decided, of course, that we were not going to join in any shenannigins, but we did need somewhere to sleep, away from the flying insects which bite so much. So we hired a large bell tent for the night, lay down our groundsheets and went to sleep, quite unaware that there were worse things knocking around than flying insects. The first was the rats. We put up with their scurrying about for a while, then told the shikar owner to get rid of them. Just like that. Amazingly, he did. So we went to sleep, feeling quite safe. I woke up next morning feeling a bit itchy, so I scratched a bit and then looked at my body; it was criss-crossed in trails of red punctures, one centimetre apart, making me look like an Ordnance Survey Hiking Map of the mountains, with the paths in vivid red dots. It was what is known as bed bugs. But it didn't hurt, so I ignored it. I was to learn more about it later.

But that morning, we set off on our real adventure. We hired six "bearers" at six rupees a day each and set off into the hills to look for prey. We were not so naive as to think that we were going to slay any tigers and we knew that elephants are not only protected but loved, including by us; but we did fancy a deer or two and some venison to take back with us. It was not to be. We trekked for miles, saw nothing, and then made camp. We ate sparsely but heartily, and then went to bed on the hard ground. We were surprised next morning to be served tea in bed by one of our bearers; he had run a good five miles back to the village and then the other five back again to get our fresh milk by 07.00 - because as is well known English gentlemen insist upon having fresh milk in their morning call tea (we hadn't, but it didn't matter; it made them feel good, and we liked it).

Someone shot a hare, I shot a pigeon, and that was about it. Not the sort of thing to make a "Big Game Hunt in India" film about, but we enjoyed the experience. Then our bearers decided to show us how to get a wild boar for the pot.

Now, your wild boar is not just an annoyed male English pig. It is a huge, muscled, hairy, one hundred kilogram plus heap of fighting machine, angry even before anyone upsets it, and looking for trouble. It has killer tusks on either side of its snout, and it knows how to use them. It has, we were told, one weakness: it is so intent upon a kill that when it charges it never deviates from its charge path.

Little Indian boy waits while his father shoots a wild boar.

So our bearer, armed with a large bow and arrow, stood right in the middle of a clearing while his compatriots went to look for a wild boar to annoy and we found a couple of trees to climb up. Sure enough, there was a pandemoneous snorting and grunting and then this huge tank of an animal came thundering out of the scrub towards the bearer with the bow and arrow in the clearing, who stood his ground until the very last moment then jumped aside and knowing the exact track of the beast put his sharpened arrow slap into the animal's chest, to the heart. It thundered on for a good fifty yards before it fell – at a place where the other bearers were already waiting to deliver the coup de grace, which in the event wasn't needed. One would have said that this was the most foolhardy thing one had ever seen, except that it was executed in such a trained, well-rehearsed manner that one could not help but admire the skill and indeed courage of those who had done it - so that the rest of them would have something to put in the pot and eat. It was actually, in short, awe-inspiring.

What could be more impressive? The next event could be. Was. We trekked down the scarp and back onto the coastal plain so that we could catch the train back to Bombay. The only problem was that although we found the railway line - which went in a very straight line for miles and miles, so much so that one could use it as mathematics class analogy for "parallel" - there was no station. Our Sikh leader came into his own, in a way that could not be guessed at. We stopped by the side of the track and had a brew of tea, and passed the time until at last someone saw a plume of smoke, far, far in the distance. It was an approaching train. I don't know if you have ever seen an Indian train, but take it from me, they are enormous. They are ex-colonial, they exude power and they make a lot of noise and a lot of smoke. And this one was thundering towards us at a rate of knots. "Where is it going to stop?" we asked. "Here." said our Sikh Chief Petty Officer. And he stepped on to the track. The huge snorting beast thundered towards us, belching smoke and the Sikh simply put up his hand with his palm facing towards the oncoming train for all the world like an English policeman on traffic duty calmly stopping cars from coming out of a side road. Onwards thundered the train. Resolute stood the Sikh. And then with about a mile to go the driver saw him and slammed on the brakes. We saw sparks flying from under the wheels and extra smoke belching from the funnel, and then more sparks, as the Sikh stood, between the rails, with his hand up. It was touch and go. The train screeched the last few yards and then finally managed to stop, some ten yards or so from the Sikh. The driver and fireman leapt out of the cab, and we thought there was going to be bloodshed.

"What are you doing, you stupid idiot...." said the driver, plus lots of other things. When this had finished, the Sikh simply grabbed him by the throat, held him up so that he was face to face, and said "Many years ago, when your ancestors were cowering in caves in these hills from the animals, my ancestors were fighting to protect this land to make it safe - even for cowards and slimy rats like you and yours. We wish to take your train, and that is what we will do. We shall hear no more of your feeble effeminate screeching". And he put him down. We got on the train, with difficulty because it was very high off the ground, and it set off again, slowly at first and then thunderingly quickly until we got back to the terminus at Bombay where we all went our several ways, with promises of keeping in touch and, on our part, the desire for a beer and a shower, not necessarily in that order. But this we did, and went on to our separate places of residence.

A couple of days later I went shopping, principally for jewellery and Indian trinkets for my girlfriends back in UK. Now, it is important to know that there are several prestigious "Clubs" around the British colonial world, mainly but not exclusively gentlemen's clubs - The Hong Kong Club, for example, the Calcutta Club, the Mombasa Club and the most senior of all, perhaps, the Bombay Club. As Officers of the Royal Navy, we were given temporary honorary membership of all of them, all around the world. Also that they do not and never have accepted cash. Everything was on "chits". The Restaurant Manager or the Golf Club Manager or the waiter brought you a book of "chits" and you signed it. A list of these chits was sent to you monthly, and you paid what you could. It didn't matter if you temporarily couldn't - they just built up: but gentlemen were expected to pay them in the end, or face the ultimate indignity, expulsion. It very rarely happened, and usually ended in the *felo de se* of any chap who had decided to leave the normal human (i.e. British) race. But make no mistake - the chits followed you around the world, wherever you were; I paid my last one two and a half years after we had left Bombay and the account had followed me through six different countries back to the UK. This was not reprehensible: it was normal and more than acceptable - as long as it got paid in the end.

(Incidentally, the Officers of the Fleet at that time were served by Messrs Gieves (Tailors) from whom one purchased one's uniform; but they did more than that. If you were in the middle of the Pacific or the Indian Ocean and you had forgotten your wife's birthday (or mother, or daughter, or whatever) you had only to send a telegram to Gieves in Portsmouth stating the cash amount and they would send a very appropriate present on your behalf and with your name on it. They too sent a monthly account which had eventually to be settled. They sometimes sent reminders. A colleague received one while we were in Bombay. It said "We would respectfully remind you that your account has now reached a total of fifty pounds and we would be very much obliged if you could see your way clear to settling at least some of it so as to maintain the very good relations which exist between us and your esteemed self". As my colleague was completely broke at the time he replied: "Dear Gieves, Thank you for your letter. Let me explain how I settle my monthly accounts. At the end of the month I put all the bills in a bag and pull one out and settle it in full. If you disturb me with begging letters again I won't even put your account in the bag"! He heard no more. But presumably he settled in due course. Or took the other course of action.)

So there I was, in central Bombay, shopping. I decided to have a Chota Peg in the Bombay Club before returning either to the ship or to my temporary place of abode chez the Normans. On the vast steps of the Club I met an Indian chap coming down the steps; we looked at each other in semi-recognition. He was a distinguished looking fellow; "Hello," he said. "Hello," I said. You know, the way you do when you meet someone but can't put a name to them. "Where was it....." he said. "I can't recall." I said. "Were you at Dartmouth?" "No," he said, "Did you do the Indian Staff Course?". "No," I said. "Did you play hockey?". "No," he said, "Were you ever in Dubai?"...... and so it went on.

We had become bosom friends and went into the Club to have a Peg with each other - and it transpired that we had simply been in the same jewellery shop together that morning. What idiots we felt! But what companionable idiots! We became even greater friends.

In a seemingly inexorable chapter of my life, he invited me to his Grandfather's funeral. It was held some days later on the great mud flats just to the South of Bombay - a huge area of stomped-down ground which could be used for any large event. And this was indeed a large event. There must have been a thousand people there. It was also a very cost-effective and effort-effective and eco-effective event. Hundreds of tables had been laid out and on each table were laid several cut-in-half or cut-in-quarter palm leaves. These were the "plates". The food (curry, of course, in various styles) was delivered on to the palm leaf and it was eaten as is the custom with the fingers. When it was over, the leaves were gathered up and chucked away. No washing up! I cannot comment on the service or the speeches because I didn't understand a word of them, but I nodded my head from time to time as if I had, and this seemed to be very much appreciated. I expressed condolences to my host, and returned home. I didn't know that the mortal remains were then taken to the "Towers of Silence", hauled to the top and laid on a rack so that the vultures could devour the flesh and the bones fall, clean, to the ground, to be gathered later. A very hygienic system, given the great heat. But I read about it, later.

Talking of health and hygiene, feeling sick one day I reported to the sick bay and ended up having a complete blood transfusion. Bloody (sorry) Lonavla bed bugs.

Eventually, of course, we completed the refit and left Bombay among cheers and tears, as British warships always do, wherever, and sailed off back to Bahrein. Only to find on arrival that we had been disbanded.

So, back to Bahrein. We sailed across the Indian Ocean, back again to our base. It was idyllic in the calm seas we encountered. I was on watch, the First Watch (20.00 to midnight) one evening when I saw the most astonishing thing. The sea was flat calm, the sun was going down, nearly gone, when I looked over the bow and saw on the horizon a great row of bright yellow diamonds appear in the sea, as if it were a necklace of bright yellow lights. As I was thinking of this, there was a series of loud reports, something like rifle fire; I called the Captain, as one was instructed to do if something unusual happened. He came immediately to the bridge and we watched as the diamonds disappeared, and then suddenly reappeared, as if we were in a cartoon film of some spectacular apparition. It was weird, a bit frightening. Then the rifle fire reports again. Then, it seemed, we reached what had previously been our horizon, and we watched, enthralled, as a dozen or so giant manta rays leaped out of the water all round us and landed again with great "Splat" noises leaving diamonds of bright phosphorescent light on the surface of the ocean. It was something I have never seen before, nor since. I felt really privileged to have seen it. It was something like communing with ancient spirits.

(It was at about that time, but not for that reason, that after considerable study and deliberation I had decided to abandon all man-made religions based on some sort of prophet capitalised upon by cliques of evangelists. "The fatherhood of God, the brotherhood of man, spirituality, and personal responsibility for what you do" appealed to me fine, and I joined the Spiritualist Church, which has been an inspiration to me ever since. Its seven Principles are so simple and straightforward).

Back to the naval base in Bahrein. The Ship's Company - officers and sailors - were serving on what was called a "Foreign Service Commission", that is to say that they were going to be abroad for a year and thus their wives and families were allowed to come out with them and take accommodation in the port where their husbands' ships were based. They then put their children in a local school (or in some cases, a British-run school), bought a car, opened accounts, and generally settled in just as one would in Portsmouth or any other naval base. We had now been given fourteen days' notice to get out and return to the UK. Imagine the upheaval! Children out of school, rental paid off, electricity bills sorted out along with gas bills and other necessities, flights home arranged, accommodation booked in UK for the families' return and so on almost ad infinitum. It was a heck of a shock but one entirely covered by the Naval mantra "If you can't take a joke, you shouldn't have joined". Or the other, more fatalistic one: "That's life in a blue suit".

One thing seemed less of a problem than the others; all these residential families had a car, of course. Not the huge Cadillac or Rolls Royce of the Sheiks, but a quite decent little car of sorts - to get to the shops and the necessary swimming pool and social facilities inside and outside the base (when one safely could). MESSINA was a tank landing ship, and as I said she could carry a huge load of vehicles. So we made arrangements for our cars to be put in the empty tank deck for the passage home so that they could be registered and used in the UK. Then came the second blow in the shape of a directive from the senior RAF officer: "We, the RAF, are responsible for the tri-service shipping of all goods back and forth from the UK to the Middle East and this means just what it says. We therefore require your deck space to return the important freight which we, the RAF, have ordained to be returned to the United Kingdom. You are to remove the private cars from your tank decks and allocate all the space to our Loadmasters." There was no reprieve, no flexibility, no option. Our senior officer was a Lieutenant Commander, the RAF senior officer was an Air Marshal, and that was that. So all our sailors had to offload their cars and sell them within two or three days. They didn't, of course, get much for them (the locals knew they had to sell them) and they were seething. But not as seething as when the RAF Loadmasters' "important freight" was brought down to the jetty to be loaded on to our ship. This load consisted not of technical RAF equipment, but of mainly duty free cars (because Inland Revenue rules stated that if you had a new motor vehicle outside the UK for six months you could bring it back and not pay any duty on it, and these RAF personnel could each buy two cars, ship one home and sell the other). Brand new. Of course, freight charges for a vehicle returned by sea were hugely expensive - but it was cheap if you could return it on board HMS MESSINA for free. All the RAF senior officers took advantage of this windfall, and we having offloaded all our own little private cars had to embark some twenty-four or thirty RAF officers' unused duty free Mercedes, BMWs, Audis, Rovers, Alfa Romeos - and one Maserati. They were all duly and efficiently strapped down in the tank deck, and we set sail for UK.

The trip back through the Red Sea was uneventful. But I remember the return passage through the Suez Canal for several reasons. Firstly, I wasn't standing on the bridge roof with no food doing penance for starsight misdemeanours. Secondly, showing the Port Authority official into the transverse gangway and his asking "Have you got rats on board?" as if any old ship hadn't, and then a huge "bang" right behind him as the Bos'n flattened a rat with a spade on the deck and his saying "Well, that's all right then". Just doing his job.

And then thirdly the Gully Gully men coming on board.

Gully Gully men come in a variety of guises. Unlike tailors, who will measure you at one end of the Canal and then deliver your suit at the other end, or the shoemakers, who can repair anything (we once gave one such a pair of brown shoelaces and told him they were a very worn out pair of size ten brogues - and received a beautiful pair of brown size ten brogues at the other end of the Canal) or Laundry Boys who will take as many shirts as you can give them (hoping to see some of them again). The Gully Gully men were magicians. They did all sorts of magic - spectacular grand feats and close up magic, but it was best not to have your wallet on you if they were doing the latter. Try as you could, it was impossible to see how they performed their tricks, and donations were usually generous on completion (except for those who couldn't find their wallet, of course).

Gully Gully Man watched by off duty crew members

The Tailors came on board with all sorts of samples and books of testimonials from previous "satisfied customers". These were invariably signed by current and previous members of the Board of Admiralty whether or not they had been anywhere near the Suez Canal as younger officers, but contained references (which the tailors professed not to be able to read) such as "Do not allow this man below decks; you will have nothing moveable left when he leaves" and "Weigh this tailor when he leaves; you will find that he is heavier" and (I presume this one was for merchant ships) "I hope you have no virgins on board; if you have, lock them away." And "This man's suits are atrocious, absolutely atrocious. I have told him, and he thinks "atrocious" means "wonderful" Signed "Admiral of the Fleet". Or "Winston Churchill". Or "Abraham Lincoln". It was wonderful reading in itself. But we bought trinkets, we enjoyed the magic, some bought jackets or ties or shoes, and everybody was happy.

We came out of the Suez Canal and turned left ("to port") to head westwards across the Mediterranean towards Gibraltar. The Mediterranean Sea may be an inland sea but it is larger than you may think and it can have some of the most ferocious storms anywhere, with perhaps the exception of Cape Horn. They can be quite devastating and even seasoned mariners have to be wary. It was unfortunate that we hit one of these violent storms a couple of days after leaving Alexandria, and even more unfortunate that because it was too dangerous to do so we were unable to get down into the tank deck to ensure that all the Mercedes's and BMW's and other brand new vehicles were still lashed down as securely as they had been when we sailed from Bahrein (knots and lashings tend to move and become less tight with time, and can become particularly less secure with movement, and they sometimes break completely). It was regrettable that our sailors had to watch from above as all these lovely duty free cars in the hold broke free of their strops in the rough weather and crashed from side to side into each other as the ship rolled, and then into the vehicle in front and the vehicle behind as the ship pitched. There was nothing we could do about it - it was too dangerous to access the area, and indeed the Captain had prohibited it (he had failed to sell his little Fiat, and had had to leave it on the jetty when we left, not, of course, that that had anything to do with it). We recorded in the ship's log that we had "endured a Mediterranean storm, but with sound naval precautions and good seamanlike practice, albeit at a cost to the cargo, the ship and its crew had survived intact."

We called at Gibraltar. It was a magical port at a time when commodities were sparse. The shops had watches and radios and stereograms such as we had never seen, and cheap cigars and tobacco. And of course the bars served alcohol at prices which we had never seen, either. But we all went to the top of the Rock and some of us visited the caves, and so on. But for Mike B-S and me it was crunch time: we had to take our "Midshipmans' Board" - a multi part oral test to ensure that we had learned sufficient to proceed to the next stage of training. It took the form of interrogation by a seamanship expert, a navigation specialist, a radio and communications specialist, a logistics specialist, a marine engineering specialist and a weapons specialist. And then a grilling from the Captain on anything under the sun to ensure that we were fit for continuation training. MESSINA had no weapons, so that bit of it was done away with. My first exam was with the communicator, and I did quite well. My next was with the navigator, and since I had already navigated MESSINA as a Watch Officer I also did quite well. The real problem came with the marine engineer, who wanted to know about the closed feed lubrication system: when I said with respect that I didn't know what he was talking about he asked bluntly "How are your engines lubricated?" and I said "Oh, I know that, Sir. The Leading Stoker gets a bucket of oil from the tub and chucks it into the engines." "My God!" he said "What sort of ship are you from?" "MESSINA, Sir" I said, "We have beautifully oiled engines and they never give any trouble, except sometimes when we go aground and they suck in sand". His apoplexy caused him to put a tick in the "First Class" box of the recording form. I was through.

After a bit of time in a UK minesweeper learning more officer of the watch duties it was September 1965 and time for all of us Midshipmen serving in the fleet to return to the Naval College at Dartmouth for a year of final academic training.

CHAPTER 4
Back at BRNC Dartmouth

The author ships his first stripe (1965),
with father, Leslie, and dog, Bess.

We now had a stripe, and we earned our pay by supervising the Cadets - and we learned all sorts of theoretical things which would advise our later decisions. Maths. Physics, Electronics, all that sort of thing. It was really an excuse for retaining all the schoolmasters who had become redundant when Dartmouth ceased to be a public school and became a naval establishment. Nonetheless, it was good stuff, good experience, and all that. We trained the new Cadets to the generally accepted naval standards.

Because I had failed Russian "O" level, the navy had no record of my ever having done it. So when I entered for the Russian Language course at BRNC I was already streaks ahead of the beginners. But I didn't say anything, and duly won the Russian Prize for academic study. I never thought that it would go any further, but it did. At the end of term we were all told to select a book prize from the table offered. My parents had come down to Dartmouth for the Passing Out Parade and I had spent the night with them in their hotel, not thinking that I might have broken my leave or even, technically, deserted. When I returned the following day there was a notice out for me to select my book prize. There wasn't much left, but there was a book called "Other Men's Flowers" by General Wavell, which he wrote and published at an appallingly difficult time of WW2 when he took his mind off the military problems by turning to poetry: "I have gathered a posy of other men's flowers, and naught but the thread that binds them is my own", he wrote.

It changed my life. Completely. Utterly. I took it to sea with me and read it and became completely enamoured of poets who could paint pictures with words. People with pens, like artists with brushes or composers with staves and clefs. I have committed most of the verses to memory and they served me well when times were glum.

CHAPTER 5
Fourth Year Courses

Our basic training was over, after three years. We logistics tyros then had to do six months' training in all of the different specialities such as Gunnery, Anti-submarine warfare, Communications and Encryption, Aviation, Submarines, and various sorts of Engineering. We were to be General List Officers. But because we were logistics specialists we then had to go to HMS PEMBROKE, a shore establishment in Chatham, to complete our professional training. Before that, at the NBCD School (Nuclear, Bacteriological and Chemical Defence) we learned how to protect ourselves against all forms of attack. But they also had a "Unit" for practical training. This was a large, steel cubicle built to represent a compartment on a ship, and we were put inside it, not knowing what was going to happen. What we did not know, too, was that that the whole edifice was on gimbals so that it could rock from side to side, back and forth or up and down. Or that it was "rigged"; it had holes in its sides to represent shell hole damage, and it had broken electrical wires which would spark like hell, and it was able to start its own fires. So there we were, ordered to stop the ship sinking as water was pumped in up to our waists. We started to plug the holes, but then the fires started, the electricity started to spark and the lights went out. We seemed doomed. But as a morale booster I had smuggled my set of bagpipes into the unit under my tarpaulin suit and as the storm rose to its worst and the fires spread and the water deepened I got out my pipes and played "Scotland the Brave" and other stirring tunes. The result was electrifying. Not only did the morale boost inspire the others to greater feats of heroism (and self preservation) but also the training crew, who had never heard this before, sent for the Captain and Commander to come and listen and we were all turfed out with (a) a strict warning not to be frivolous and (b) a commendation for our morale and for sorting out the posed problem. We were through with flying colours.

In ship-preservation classes we were told about heavily damaged ships which had succeeded in returning to port, and it was most edifying. We had a lesson on wooden plugs from an ex-Chief Shipwright, who was an expert on stopping ships from sinking and indeed had done so in WW2. He was avid about plugging holes, which might sound naff but of course is actually crucial.

He talked to us about wood. "The woods what we use in the Navy are Hoak, Hash and Helm. Hoak is a dense wood what has a weight of forty-two pounds per cubic foot and is used for upper deck fittings."

"Excuse me, Chief," said a languid upper crust voice from the back of the classroom, "Don't you mean "eoak"?

"That's right, Sir" said the Shipwright, "Hoak" "Now the next wood is Hash. Hash 'as a very straight grain and is used for splints and strakes."

"Excuse me, Chief," said the same voice, "Don't you mean "eash"?"

"That's right, Sir" said the tolerant and patient voice of the Shipwright. "Hash".

"Now the third kind of wood what we use in the Navy is Helm, which is principally used for making piles for piers, and before the gentleman at the back corrects me I want to make it clear that when I talk about "piles in piers" I am not talking about 'aemerroids in the harseholes of the haribloodystocracy".

We went on from there to the naval station at Portland to learn about computers, which were just coming in. It was interesting. Just about. But we were there over Easter, and there wasn't much to do during our evenings off. Then one of our course, reading the Weymouth Gazette, or whatever it's called, said "Hey, there's an advert here for ballet lessons, first lesson free!". An offer not to be ignored by twenty or so red-blooded young men, and so we all signed up. We put on our best parade boots and tried our hardest to look like Nijinski for an hour or so. It didn't work, but we didn't half pull some birds.

At HMS PEMBROKE, we did all the boring stuff in the classroom, like learning how to do pay sheets, learning how stores were accounted for, learning about supply chains and so on. Some of it was quite interesting: we learned how to do emergency catering ashore for devastated communities - say after a tsunami or other disaster - and how to get oil drums cut in half to make cookers, and how to make vegetables fit for eating; and of course how to account for it all. We did a "practical" in the dockyard and made two hundred pasties, which went to the dining hall to be eaten afterwards. Then, having 10lbs of pastry left over, we made a solid pastry pork pie (no pork, nothing else) and sent it to the Wardroom for consumption. It looked beautiful - glazed and shiny - but it was just a lump of dough, and brought much surprise.

The staff at Chatham were actually wonderful; very understanding and tolerant. They were mostly ex-RN people, most of whom had been through the war and were therefore unfazed by minor details. Such as when the young officers came back at 03.00 from a party and were then woken by the screeching peacocks on the lawn outside at 04.00 and went out and wrang (wrung?) their necks.

During the course, we went to the Army Catering School at Aldershot to see how they do it. It is the only British catering organisation, perhaps the only one in the world, which takes food from the field to the plate - that is to say they have their own cattle, their own abattoir, their own butcheries and their own caterers and chefs. We had been invited for an abattoir visit. But Army hospitality being what it is, we were invited to arrive p.m., get settled in, then attend a formal mess dinner. The abattoir visit was the following morning. We were wined and dined well into the night and then staggered off to bed. After about three hours' sleep we were woken, put in a bus and taken to the abattoir, where within minutes we were watching poor cattle being stunned, having a shot put through their heads, and then being bled over a trough before being taken away to be butchered. Not good for a post-prandial stomach. But we survived.

The officer in charge of the abattoir, incidentally, was a keen vegetable gardener; he drove a VW Beetle and used to take home from time to time a bucket of blood (very good for the tomatoes) covered in clingfilm and wedged under the bonnet of his VW Beetle (which of course was at the front). One day, going through Aldershot at about 10 mph in the traffic he was in collision with another vehicle. Only a bump and a scratch on the front wing, and the other car likewise, but his bonnet sprang open and spewed a gallon or so of blood all over the road. When the police arrived, they found two broken headlights, two unharmed people and a road awash with blood. I'd love to have seen their report.

Extra-curricularly, we had a lot of fun. Sometimes we went to a "Grab a Granny" dance at the "Nite Life Club" (sic) in Gillingham where we were to dance to the enchanting music of Herbie Goins and the Nightimers. The Nightimers were not very good, and Herbie Goins never made it to the top hundred either, but there were two things of interest. I danced with a hopeful granny in a strapless, backless evening gown, and in order to get some sort of a conversation started (you could still talk to your dancing partner in those days, as they were in your arms) I said "I do like your make-up, it's very pretty, and I can feel that you've got make-up all down your back, as well."

"Nah." She said "I work in a chippie".

The other thing of much more import was that we somewhat impecunious young officers, who shared double (or quadruple) rooms in the Mess had nowhere to take our girlfriends when we had wined and dined them. So some genius decided we should open a Mess account in the fictitious name of H. Goins (see above), Sub Lieutenant. He was allegedly a young hydrographic officer from one of the hydrographic survey ships in the port, and was thus always in an out of the Naval Base and the wardroom mess, and nobody could say where he really was. But being an officer (not on course) he was allocated his own cabin. Of course, he did not exist, but from time to time each of us would go into his cabin early and rough up the bed and put some toothpaste on the washbasin and we left items of clothing around as well. So any young blade who wished to entertain a young lady late could use the cabin, for whatever. The scheme went swimmingly until there was a big problem. Somebody used "Herbie Goins'" mess number to buy a drink at the bar, and then forgot to settle the monthly account. Sub Lieutenant Goins was sent for by the Commander to account for his failure to pay his messbill and of course since he didn't exist he didn't turn up. There was a huge Hoo-Hah and we were all invited to pay the penance. But we survived the training and we were all given a Commission and sent to sea. A scrape or two. An escape or two.

Now, when I say "Given a Commission" it is a misnomer. The last time I knowingly used this expression was fifty-five years later when I went to the funeral of an older naval colleague who had spent his last years in the Service working with the Royal Marines. There were three splendid RM Sergeants at the funeral, and we were talking afterwards. When I used the above expression they were horrified. "No," they said. "You weren't given a commission, you earned it." Surprisingly, I had never thought of it like that. (Because all Royal Marines, of whatever rank, can run fast, climb quickly, shoot well and endure all sorts of privations. Their Powers That Be decreed that they should all undergo the same basic training in footslogging and lifting heavy weights and shooting things, but the officer trainees had to achieve a 10% better rate at everything than the marine trainees: so if an endurance course had to be completed in sixty minutes, the officer trainees had to do it in about fifty minutes or so. And so on. The system worked, and as far as I know, still works.) I suppose that after four years of being judged at every stage I really did "earn" my commission. I just never thought about it like that.

The author at home on leave before going back to sea

CHAPTER 6
First commission at sea

The next thing that happened was that we all received details of our next appointments - our first commission - including travel details. Mine were to report to HMS AJAX in Singapore and take over as Squadron Secretary to the Second Destroyer Squadron, Far East Fleet. At that time, there were sixteen RN frigates and destroyers in the Far East based in Singapore - more than the whole Royal Navy has in operation now. I took over from another young officer and settled into my cabin and my office on board and thought "I haven't a clue what I'm doing". The Captain, who was in charge of not only the ship but the whole Destroyer Squadron was a splendid man called George Kitchin - George Armand de Gavardie Kitchin. He had been through the war and had already commanded four other ships, so he was what people would nowadays call "laid back" - but nonetheless very competent, and an excellent leader of men; the ship's company would do anything for him. This is an interesting concept; he was the Captain, so in fact everybody had to do everything he said. But he was such a good leader that everyone wanted go that extra mile without being asked.

I joined early in September 1967. Our new doctor, straight from medical school and a few weeks' induction training on how to wear a uniform and whom to salute and who was responsible to whom, joined the day after I did. Two days later, we sailed for the Java Straits and a patrol round the Indonesian Islands - which was to be delayed. Within two days of sailing we received a "Flash" message. (Naval messages are divided into security categories, and in importance from "Routine" through "Priority" to "Flash" - which means "Drop everything else). An RAF Shackleton aircraft (they looked just like Lancaster bombers) en route from UK to Singapore had ditched in the Straits of Java and we had to go and assist. This was jolly exciting to someone three days into his first job and just out of school and training, to think that we were going to rescue people, but it was not to feel like that afterwards. We sped towards the site of the crash. We arrived in good light and the first thing we saw was liferafts bobbing about on the surface of the sea. We were optimistic. But the first two liferafts were completely empty. The third contained two crashed airmen: one was quite severely injured, the other literally just had a scratched cheek. We got them on board and in true naval tradition gave the fit one a tot of rum. The doctor was less sanguine about the other. He ordered a message be sent to the nearest UK base saying "Send blood serum and all other necessaries" and took the seriously injured airman to the sick bay. Within a few hours two things had happened: first was that an aeroplane had appeared out of the sky and parachuted down blood serum and other medical things necessary for the man's survival. Good. The doctor laboured without a break for forty-eight hours and undoubtedly saved the airman's life. The second was not good. The man on upper deck watch shouted that he had seen something in his binoculars and it looked like another airman floating in a Mae West near the horizon. We put on full speed and went to pick him up. As we approached, all watching over the ship's side, it became clear that it was indeed a British airman in a Mae West, but he looked unconscious so we lowered a man on a davit to put a rescue hook on his lifejacket and pull him up. As the winch started and he was pulled out of the water several onlookers retched or were actually sick - we had pulled out a head and shoulders and some chest but not much else except dangling entrails - he had given a shark a nice meal not long previously.

We did what we could, and everything was done reverently. But the (half) corpse had to go into the huge fridge which also held our food. Well wrapped up, of course. The Chinese laundrymen stopped eating. (Each ship had its own crew of Chinese laundrymen from Hong Kong, and very good they were. Bigger ships had a Chinese tailor as well, and the messdeck joke was that the tailor paid the laundrymen to smash the shorts buttons so he could supply new ones and sew them on). They were very superstitious, or religious, take your choice, and wouldn't eat anything from the fridges. So we returned to Singapore, dropped off the airmen and such evidence as we had, firecrackered the fridges to get rid of the spirits, and returned to our patrol. We had to go North. To the Hong Kong area. At that time Chairman Mao was wielding influence, purges were taking place in China, and there was a great threat to Hong Kong, a British territory, by Chinese invasion. So it was important to maintain an RN fleet there, and on shore, to have a lot of British troops, including the Gurkhas. We carried out our flag-showing patrol for a few days, and then berthed in HMS TAMAR, the RN base right in the centre of Victoria, the capital of HK. Opposite Kowloon, the landward side of the province, and right underneath the Peak, as it was called - the mountain which rose out of the sea on Hong Kong Island. TAMAR was surrounded by city, and by high-rise blocks, although at that time there were only two actual skyscrapers. The Mandarin Hotel and the Hong Kong Hilton. The whole of the naval base could be seen from all over the Peak, especially when the ships were floodlit, as they were on public holidays and when it was important at other times to do so. To floodlight, you hang booms over the side of the ship with powerful lights on, shining inwards towards the ship. The whole ship is bathed in light, and every detail can be seen for miles around. A real appearance and show of power. Thus it was on Wednesday September 27th,1967, a date forever etched on my heart and mind. I was twenty-one.

I had been on board for just a few weeks. It was my first ship as a qualified officer. We were alongside in a British dockyard contained within a British naval base, in a British territory. We could not have been more secure. What could go wrong?

What went wrong (for me) was that I was selected to be the duty officer. The only duty officer. It was my first time. For real, not training. And because Hong Kong is so beguiling, the vast majority of the ship's company had gone ashore, leaving me alone in charge of a warship and two hundred and fifty men. No problem. What? The only thing to disturb the peace was that it was reported to me that a sailor had been drinking too much. So I sent for him and for the Leading Seaman of his mess, and spoke to them both, as per rules. It was apparent that the sailor had been drinking, but he was certainly not yet drunk and so I put him in the charge of his Leading Seaman not to drink any more and to see that he got into his bunk at "Lights out". So far, so good. This we had been taught at Dartmouth. A light touch unless a sailor was actually drunk, in which case - Jankers. Some hour later, when I did evening "rounds" (an inspection of the living quarters of the ship), I visited all the communal spaces and all the messdecks to receive reports that all was well and to satisfy myself that this was so. It is a tried and tested procedure which has been going on almost forever. It is formal and serious. And it ensures good order and naval discipline. And when it is over everyone can relax. Half way through rounds, there was a "pipe" over the main broadcast, throughout the ship: "Officer of the Day requested to come to the gangway". Even I, the newby, knew that this was unusual - and it should not have happened. So I ignored it, and made a mental note to have a word with them not to interfere with Rounds. One minute later, there was a double volume explosion on the main broadcast "Officer of the Day, Gangway, Now!" This was tantamount to a sailor giving an order to an officer, so I knew something really serious was wrong. Indeed it was. I could hardly have been more correct. I sped to the upper deck to find the duty crew mustered by the gangway, pointing upwards. They couldn't speak, just point. They were shivering, shaking. I looked up. There, hanging by his neck from the ship's yardarm, fully floodlit and in clear sight of every single person in Hong Kong on that side of the peak, was the sailor whom I had formally certified and recorded as "having been drinking, but not drunk". Just as in cowboy films, he hung limp, with his head to one side. While I was rapidly thinking and planning, my duty Petty Officer, a very experienced man who was going through the selection to see if he could become an officer, without instruction or hesitation, ran to the ship's mast (which was hollow), climbed up inside, as had the sailor, edged out along the yardarm with a rope with a lasso loop on it, lowered it over the suspended body, drew it up around his armpits, hoisted him up a bit, cut the rope by which his neck was hanging, and lowered him to the deck - with enormous difficulty because he had to take the whole strain himself. He had achieved astonishing, adrenalin charged, reserves of strength, and had succeeded. While he was doing this, I had called the ambulance and the police, and the duty naval base people, and turned off the floodlights, and started a general recall. He was given CPR and mouth-to-mouth. The ambulance then took the man away, and order was restored. The whole ship's company came back on board. I spent the whole night taking statements and having them witnessed.

The sad start to this event was that it was the sailor in question's 21st birthday that day. He had not received any recognition of this milestone in his life; his estranged father had not sent any communication at all and his only other relative in the world, his mother, had not sent (or caused to be received) a twenty-first birthday card. He had, quite simply, decided that nobody loved him and had decided to end it all.

There was, of course, a full and formal Board of Enquiry. This established beyond doubt that to shin up the inside of a ship's mast and then climb out along a wet and slippery yardarm with a coil of rope and attach it as he had, in precarious conditions and in drizzle, could not have been done by anyone who was drunk - they would simply have fallen at some stage or another. So I was exonerated from any blame. Indeed, commended for the action we took. The Petty Officer became an officer very quickly, having become famous for his daring feat, and the only worrying feature of the whole sad event is that to this day I do not know how long the hanging man's brain had been without oxygen and whether it was kindness to save his life or not; neither do I know where he had been taken to, or what his state of life was thereafter.

HMS TAMAR was a wonderful base, with all facilities, professional, personal and recreational. It had its own swimming pools, as had HMS TERROR in Singapore, and its own clubs for the various ranks. My abiding memory was of one traditional competition which took place in the officers' swimming pool every so often: a bicycle race from the shallow end to the deep end. Easy at first, more difficult later. I don't think I need to say more.

Later, back in Singapore we had a few days' rest and recreation. We were sitting in the Wardroom mess one evening when one officer, Francis-Jones, started to slag off another's car. "It's a heap" he said. "You're lucky it gets you from your home to the dockyard, let alone anywhere else". The owner, Dibble, protested that it was a Humber Hawk, the finest example of British engineering, and it would go on for ever. "I bet you," someone said, "It wouldn't get as far as KL without breaking down". "It would get to Thailand and back without breaking down." said its owner. "I'll bet you a bottle of Dom Perignon it wouldn't" said another. "Now" said a third. So the bet was laid, and the bet was accepted. That the old Humber Hawk would get to the Thai border and back by midnight the following day. The Captain was called from his slumbers to witness the bet, we all had a gin and tonic or a Horse's Neck or two until midnight, and then the intrepid two (owner and collaborator) set off from Singapore dockyard to get to the Thai border in the Humber Hawk, and back again. They did it, and got their passports stamped accordingly, to the surprise of the border police who saw them just turn round and come back again. But they did it.

In the meanwhile the Captain, George A de G Kitchin, was relishing his invitation to the Wardroom. Traditionally, the Captain has his own "mess" and is not a member of the Wardroom and can therefore only enter it by invitation. He had been given that invitation, and so proceeded to entertain us by introducing us to the "Brummel". You have a glass of brandy ready, then you heat up a glass of kummel (liqueur) and set fire to it, then pour the flaming kummel into the brandy and drink it. If you are quick, it doesn't hurt at all. If you hesitate half way through you have lips on fire and if you have a beard you have a beard on fire as well. A real test of manliness. Only men would believe this; women would think it completely silly. Hmm. Make your own mind up.

Our next task was to participate in the withdrawal from Aden which at that time was a "Protectorate" which had become a hotbed of violence and mayhem as opposing tribes and factions fought for control but joined together in wanting the British out so that they could impose their own rules – of benefit to themselves, of course.

Incidentally, the term "Protectorate" invokes a statistic which not many people today, Brits included, know: that of the one hundred and ninety-three sovereign nations acknowledged to exist by the United Nations, one hundred and seventy-seven of them have at some time been owned by, ruled by, invaded by, lost a war to, been conquered by or had had some form of mandate imposed over by, or been legally subservient to in some way or other, or part of, England or Great Britain. One hundred and seventy-seven out of one hundred and ninety-three. Just think about it.

However, in this case, the warring factions were trying to try to win this three-way battle. In the meanwhile the British Government had decided that enough was enough and we were going to pull out, in as orderly a way as we could. We tied up alongside for a while, and a group of us were invited to the Army Officers' Mess in the hillside camp for dinner before we got down to the serious work of withdrawal on the morrow. We were picked up by armoured Landrover and driven through the city and then off to the base. Now, sailors make fun of the bewilderment of soldiers when they are on their ships, and I got a taste of the reverse: our army officer escort was quite relaxed, as was the driver, but I must admit I was quite disturbed by the explosions I heard en route to the camp, and the sound of what was quite clearly powerful rifles. Not to mention the "crump" of the odd mortar discharge. They took it in their stride, delivered us to our destination, and then waited to take us back again. In the Mess, sweltering in our white tropical mess jackets, we were well entertained and finely dined, and when we drank the Loyal Toast it was quite moving to hear the Colonel say "Gentlemen, that is probably the last time a Brit soldier will ever toast Her Majesty in this country."

We returned in the same Landrover. The mortars were still bashing away and the bullets were still flying, and we RN officers ducked down in the back while the Army chaps drove blithely on as if it were a bit of pother at Wimbledon, or outside Lords.

The 2nd Frigate Squadron, Far East Fleet, with its anti-submarine helicopters 1967

The next day we escorted hordes of landing craft and Royal Fleet Auxiliaries as they took loads from the British bases on shore, made on-the-spot decisions about what was reusable and what wasn't, stored the "reusables" in their holds and simply threw the remaining items over the side into the deep ocean: lorries, radio stations, kitchens, sports equipment, safes, whole office suites, the lot - it was all taken and either saved or ditched. It was a salutary lesson in not aiding the enemy - as the call it what you want had become. We were getting out, and that was that. But to see a nice Vauxhall being chucked over the side was a bit galling. Not our business.

Servicemen are paid to obey political orders. Not a lot of people know that - or even think about it, which perhaps they should.

Withdrawal from Aden 1967

Then we had a long passage South across the Indian Ocean to get to our patrol. It was called the Beira patrol. It was highly political. Ian Smith and his government in Rhodesia had declared UDI (Unilateral Declaration of Independence) and the British government did not like it. So they put an embargo on the import of all goods into and out of Rhodesia, which by sea had to be through the port of Beira in Mozambique. (Sufficient quantities for any whole country can never be delivered by air; it is significant, for example, that for the United Kingdom 96% of everything that is imported or exported travels by sea, hence why we need a Royal Navy.) But before we started the patrol we had a break, a few days rest and relaxation, in the port of Mombasa, which at that time was extremely beautiful, well ordered, with lots of flower beds surrounding very clean open squares and completely safe and law abiding. We were there for about seven days. Unbeknown to me, the captain had a sister and brother in law living in Kenya. They were called Hunter. They owned and ran Hunters Lodge in the Tsavo Game Park. The captain asked me to fix him up with a

Landrover and get the steward to fill it up with provisions and gin, to be ready the following morning so that he could go and see them. This I did, of course. When I reported to the captain that all was ready he just looked at me and said "Aren't you coming?" He was teasing me. This had been his plan all along - teach the young officer about life abroad. I had ten minutes to pack, and then we were off. We drove up the main highway out of Mombasa and towards Nairobi, and then turned off to go to Hunters Lodge, where we were given the most wonderful welcome. We ate and dined well, and then slept well. The next morning we re-packed the Landrover and set off to look at the wildlife. We had been sent in the right direction, of course. Once, when Father (as good captains are affectionately called) was driving I was standing at the back with my binoculars looking behind us when the Landrover stopped. "See anything?" he said. "No" said I. "Look out the front" he said. Our way was blocked by a mother elephant and a junior, at a range of about twenty yards. There were also several giraffes looking on. It was real wildlife, and I had nearly missed it. We also came very close to hippos at the water hole (which we had been advised to avoid because they are more unpredictable and dangerous than most other animals) and rhinos staggering about on our track. It was a wonderful experience, all the better for not being an "organised tour". We watched the zebra coming into the watering hole outside Hunters Lodge as we sipped our evening drinks, and retired to peaceful slumber. On our last morning Father wanted to check that all was well on board his ship, so at a village on the way back we stopped and made a phone call. The operator called and said "I can't get through. What number should I tell them to call back to?" The owner of the 'phone gave us his telephone number. Makindu 3. I've never forgotten it. Must ring it some day to see what happens!

The other thing I remember about Mombasa was that one day I was duty shore officer (as opposed to duty onboard officer) with the shore patrol and we were called to an affray at the Nyali Beach Hotel where a stripper from Wigan had been entertaining the guests dressed only in a large snake when one of our Stokers had climbed on to the stage, snatched the snake, and tied a big knot in it. He had been hauled off, and it was my duty to get him back on board, which I did. With a straight face. Difficult, bearing in mind she was from Wigan.

We had time to spare on our passage across the Indian Ocean. So, in accordance with the true customs of the RN we stopped when we came to our first "desert island", dropped anchor for the afternoon and had a banyan. A "banyan" just means a beach party. So you find a palm tree fronted tropical island and go ashore with BBQ equipment and all ranks enjoy a good relaxing, beach party, and swim. It was wonderful. We took the large half-drum fires ashore, together with all the ingredients needed for a barbecue, everyone took their beer ration ashore, and we all enjoyed ourselves. Except for the Supply Officer, one Jake Francis-Jones, more of whom later, who at that time was a Lieutenant. We all took KFS ashore with us (knives, forks and spoons) and had a brilliant time. We then ate our BBQ food and drank our beer and returned on board. The only problem was that the KFS tended not to come back. It belonged to the government, so it wasn't important. This drove the Supply Officer potty, because there was a ration. So he got the Welfare Committee (the ship's voluntary fund) to buy plastic KFS. The next time we had a banyan ashore, all the plastic KFS was brought back on board. This taught me a valuable lesson: if something is given to you for free, people abuse it. If they have to contribute to its cost they care about it passionately. Think on, NHS.

Back to the Indian Ocean. We had this wonderful banyan and then sailed westwards towards Beira. On the way we stopped at the Farquhar Islands. These are small islands off the Seychelles, where islanders grew and cultivated and cut and stored just coconuts - nothing else. They came from the Seychelles, stayed for six months, and then returned. We anchored off, sent boats ashore, and offered them things we thought they might be short of - tea and coffee, sticking plasters and bandages and other "comforts". In return, they said they would give us a suckling pig. After a while, a canoe came out and offloaded on to us the said suckling pig. It was still alive. So we had a problem. The Bos'n said he would resolve it by shooting it in the mortar well deck - an enclosed area near the stern. So he armed himself with a wardroom pistol and approached the young pig. Which did not want to be looked at, let alone be shot. But it couldn't get out of the well deck, and so we all crouched around the lip of this deck and we heard a bang, then "Bugger. Missed." Then another bang and "Bugger, missed". And with the third shot, the ricocheting bullets having flown all around us, he got it. I have to say, it was delicious.

The other interesting thing about the Farquhar Islands, which I have never seen anywhere else in the world, was that we anchored off in completely calm weather and water, but when I later stood looking over the ship's side into the beautifully clear water I discerned that I could see the ocean bottom in great detail - coral and crabs and starfish et al. Then, to my horror, there seemed to be a volcanic eruption right underneath us - the seabed was coming up towards us at a slow but steady rate. I thought that we were about to be evaporated by a volcano, and was just about to run to the bridge to alert them when the seabed slowly started to go down again. I was gobsmacked. But the explanation was simple. It wasn't the seabed which was moving - it was us. There was a huge swell across the ocean - very slow and with a long period but some twenty feet high and we were simply rising and falling on the water. We took up the anchor and sailed on.

In his routine report to the Admiralty at the end of the month the captain was constrained to say, having misidentified the head of the Farquhar Island natives, "He wore nothing to show that he was their leader". I hope Their Lordships understood.

We were going to the part of the Indian Ocean off the port of Beira, through which all goods had to go to get to Rhodesia. We had to blockade it.

We were to take over from HMS MINERVA on Beira patrol,

and she was due to return home. In the leisure hours before we joined them, another young officer called Quentin Banting and I dreamed up a spoof, which was a huge success. We announced that there would be an "Inter-ship Quiz" over the radio, with teams of four answering general knowledge questions, put out over the ship's tannoys. Our question master was to be me, and HMS MINERVA's question master was to be their Padre (who didn't exist, because neither did our radio link with HMS MINERVA - it was all a spoof). We had a prearranged script, with "Q" at one end of the radio room with a voice changer and me at the other and the whole thing was going out on our ship's internal broadcast, which it did at recreation time one evening. First I asked a (fictitious) member of the AJAX team a question so complicated that no-one could have answered it, and then the "MINERVA Padre" asked one of their team a very simple question which "he" got right. Then I asked "our team" the value to "Pi" to four significant places and "he" said "3.1411" and I said "No, I'm afraid that since the next digit is 9 it has to be rounded up to 3.1412. So no points there". And the "MINERVA Padre" asked "What is the speed of light". The answer from "Junior Seaman Smith" was "100,000 miles per second" and their "Padre" said "No, actually it's 186,000 miles per second but that was a very good try and you're very young so I'll give you the point". And so on. By this time, the messdecks of HMS AJAX were heaving with indignant sailors about the bias and iniquity of this intership quiz, and what they were going to say to that bloody Padre when they met him and there was almost but not quite a riot. It took our Officer of the Watch to come on the broadcast and tell people it was all a spoof, while Q and I retired to somewhere safe for a while.

We moved on from there, closing Beira to take over from the real HMS MINERVA. It was March and near the end of the MOD financial year. We had several mortar bombs and one depth charge to use up before the end of the financial year, so we went fishing. Strictly team practice, you understand. It had to be done to train the crews and keep them up to date. Off the African coast, we fired a circle of Mortar Mark 6 bombs, each containing some 600lbs of Amatol, and our helicopter dropped his remaining depth charge into the middle of the circle. The explosions were enormous. We expected to get at least some very large fish for the galley, but nothing happened. Great blast, but no fish. Why? We waited and waited and then after about an hour and were just about to go when a large patch of the sea turned golden - thousands of golden fish. Raised to the surface very slowly as they achieved positive buoyancy. We hoisted in basketsful, because the Chief Cook proclaimed that he had an infallible method of telling whether things from the sea were poisonous or not - which was to fry them in a pan with a silver sixpenny piece in it - if it turned black, there was poison. He said. I didn't say anything. I just waited until several other people had eaten the fish. They were actually delicious.

There was another four or five days in East African waters. It was a very peaceful passage - not a single ship on the horizon, and indeed we had not seen another ship for over a week. We all got on with our administrative work. One evening after dinner the Captain sent for me. This was unusual, and I wondered what was up. "Alan" he said, "I want you to type a memorandum and deliver it to the Master at Arms" (the ship's most senior rating). I was about to say that I would get the typist to do it straight away when a saw a smile on his lips. He handed me a handwritten piece of paper which of course I read. It said "To Master at Arms. 09.00 Tuesday. For exercise, for exercise, for exercise, all the officers on board including me have eaten some fish which has turned out to be poisonous. We are all dead. You are to take over." "SAFEGUARD: I will be on the bridge just in case, but for the purposes of this exercise I am "dead" and you cannot ask me any questions. Exercise ends in twenty-four hours exactly".

Next morning was one of the most interesting I have experienced. The memo was duly delivered, by me, and the Master at Arms said "Is this serious, Sir? What have we got to do?" and I replied "I don't know. I'm dead. You are in sole charge of the ship". And he said "Bloody Hell!" But to his credit, he got all the senior Chief Petty Officers gathered

together and sorted out who was to do what, and who was in charge of what, and what he wanted to be told about and what he wanted to be asked about and so on - which, if you think about it is what any good Captain or indeed any good leader would do. I retired to my cabin to write some reports in complete peace, then to have a coffee, then to do a crossword before lunch. At about 10.00 (i.e. 10 o'clock) our Chief Petty Officer Storeman knocked on my cabin door and said "Sir, the daily rum issue. It's got to be properly supervised - we can't risk anything going wrong, and you're the Duty Officer." and I said "Sorry, Chief, I'm dead. You're in charge of that". And he said "Bloody Hell!" and departed to get on with it in the highly professional way that I knew he would. It was the same for all us officers: we had to face the acceptance that our highly skilled senior ratings would perform in the way that was expected of them, and give them licence to do so, and they had to accept that responsibility was both onerous and important and that duty required a proper outcome. It was without doubt the most successful man-management exercise I have ever seen, before or since. And we all - top to bottom - learned even more respect for each other than we already had. There were a few hairy moments, such as when a signal in French came in and they couldn't find anyone to understand it, but they got round the problem well; and I have to say that not one single drop of rum was allowed to pass out of the rum store without the most rigorous scrutiny there has ever been, nor was a single drop "spilt", as it so often had been.
.

Soon, we took over the Beira Patrol from HMS MINERVA and settled into a quiet routine of sailing up and down the coast to ensure that no illicit goods bound for Rhodesia could enter or leave the port. I will not comment upon whether this was right or wrong, I will merely say that we succeeded completely. But it was a very boring routine and we went to great efforts to relieve the tedium. We had our own quizzes, we had kite-flying competitions, we played deck hockey, and deck cricket with the ball on a string, and sometimes we swam (it was an amazing feeling to be over the side in the Indian Ocean swimming just for pleasure, and an interesting one to know that the nearest land was just a mile away - that is to say 5,280 feet away - downwards.) A bit different from the deep end of a swimming pool. But we did have a Lifeguard; he sat on top of the bridge with a high-powered rifle just in case some nasty sea creature arrived, and he had a whistle. In all my days I had heard such blown only once - and to behold the speed with which a hundred men or so got out of the water and up the ladders was astonishing!

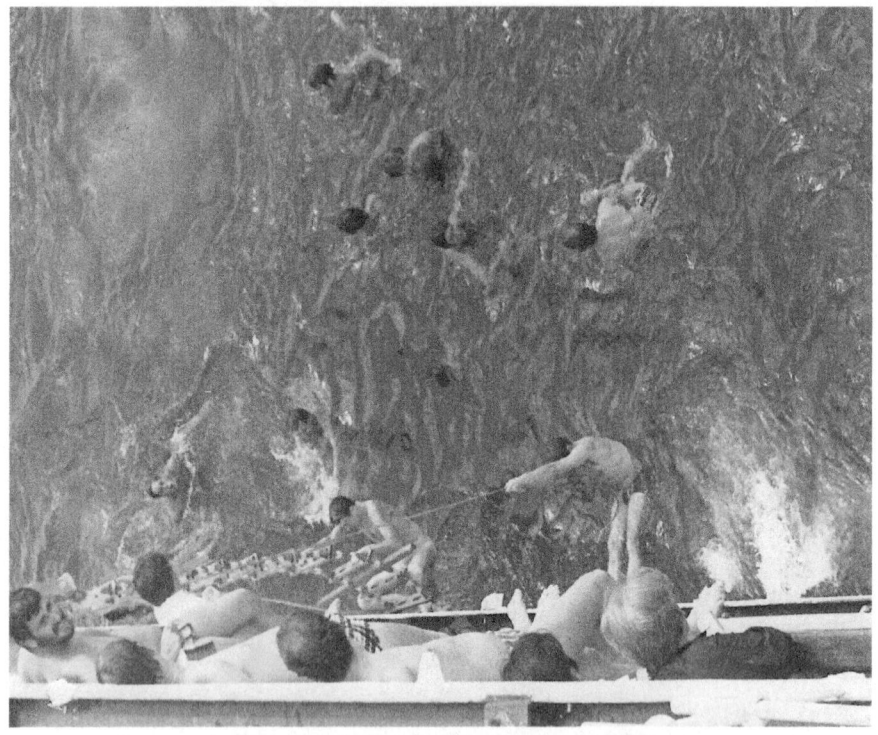

"Hands to Bathe", off Beira, 1967

The other thing we did was to have a "Sod's Opera". Perhaps I should explain. By tradition, this is a sort of outdoor Music Hall/Variety Show type event, with a stage rigged on the aftermost deck and rows of seating in which sit, in true naval tradition, the Officers in the front row, including the Captain, then behind them the Chief Petty Officers, the Petty Officers, the Leading Hands and so on. It is also tradition that "anything goes" and it is permissible for anyone to poke fun at anyone else on the grounds that the following day it will all be history. Danger apart, almost anything can happen. It takes place in late evening after dinner and supper. People will have taken drinks, but do not bring drinks.

Perhaps the most important requisite is the compère. By mutual consent the HMS AJAX compère was a Petty Officer Electrician called ....I don't know what; he was one of those most unusual people in a disciplined service who was just called one name by everyone of all ranks. Ours was just called "Angel". Because it was the name under which he entered wrestling competitions when he was back in UK and ashore and trying to earn some extra money. He was a big softie, really, and wouldn't harm a fly; he used to tell us that when he was home on leave his wife and her big family would dump all their multitude of children on him and go off clubbing in Portsmouth and the only way he could control the children was by dipping their fingers in syrup and then slitting a pillow and sticking their hands in, so that they spent hours trying to get the feathers off. But he was an accomplished wrestler, even if it was all fixed. He was also an accomplished raconteur and compère.

I hope I have set the scene. Indian Ocean sun going down, lights on, all seated in rows expecting great things. And one always got great things. There were songs about what certain officers should have done yesterday, and skits on naval traditions including a most moving but also hilarious "Death of Nelson", spoof weather forecasts, drunk acts, clog dances, cutlass swinging acts, everything you could think of. (As an aside, I have to record that most of these acts were quite lewd. Also that it is quite astonishing how much female attire, particularly of the underwear nature, that there is on board an all-male warship. Ah, Well. Helps to pass the time, as they say). As compère, Angel was magnificent. In the gaps between acts he told jokes, made innuendos and kept everyone attentive while the next act was prepared behind the arras. He also did magic tricks, at which he was quite good.

Unfortunately on this occasion, one of our more gobby ODs (OrDinary Seamen) had overcelebrated his birthday, and after nearly every trick by Angel he would call out, or rather slur out, from his seat at the back: "Seen it. It was up his sleeve" or some such. Angel waited patiently. He was a patient man, and put up with quite a lot of it. Most of us were finding it rather tedious and wondering what to do about it without either creating a major incident or destroying the ambience. Angel did it for us. After a rather good juggling act he stood in front of the curtain so that the next act couldn't get out and announced that he was going to do the most difficult magical trick in the history of the craft. He had done his homework. He knew that his victim would volunteer himself. "I am going to ask a member of the audience to give me his watch, put it in this velvet bag, and smash it to smithereens with this hammer," he said. "Then I am going to say the magic word "Abracadabra" and reconstitute the owner's watch magically for him". We had a suspicion we knew what was coming. "But I do have to say, in all fairness," said Angel, "That sometimes this trick does not work". Tension was building. Some of us, those who could see what was going to happen, had to stuff handkerchiefs into our mouths and bite on them to keep quiet. Then from the back: "I got a watch. Seiko. New in Singapore. One hundred dollars. You can have it. I know wot you're going to do. You got another one 'idden somew'ere. 'Ere" and our OD stumbled to the front, taking his new watch off. The next few seconds flew by. Angel took the watch, put it in his velvet bag and smashed it to smithereens on the steel deck and poured out all the cogwheels and broken glass and twisted metal into the OD's hands and said "Sorry, Sir, I did warn you it doesn't always work. Now the next act is a musical parody on.........." We didn't hear the rest. We were in paroxysms.

I got back to my cabin after it was all over to discover that my sick parrot, Sam, far from being better was actually much worse. The poor thing could hardly stand, let alone perch, and I was very worried. I should have explained that I had obtained permission to bring a pet on board - small pets were generally accepted; mine was modest, and suffering in a bad way. Logic told me I needed a vet. We had a doctor, but not a vet, obviously. Where was the nearest vet? In South Africa. So I made (and paid for, it cost me a fortune) a radiotelephone call to the Capetown telephone exchange. "Whom do you want?" they said, "I don't know," I said, "I'm out at sea and I need to talk to a vet, any vet". "Plees wait and oi'll putcha threw," she said. True to her word, it was just seconds before another heavily accented South African voice said "Yis?". I described the situation and all the symptoms to him. Fortunately, he was a small animal vet and quite well versed in the avian world. He had diagnosed the problem in seconds. "Greet" he said. "Greet?" I asked. "Yis, greet," he said. "Birds need greet in their crop to groind up the seeds which they eat. With'aat greet the seeds pass roight through them and they don't get nourished and they die. Greet. That's the answer. Greet. G.R.I.T.". The prognosis and the solution dawned on me. "Thank you very much," I said. "But we're miles out at sea, where am I going to get any grit?", and he replied "O'im sorry. I can't hilp you there. That's your problim". And that was that. I scratched my head.

The following morning I had an idea. At lunchtime I engaged the First Lieutenant (Second-in-Command of the ship) in conversation about morale and suggested that we have a fishing competition (sailors are often keen fishermen, and usually have their tackle on board with them. He declared the following afternoon a "Make and Mend" (i.e. free afternoon) and got the Navigator to find a nice sandbank to stop above. All the sailors came out with their tackle and having got bait from the Chief Cook in the galley, proceeded to lower their hooks some fifty or sixty feet to just above the sandbank. In the meanwhile, I had got the Chief Bosn's Mate to lend me ten fathoms or so of rope, and a bucket. Much to the amusement of the sailors, I started "fishing". When my bucket hit the bottom, I dragged it a bit, and then brought it up. Repeatedly. Eventually, I had accrued a small pile of sand and small pieces of gravel which I carefully decanted into a drinking glass and returned to my cabin. I washed it in fresh water and put it in the parrot's cage, along with more seeds. To say that the result was spectacular would be an understatement; within an hour Sam was jumping around on his two perches, scratting in the sand and eating his seeds like a man demented, or rather, a parrot demented. Which I suppose in a way he was. He didn't actually say "Pretty Polly" because he couldn't, but he chattered like billy-o and I have to record, lived to an old age. (I took him home to my parents' house, where he lived for a year or two, but then he began to peck out all the feathers off his chest, which apparently is a sign of parrot boredom; so he went to a pub, where he was kept well entertained, grew his feathers again, and lived for a long time).

The ship's company of HMS AJAX actually had their own parrot, much larger than mine. A macaw. It lived in a cage on the upper deck, sheltered from the wind, but was brought in when the weather was cold. Earlier on, I mentioned the "lifebuoy ghost"; a warship also has a "watch on deck" to cope with unforeseen problems. They stay on the upper deck, watch after watch, all the time the ship is at sea, and they can be deployed as lookouts at a moment's notice, or be sent to a fire or an incident. But mostly they do nothing. Except, in this case, teach the parrot to speak. Hour after hour they would delight in regaling the parrot with filth which, of course, it eventually learned to regurgitate. In the end, you would go up to it and it would say "Pretty Polly. Filthy bastard get off my messdeck. Up your arse. Sod you, too." And a whole load more, much worse. But when the ship decommissioned in Devonport and the ship's company tried to sell the parrot to a pub, no publican would buy the thing. A parrot condemned. I never found out what happened to it.

Our last port of call before the inevitable call at Gibraltar on the way home was a most unusual one. We stopped at St. Helena. It isn't (or wasn't) possible for a ship to tie up alongside at St. Helena, nor was the continental shelf big enough for one to anchor very far off the harbour, so we dropped anchor where we could. We all had to go ashore by seaboat. Now, St. Helena can suffer an enormous swell, so the harbour wall is enormously high - and strong. It is the only portal for a ship to arrive or depart, to deliver goods and to take things away. When my duty on board had finished I went ashore to explore, as did many others. The seaboat took us alongside the huge jetty, and we stepped off as the seaboat rose to jetty height and then waited for the swell to take us down again and then up again, and then more people stepped off. It was a bit hairy. The sailors mostly went to the single tavern in Jamestown, the capital, named after James Duke of York/James II of England, where they could relax and get a drink, but I was determined to see the Governor's residence and the house in which Napoleon was interred while he was on the island - Longwood House. In reverse order, then, the taxi took me up to the Napoleon house. It was quite remarkable, for two reasons. Firstly, the house was dredged in character; unlike so many museums and "historic sites" and National Trust houses around the UK, it seemed to have been completely untouched since Napoleon was there. It was a bit damp and a bit dingy, and one could easily imagine that an old creaky door would open and Napoleon himself would walk in. It was, in short, a bit spooky. Including the fact that it is generally thought that Napoleon died from poisoning from the arsenic in the wallpaper in this spooky house. But another interesting thing was the island itself: if you can imagine a huge sea with a tiny volcanic island sticking up through it you might imagine a cone - which is what St. Helena is. And at St. H you can experience your own climate: down at sea level, it is arid - dry and dusty and with cactus and succulent plants only; higher than that, it is quite temperate: fields and streams and a bit like England; and at the top third it is like tropical jungle - large broad leaved plants and trees, dripping with moisture.

Having experienced all this, we went down to the Governor's Residence, Plantation House, which, although a private residence, was just about accessible to all. And in the grounds, there was a giant tortoise. Called Jonathan. He was about one hundred and thirty years old. He gave me a short ride. Google him if you wish to see just how big he is! I was quite moved, because when I wrote home (no emails in those days) to tell my parents I had done so, I got an emotional reply from my father: in about 1929, on a merchant ship travelling to South America and then India before coming back to UK he had contracted some tropical disease or another (no penicillin then) and had been landed at St. Helena, effectively to die in peace in British hands. In fact, the Governor's wife fed him on Guinness and vegetable soup, and he survived. He informed me that forty years before I did, he had also had a ride on Jonathan! I did something else my father had surely done - I climbed the six hundred and ninety-nine steps of Jacob's Ladder which led from Jamestown to the fort at the top of the hill. Exhausting, but it had to be done. Then back to catch the seaboat back to the ship.

By this time, some of the ship's company had imbibed copiously, and as we stood on the huge jetty watching the seaboat come up and down on the swell it was apparent that one had to step off into the boat while it was at its zenith - before it disappeared down into the depths again. The seaboat crew did what they did to help, but a few sailors stepped off the jetty at the wrong time to disappear downwards and land with a "crump" in the boat. The ship's medical attendant was, as usual, very good, and there were no actual broken bones - or fatalities.

We arrived back in UK for a winter refit, ready to go straight back to the Far East again early in the following year. I needed transport, but I wasn't going to spend thousands on a car which I needed only for four months. On leave, I wandered the streets of Manchester, where competition to sell is fierce, and passing a Rolls Royce garage noticed on the forecourt an A35 van, grey, as they all were. £55. I said to the salesman "Why?" and he said "a customer won the pools and wanted a Rolls Royce, but only if we took his vehicle in part exchange. That's it." I bought it and ran it for four months and the only thing I did to keep it going was to put petrol in. Except for the time I was visiting my girlfriend in Paignton for the weekend and the brake linings fell off and I had no brakes - but I drove carefully back to Portsmouth using only the handbrake. The things you do when you're young. I have to report, too, that rust later removed the rear wheel arches, so I had pop-riveted a semicircle of marine ply on each side, but on the way back the rear spring burst through the floor and the vehicle tilted twenty degrees for the rest of the way back. I sold it for scrap for £5. Good service from Austin, I thought.

So we were in dockyard hands for a few months. We who were on board carried on with our normal administrative jobs - mine to ensure we had all the necessary authorisations to proceed, and to deal with day-to-day changes (including Able Seaman Murphy, who was known, of course, as "Spud", which he hated, because he was a Welshman, so I helped him change his name by deed poll to a suitably non-Irish name; he immediately became the only "Spud Johnson" in the whole navy. And another AB who came to the admin. office and said he wanted to change branches. After explaining the necessary procedures to him I asked what branch he wanted to change to. "Roman Catholic, Sir" he said, "my new fiancée's a Roman Catholic.)

The Supply Officer had to get three months' supplies and spares on board, and continue to pay the crew, the engineers did all their repairs, which is what a refit is all about, and the warfare team prepared their exercises and contingencies ready for anything operational. We also had a change of staff. The most important of these was the departure of our Captain, who was a gentleman, replaced by a man who was most certainly not. We had a new Bos'n (to replace the one who shot the pig) and a new gunnery officer. Also a new Midshipman, called Charles. We had just moved back on board, and only the duty people stayed after normal day's end work had finished. Charles and I were the only officers at dinner that evening, but we still, in naval tradition, dressed for dinner. There was just one cook to cook for us and one steward to serve us. At first the meal was uneventful but then Midshipman Charles, wanting something, flicked his fingers to attract the steward's attention. I quite mildly remarked that officers don't do that, but Charles did it again. The steward was getting quite annoyed and agitated, but of course couldn't do anything. I rebuked Charles again, in fact I said, after the third flicking "Charles, that is not the way officers behave. If you do it again I'm going to do something nasty to you with that bowl of sherry trifle". Unfortunately Charles did what he wanted, and I did what I had said. The steward fled, as I knew he would. Stewards do not wish to witness acts of violence by officers in case someone legal asks them if they saw anything. So they make sure they don't see anything. Charles was abashed, and I thought he had learned his lesson about being pretentious and doing what he bloodywell wanted. I was wrong. It gives me no satisfaction to record that Charles was recently jailed for seven-and-a-half years for doing things which involved touching other (subordinate) men, having ignored all the lessons that people have tried to teach him.

Another new arrival was our new sick berth attendant. He was a splendid bloke with a whole series of impeccable reports who quickly was to become respected for his knowledge and his practice by everyone on board. On the day he joined, he strode to the hatch which led down to his mess and called down "Hey, you got any black men in your mess?" and the reply came "No." He threw his kitbag down the hatch into the mess and called "Well you have now!" He had started as he meant to continue, and he became one of the most reliable members of the crew. We all loved him.

So we finished the refit and sailed again for the Far East. We were saddened by the news that RFA Ennerdale, a Royal Fleet Auxiliary oil replenishment ship displacing 47,470 tons deadweight, had struck a completely uncharted rock near the Seychelles and sunk in twenty minutes, fortunately without loss of life. In waters we were about to sail through. And of course as a tourist destination, the Seychelles waters teem with cruise liners. How little we know about the oceans; it is a fact that, statistically, we know more about the moon than we do about the deep sea.

On the way out, we had to scatter the ashes of a departed naval officer in the English Channel. We had embarked a padre, and the urn was safe in the Wardroom. Or so we thought. It was in the Wardroom, but it wasn't safe. Because one of our officers, I don't remember who, said "I served with that bastard - I want one last look at him", and he opened the top of the funeral urn, and tipped it to look inside. Just at that moment, someone flung the Wardroom door open, he jumped, and a huge gust of incoming air whipped the contents of the urn out and onto the carpet. The Petty Officer Steward solved the situation in a flash by fetching out the vacuum cleaner and hoovering the poor dead officer up. Unfortunately the vacuum cleaner had been used previously in a smoking area and so when the Padre got to the "dust to dust, ashes to ashes" bit he also threw out into the ocean a quantity of fluff, dust, ashes and cigarette ends. It wasn't quite as planned. Fortunately, the family weren't there, and the whole thing was left to rest.

If you were "duty ship" you had to be prepared to sail at short notice. Our sister ship, HMS DIDO, I think, was called upon to do just such a thing; a dismasted yacht had been sighted miles away down the Western Approaches, out of reach of the RNLI, so DIDO was dispatched. They found the yacht, with an unconscious body in the cockpit, wallowing around in heavy seas. The weather was too bad to launch the helicopter, so an experienced seaboat's crew was selected, and these brave fellows were lowered into the raging inferno, content only in the knowledge that a well tried and tested boat bobbing around like a cork on the roughest sea is actually relatively quite stable and safe - as long as you are not washed out of it. Or broached. After painfully slow progress, they finally got to the stricken yacht, and, showing great bravery, the Leading Seaman managed to drag the unconscious sailor into the boat and get a lifejacket on him. They were winched back safely, The seaboat's crew, exhausted, all retired to their messes to rest. The unconscious man was taken to the Captain's day cabin, where he was dried, given a bunk, and seen by the ship's doctor. The Captain was with him when he came round. He was told where he was. He replied "Have you got my yacht in tow? She's worth a million quid and if you don't recover her, I shall certainly sue you". The Captain's reaction was instantaneous: he reached for his microphone and gave the order "Stand by to use ship's main armament. Guns crews to their stations. Surface to surface bombardment. Target: one million pound white fibreglass yacht, which is a hazard to shipping and a danger to life." The sailor in the bunk was apoplectic, and said "You can't do that!" (or words to that effect). The Captain said "Hazard to shipping. Very dangerous. I must do my duty" and gave the order "Open fire when ready." You may imagine the rest.

We joined in several exercises on the way back out to the East, with various other authorities, and then returned to Singapore naval base. We had a few days there, during which we carried out all the necessary checks on equipment and stores and then one morning came the news that the NAAFI store had been broken into and a large quantity of cigarettes stolen. Who on earth? You can't hide anything larger that a bottle on a warship - it couldn't have been a member of the ship's company. The police were called and after a short while they said they would like to fingerprint us all. We all volunteered without being pressed (no pun intended). They took me to one side and said "We've found your thumbprint in the NAAFI, and it's upside down; how do you account for that?" I thought hard and eventually it dawned on me that one of the checks we had carried out prior to our arrival was a muster of the NAAFI stores, during a storm at sea, when I had to stand on a crate and put my hand up, fingers outstretched, on the bulkhead to avoid falling over. The police were entirely satisfied by that. I was hugely relieved. I was worried about something else completely.

We sailed for an exercise in Philippines waters to show solidarity among SEATO forces (South East Asia Treaty Organisation), chiefly UK, Australian, New Zealand and United States. We anchored off Manila for a few days before the exercise started. What reminds me of this was that our young Midshipman (the other one) went ashore and was persuaded to buy "feelthy books" and when he got them back on board he found that not only were there no pictures, but also that they were written in the tagalog language - which needless to say, he could not understand. That's foreign porn for you. Rubbish. Absolute rubbish.

Sadly, this exercise was to be one of the most dreadful experiences of my whole life and career. We were moving an aircraft carrier force across the ocean. Whatever some politicians tell you, aircraft carriers are of no use, indeed are exceptionally vulnerable, without an escort of anti-submarine and anti-air-attack frigates and destroyers around them. Carriers can thunder along at speeds in excess of thirty knots but like huge oil tankers they can only slow down or change course very slowly and gradually. So the circle of support warships has to keep well clear, and if ordered to change places for some reason or another they have to dodge around the stern of the carrier. The rule is very simple: you never, never cross the bow of an aircraft carrier. There was such a change during this exercise and the officer-of-the-watch of the USS Frank E. Evans thought he could get from one side to the other without difficulty by just cutting across the bow of the carrier, HMAS MELBOURNE. They didn't make it. The carrier struck the frigate almost exactly amidships and sliced her in half. Literally. One half of the Frank E. Evans remained afloat, and the other half sank, taking a hundred or so men to the bottom. There was an immediate Mayday, the exercise ceased on the spot, and everyone went to the scene to salve what they could. It was one of the most dreadful sights I have ever seen - to come up over the horizon and see half a ship bobbing around on the waves. A half ship that might or might not have on it the fellows one was dining with and swimming with or working with just a day or so before. Everyone did what they could, and a lot of people were saved, but the repercussions were pretty terrible. Anyone who has ever served at sea in a warship will tell you: you never, ever, in any circumstances, cross the bow of an aircraft carrier. And there is no point trying to lie your way out of it.

It was during this exercise, too, that we had confirmation of what a tyrant of a captain we had. It was dark in the Ops room during exercises, so that people could see their dials on radars and other instruments, and the Bos'n, who sat next to the captain's chair and controlled the helicopter and the anti-submarine operation, got fed up of the captain, impatient for information which wasn't available yet, hitting him over the head with a large plastic 18" ruler and shouting "What's happening?" So the following watch he turned up with a steel helmet on, and in the dark the captain broke his baton over it. The sailors thought it was hilarious, but the captain never forgave the Bos'n. (He was certainly a megalomaniac; he sometimes came into the Wardroom uninvited, at which the officers quietly excused themselves and went back to their cabins, leaving him on his own).

Take heed of the reason for which I lost all faith in him and just joined the others in obeying his orders without putting any other effort into anything. (And this man became an admiral!) Earlier, we had been alongside the jetty in Singapore, and because it was a public holiday and because all the off-duty officers were at a party ashore I happened to be the only officer on board. It was very quiet. Nothing happening. And then the duty radio operator came to me bearing a piece of paper, on which he had taken down a private telegram, in his own handwriting. It had not been typed. It was for the captain. It said "David, I can't stand it any more. It's the end. I'm leaving. I'm going to stay with my mother until it's all sorted out". End of message. I was shocked. "Who else has seen this?" I asked. "No-one, Sir" the young radio operator replied. "Well," I said, "I'm going to tell you one thing and I'm going to order you to do another thing." (This was unusual; contrary to public opinion, officers do not actually give many direct orders - I've only done so two or three times in my whole career - they normally adopt the more managerial "Would you..." or "I'd like you to...." unless of course it's an emergency.) "I'm going to tell you that only you and I in the whole world have seen this telegram, so if the information gets out - I'll know it's you. And I'm going to order you to give me that piece of paper and forget about the whole thing; leave it to me. It is now my responsibility." The captain may have been a stinker, but I wasn't going to let another human being suffer for his private life, even if I detested him.

I stayed up well into the night until the captain came back on board at about 2 a.m. I intercepted him and in the privacy of his cabin I gave him this piece of paper. He read it. He looked at me with contempt in his eyes. "Why hasn't this been typed up?" he said. "I expect things to be typed up properly, and recorded. This is typical of the shoddy work I'm trying so hard to improve." I was gobsmacked. I had tried to help and it had been thrown back in my face. I slunk away. (Slank away? Slunked away?) It was only later, much later, that I discovered that his wife had been waiting at RAF Brize Norton for a families passenger flight out to Singapore, had been waiting for two days, had got fed up of waiting and had gone to stay with her mother who lived nearby in Oxfordshire until another families flight could be arranged. Not leaving him at all. I spent a long time licking my wounds.

We had a trip to Japan, a friendly visit to show that our countries were rebuilding their relationship. We first went to Muroran, on the North Island, and had a most fruitful and enjoyable time; the captain called upon the local dignitaries, and they in turn were invited to visit our ship and have drinks and dine on board. It wasn't quite so easy for us ashore. Although the vast majority of people in most of the far eastern countries - at least in the cities - speak some English, the Japanese tend not to. We got by, of course, as sailors the world over do, with hand gestures, but it was not easy. The only thing that I heard repeated in English by those with a few words was quite amusing. In those days I had a large ginger beard. Few Japanese men grow a beard at all, and then in age they tend to be wispy. All the women I met - of whatever social standing - would point to my beard and then to my crotch and say "Same same?" I didn't take offence. They do things differently in the East.

The author taking part in Noh Theatre performance, Japan, 1968 in Japanese costume - and naval tie!

Despite, or rather because of this lack of English, the British Embassy had given us all little slips of paper to give to taxi drivers for any trip back to the ship, which said "I am a Royal Navy sailor from HMS AJAX. Please take me back to Ujina Wharf No.3 in the Muroran Docks (Central)" and all we had to do was hand it over. It worked wonderfully. We travelled around, we learned a great deal about Japanese history, including the Ainu aboriginals and their culture during our stay, but then it was time to go. We sailed, carried out some exercises, and then called at Yokosuka, on the South Island (Honshu). Much more urbanised, but still not a lot of English.

But with all the Japanese traits, nonetheless. For example, we were tied up alongside a huge wharf. We were to open the ship to visitors at 11.00 so that they could tour the upper deck, but this being such a rare occasion there were several thousand people milling around on the jetty long before 11.00.

It wasn't looking good, so the police were called. One car arrived. We were dubious about crowd control - just one car? But a policeman got out, climbed onto the roof with a megaphone and shouted something out which of course we couldn't understand - and within about thirty seconds these several thousand people were all standing in neat East/West lines on the jetty, waiting to come on board. What a lesson in civil compliance!

Another Japanese trait - precision: at sea, we had broken the crankshaft of a diesel generator, so the engineers had arranged in advance for another to be manufactured; so that their engineers knew exactly what it was like, the broken crankshaft, in two pieces, was sent to the factory - where they made another one, exactly the same, as ordered, in two pieces.

But we had a spectacularly successful visit, and all went ashore, wined and dined, and then got into our taxis for the return to the ship, handing over the new pieces of paper written in Japanese script which the Embassy had given us, and expecting our taxis to return us to the ship. Unfortunately, owing to an administrative error, they gave us *exactly the same slips of paper which we had been given in Muroran, on North Island.* For most of us, this caused consternation and altercation with taxi drivers which was quickly sorted out and we were eventually taken to the dockside in Yokosuka where AJAX was tied up. Unfortunately, a group of Stokers, all from Glasgow, on hearing the protestations of their taxi driver, said words to the effect of "See you, Jimmy, that's what it says, that's what you do - OK? Don't give us any........." and then fell asleep. They all woke up in the taxi on the ferry between South and North Island when the weather got a bit rough. When they hadn't returned on board, and when we found out what they had done, from the taxi company, I was sent to get them back. I got in touch with the Japanese equivalent of the RAC, who took me to the port and arranged for me to meet the recalcitrant sailors when they disembarked back on to South island territory. After a lot of negotiation - although to be fair, the taxi driver had to be paid in full, and the Stokers had to find and hand over large sums of money - the whole thing was solved without diplomatic incident. A lesson for all. A bit of a scrape, that.

On our way back to Singapore we took a detour to call in at the US Navy base at Subic Bay. Outside the huge base had grown up a whole town, called Olongapo. It had one long straight main road leading North East from the gate of the naval base. On either side of this road, which had wooden sidewalks such as they have in Western films, were nothing but bars, eateries, saloons, nightclubs, tattoo parlours, godowns, places to drink alcohol, blue film clubs, shebeens, massage parlours, boozers and brothels. I would not have seen it had I not been Duty Shore Patrol Officer for the weekend.

I did not want to be shore patrol officer - no-one wants to be shore patrol officer, but it has to be done. It involves going ashore with the patrol in uniform and ensuring that our sailors are acting with decorum. When did sailors ashore ever act with decorum? So it mostly involved getting the duty ashore patrol ratings to arrest the most serious drunkards/miscreants and get them back on board. The officer was there to make sure justice was done; he did not get involved - indeed, all officers are trained never to get into a position where a sailor can take a swing at them, because that is such a serious offence: "Don't let them get in more trouble than they're already in."

But this was different. We were in Olongapo, which is US territory, and it made sense to defer to American practices, so long as they did not outrage ours. We, the RN patrol (me, a Chief Petty officer, a Leading Seaman and an Able Seaman), therefore turned up at the US Provost Marshal's Headquarters at 18.00 in full tropical (white) uniform to be briefed on the night's work. The duty US officer was a Lt-Commander; I was a Lieutenant. But he said with the utmost respect "Sir, I don't think you Brits should go out there tonight on your own; we usually have one death by stabbing or shooting per night down the main street, and we have experience of how to deal with this and so perhaps you would consider deploying yourselves among ourselves?" It seemed like a good idea to me. My Chief just nodded - so I knew it was OK. "Your guys can split among our guys," he said, "and you, Sir, can choose who you go out with." I looked at the US dutymen, all armed with their "night sticks". There was one patrol I liked the look of: two large black sailors with bulging muscles everywhere and a pretty hard look on their faces. But next to them were two white men who actually dwarfed them, and looked particularly mean and tough as well. I pointed. "I'll go with those two." I said. A voice alongside me said "Beggin' your pardon, Sir..."

Now, some explanation is needed. When an experienced senior naval rating says to a young officer "Begging your pardon, Sir....." it actually means "Sir, you are about to commit a blunder", and all officers worth their salt will listen and carefully consider. If he says "With respect, Sir......" it actually means "Sir, you are about to commit a Monumental Blunder and I don't want to be any part of it." These things wise officers learn. "Yes, Chief?" I asked. "Well," he said, "If you and those two huge Americans and you get into a scrap with some locals, it won't be them two big Americans the buggers go for......." so I said "Thanks, Chief" and chose a somewhat smaller couple.

We, the three of us, embarked in a paddy wagon and off we went to patrol the streets of Olongapo, chiefly the main street. We passed the bar where they have an artificial pond in the middle of the room which contains small alligators and when you are all drunk you chuck your mate in and have a good laugh. And another one where they breed baby ducks and one of the girls pulls out the front of your trousers and underpants and shoves a baby duck in. All good fun. As time passed and more alcohol was consumed (by the revellers, not by us) we watched in the (open) Gents of a bar where one sailor was urinating into the pocket of the bloke at the next urinal, without his noticing, and numerous liaisons taking place and arrangements being made. But no-one had actually committed any offence - so we had nothing to do. If people don't mind swimming with alligators or pouching baby ducks or having their pockets urinated in, then no law had been broken.

Later on, of course, it was, and we were called to a large bar where there was much disturbance. A British sailor and a US sailor had exchanged shirts and caps and were then duly insulted by the others and a fight had broken out. We arrived to see about a hundred people scrapping. The two US patrolmen drew their night sticks, and looked eager to get in there. I put my hand out to stop them. I said "Look, you can do what you want to US sailors, but I want my sailors in one piece tomorrow, not in the sick bay. You deal with yours as you must - I'll deal with mine." The US patrol laid in and quite needlessly started bashing US ratings with their truncheons. I noticed one or two RN ratings trying to help the sailors who were being bashed. Then, as it started just to quieten down a bit I shouted "Silence!" and miraculously there was silence - both from those who were lying unconscious and those who were still conscious, including all the Brits. I looked at them; they all looked very young - even younger than me. Then I saw a Leading Seaman called Davis. I called him over. He squared himself off, straightened up, and stood silently and reasonably steadily in front of me. I knew my man. He was a good man, usually of sound character, and a keen cyclist who had been given permission to keep his bike on board. He was the least likely to give trouble, and I didn't want trouble. In front of two incredulous American patrolmen I said "Davis, you've let the side down a bit. Retrieve the situation and go straight back on board." He squared himself up again. "Aye, aye, Sir," he said and set off for the door. "Rest of you," I said, "Either go back on board or behave your bloody selves." One of the US patrolmen said "He'll never go back to his ship." I said "He will, you know. I've told him to." The patrolman said "I've got ten dollars says he don't". "And me" said the other. They laid their notes on the dashboard and I laid mine alongside. Davis wobbled out of the bar, turned left (all naval people, in whatever state, know exactly in which direction their ship lies) and off he went back along the main street, slowly at first, then speeding up as his legs got a bit stronger. We followed in the wagon. He successfully cleared the main gate sentries and pointed himself towards the jetty where AJAX was. Subic Bay is a huge base, and he still had over a mile to go, but he did it, sobering up as he walked, then squaring himself off at the bottom of the gangway, going up it, saluting the quarterdeck at the top, and disappearing to his mess. "Well, I'll be goddamned!" said one US patrolman, as they both handed over their 10 dollar bills. "Never seen anything like it". "That's real discipline." I said, and promptly felt a bit smarmy. Amazingly, there was no more trouble of any import that night. But we did hear that one Phillipino drug dealer had stabbed another to death, which, of course, wasn't our business.

After a while, we returned to Singapore. We had a bit of a break. The naval base there was huge, too big to walk round. But there were authorised taxis, who quite simply charged one Singapore dollar (about 14p) to take you anywhere in the base. So life was quite simple, and relatively cheap. There were leisure clubs around the place in addition to the formal naval messes: the officers' mess at HMS TERROR (as the UK barracks was called) was quite formal, with strict rules of conduct. The Officers Club - open all hours - was much less formal: a dining area (open all hours), a bar (open even more hours) and a swimming pool (also open all hours). About the only rule was that you had to have some clothes on. The Senior RN ratings also had a mess and a Club, as did the Junior Ratings. To civilians, this might seem a bit parochial. But the fact is that everyone felt more at ease among their peers.

We worked "tropical routine", which meant starting work at 06.00 and working through to 14.00 without a lunch break - just a coffee break. It was immensely popular: one worked (mostly) before the might of the sun had made life difficult, and one went home in the early afternoon and had the whole of the rest of the day off. (Later, during the UK "three day week" the UK shore establishments went on tropical routine - it got the necessary eight hours in, but it gave us all two days and five afternoons a week off. It was difficult and unpopular to get back onto a normal routine in due course)

So we spent most afternoons at the pool. This was wonderful. One could have a naval lunch, or not, and then sunbathe, or not, with a Tiger beer or whisky sour, or not, and laze the day away without feeling in the least guilty. The married guys had rented homes outside the base, and had a different life. Renting a house was not difficult; getting the right Amahs was. You needed a Cook Amah and a House Amah; the latter had to be able to keep the house clean and to babysit, and the former had to be able to cook. The test of the former was durian. It is the most delectable and inspirationally tasty fruit, when cooked. But raw it smells of pig farms and sewers in hot weather. Unless it is cooked properly (you can't eat it raw - the smell would drive you to the next street). Or you could have a good cook who could do anything except durian.

On days off, we single blokes tended to dine in the mess at lunchtime and then go to the pool at the Officers' Club. The Officers' Club was run with an iron hand by Mr. Tan. Mr. Tan was a Singaporean Chinese who had achieved his position in the 1930's and wasn't going to lose it for anyone. I expect he was rather hard on his staff, but I also think he was probably quite fair, because staff tended to stay for a long time. Mr. Tan was lugubrious, with the biggest capital "L" you have ever come across. "Hello, Mr. Tan," you would say, at any hour of the day or night - he was always there on the premises - "How are you?" and he would say "As well as can be expected, Sir" as he had done for thirty years that I know of. The only time he had ever left the premises was during the Japanese WW2 invasion and occupancy of Singapore, with all its atrocities; he fled into the jungle and waited for it all to be over. Then in 1946 he came back and took over where he had left off. He was the most wonderful man - totally and utterly reliable, and discreet; no-one ever heard a bad word from him.

We used to "go ashore" in the evenings (a naval term for going into the town; even if you were on shore, you could still "go ashore") and then return "on board" (the reverse, it didn't matter if it was a shore base) and perhaps have a final "wet" at the Club before turning in.

If you didn't want to go all the way into town, you could amuse yourself perfectly well in the local village outside the gates of HMS TERROR - a village called Sembawang village. It had just one street, long and winding. All along the street were "restaurants" - open air food selling places, where oil drums had been cut in half to make barbecues and Chinese woks were in abundance over glowing fires, and if you wanted food you said what you wanted and it was thrown into the wok and one minute later, sometimes two, your piping hot food was served to you on a sparkling plate. The smell of cooking was pervasive and beautiful. You might think that outdoor cooking and eating was an invitation to food poisoning, but in my time nobody ever, ever, had even the least of tummy trouble; it was always cooked at searing heat and served immediately. But what really interested me about Sembawang village was the atmosphere: the Brits went there for the beer and for the food, and when they had had enough they staggered home. US sailors seemed to go there to fight with other people. The Australians seemed to go there to fight with each other. And the New Zealanders seemed to go there to sing - loudly and lustily and with great force. It was a wonderful experience, quite magical. And then when it was all over any remaining Brits would engage in "minesweeping" - going round the tables and "sweeping up" any drinks left in the bottom of glasses. All good natured banter.

One evening, I remember, we had moved ashore because the ship's air conditioning was being replaced and one couldn't live on board - we were domiciled in the shore messes at HMS TERROR - and each of us had a single room in Far Eastern style: a chest of drawers, a sink, a mirror, a telephone extension, a ceiling fan and a bed that looked like a "four poster" not because it wanted to be Elizabethan but because it had to have mosquito netting hanging around it. This was essential. One night I had arranged to telephone my then girlfriend (now my wife, Pat) and because we were ten hours ahead in time the pre-booked call (remember, there were no mobile phones in those days) was arranged for 5 a.m. The call duly came through, but because of the noise of the ceiling fan I pulled the telephone under the sheet and we had a lovely, quite long, endearing conversation. I had to keep turning over under the sheets to keep one side and then the other cool, and disturbed the single sheet quite a lot. Do you remember I told you that our staff were wonderful - both able and discreet? When I came out from under the sheet, my Chinese steward, observing all the movements of the covering sheet, had left two cups of morning tea at my bedside.

Our stewards were indeed wonderful. On board, we had Hong Kong Chinese, because they were British. In Singapore, the Chinese were allowed only to serve on shore, which they did with immense professionalism and dignity. On board, my steward, Thomas, was quite astonishingly good. (If you wonder why a Chinaman should have an English name; this was because we couldn't say their Chinese names properly, and they chose their own English name on joining up). I was privileged to be invited to the home of my steward for a meal - very formal - and he went to great lengths to tell his family that his professional name was "Thomas". They adored him, as I did. The only day I ever saw him flustered was when my parrot escaped and flew around the Wardroom flat - "atrium" - and refused to be returned to his cage. But on the night I agreed to play my bagpipes for a Burns Night dinner and was heavily plied with Glenfiddich, which I am not used to, and returned on board in my full highland gear, with belts and buckles and spats and everything, and couldn't get them off and therefore went to bed in full uniform, having tried very hard and made a bit of an upheaval in the process, Thomas turned up exactly at 07.00 next morning and just announced "It looks as if in your cabin a very big bomb has dropped".

Talking of Chinese inscrutability, I left the Singapore naval base in 1971 as the Brits were withdrawing from the Far East and in order to protect interests the ANZUK had been formed:

the Australia, New Zealand, United Kingdom force, for which we had to provide just one ship, to show that we were still there. But in effect, the Aussies took over the naval base, and we swanned around. I returned briefly in another ship. One day, when we were having a break from patrolling, I went to the Officers' Club - and there was Mr. Tan! Goodness me!" I thought. "Hello Mr. Tan," I said. "Do you remember me?" "Of course, Sir," he said. "From HMS AJAX five years ago." I said "Amazing, Mr. Tan. And how are things now, under the Australians?" And he thought for a moment, and then said "It is marginally better than under the Japanese". What impressed me was the stress on the word "marginally". I don't think he was very impressed by the Aussies.

We "pulled out" of Singapore, and effectively left the Far East, in 1972. In the meanwhile, I returned to the UK for my second appointment, which was to HMS DRAKE, the naval shore establishment and barracks in Plymouth, or rather Devonport.

CHAPTER 7
HMS DRAKE

It felt strange to come back to a settled job in the UK. To wear long trousers all the time and lose the hair on your knees, and wear a white collared shirt and a tie (in summer) and a "woolly pully" in winter. My thoughts were both about getting a good job done and a reputation built and about getting out to the Far East again. But for the time being, it was Devonport.

HMS DRAKE was the shore barracks in Devonport, next to the dockyard gate, and provided accommodation for those on ships in refit, and for single personnel working in the Plymouth area. It was also the administrative base for all the smaller ships which did not have their own accountancy staff, a transit base for those going overseas but not yet, a recreation centre, a gym and fitness organisation, a cinema, medical facilities, and meeting halls. It also housed the South West Welfare Section, the Provost Headquarters, the "alcohol drying out" unit and the Wives Clubs. It was, in effect, a small town in itself.

I was appointed Assistant Secretary to the Commodore. The Secretary did all the Commodore's paperwork for him, so that he could concentrate on his main military task and just had to sign any papers the Secretary prepared for him (so long, of course, as he trusted his Secretary). The Secretary was therefore doing the Commodore's admin, and I was doing all the rest of the paperwork. There was also a delightful Personal Assistant called Millie (I'm afraid I've forgotten her second name) who was a Third Officer WRNS. She looked after the Commodore's (and his wife's) diary and social life - which was particularly important in this politically sensitive area of the UK.

An aside here about the WRNS (Womens Royal Naval Service). It was an astonishingly successful organisation, first formed in 1917, then disbanded in 1919, and then re-formed in 1939 for WW2. It was a typically British anachronism, and largely successful for that. It ran itself. It provided female personnel in all branches of the Royal Navy to support the military effort. It was in no sense a "second string" to anything or anyone (if you had met my Chief Petty Officer Wren Writer who ran the Admin. Office at DRAKE you would have been as much in fear and awe (and admiration) for her as I was; she could shrivel a hairy Able Seaman or a Commander or Captain with equal ease, but also with a charm that had to be witnessed to be believed.) Astonishingly, the Wrens did not come under the Naval Discipline Act (an act of parliament which has to be renewed each and every year in order for a Royal Navy to exist at all - part of our country's amazing ability to keep us from becoming a military dictatorship and which therefore required there to be RN Articles of War as well as a Naval Discipline Act.) You were free to join the WRNS (provided of course that you could pass the stringent entry tests) either as an officer or as a rating - effectively, you could choose. Then, even more astonishingly, you were entitled to put on the uniform and go and perform an appointment or any other posting - but as you had not signed anything, you were not bound to do anything, and you could leave at a minute's notice just by telling the Senior Wren that you wanted to go home and by handing in your Identity Card. The system worked. It worked so well that it was universally admired. Except by some equality activists. Eventually the powers that be gave in and told the Wrens that they had to either join the Royal Navy or leave altogether. It was announced without consultation, and caused enormous grief and sadness. The end, overnight, of a beloved, efficient, dedicated and highly professional service. Many of us, not least every single one of the Wrens I knew, thought it was an absolute disgrace. People repeated the maxim "If it ain't broke, don't fix it". But it was too late. The WRNS was no more.

Back to HMS DRAKE. The offices were on the first floor of the Admin. Block, near the Main Gate which opened out onto the road from Devonport to Plymouth. It was a large, Portland stone building, very imposing. The Secretary (my boss) was a kindly English gentleman, and we worked well together. He trusted me, and I trusted him. We both trusted Millie, the PA, who shared an office with me, next to his and next to the Commodore's. I recall two things about him, and one about Millie. The Secretary went on leave, and while he was away I planted a marrow in his window box. Then when I went on leave, I asked him to water it assiduously. Needless to say, it grew and grew, and eventually produced a marrow which broke off in a storm, fell, and nearly flattened somebody. But it was a great hoot. The other was that he invited my wife and me to dinner out in Tavistock, where he lived, and it was a very pleasant evening. He had two children, but one morning couldn't get in through the main gate to work because he couldn't find his ID card. He received a replacement (and a reprimand for losing it, as we all did, for losing an ID card, from whatever cause) but it turned up some weeks later in his little girl's sock drawer; she had taken it and hidden it "so that Daddy couldn't go away to sea and leave us again". On hearing this, the Commodore unreprimanded him.

There was an annual Pantomime in HMS DRAKE which had become so famous and so professional that people flocked from miles around to attend its amazing seven day run. I had a minor part as Gaffer Trout, a rustic who introduced the scenes by saying "Oi remember......" and it was an amazingly good and slick show. It raised the roof at the end, and people always wondered how it got better and better as the years went by. But there was a bit of a backlash (for me). There was an annual Royal Navy Amateur Dramatic (AmDram) competition in which all the naval shore establishments competed. That Spring, HMS DRAKE had no-one who had volunteered to put on a performance. The Commodore was worried about DRAKE's reputation, and one afternoon he breezed into my little office; the Commodore was a veteran - he had been to war and he had seen others die when he hadn't, and the "stresses" of peacetime beaurocracy didn't faze him one little bit; so he never came in to work in the afternoons - he used to say "my staff can cope and do the work and they don't want me looking over their shoulders - they're perfectly competent, and I'm here on site if you want me". So we all got on with it.

But there he was, in my office. "Alan" he said, in a kindly tone, "you were in the pantomime, weren't you? We haven't got a play to enter in the AmDram - could you fix something?" Now, as I believe I mentioned earlier in this tome, despite what civilians may think, few direct orders are issued in the Services unless there is a crisis - or on the parade ground. So what the Commodore actually said was not so much a question as a demand, and I treated it as such. Rescue our honour and put on a dramatic production (a play) in the competition. I sat down and balanced my limited and untested directorial qualities against the limited resources available and decided to put on a simple play called "The Bald Prima Donna" by Eugene Ionesco, a black comedy which I only partially understood. I gathered a team. Millie, bless her, faithfully joined in, we put on the play, and we came last out of fourteen but, we were told by the adjudicator, a very worthy and honourable fourteenth. Since then I have won one personal "best actor" award and been in one "first prize" production - but not as director, at which I was not very good.

They stopped "the tot" (rum) while I was at DRAKE. A very old Royal Navy tradition had come to an end. It destroyed a way of life and a tradition going back more than three centuries. The Tot was a form of currency, and a matter of protocol and pride. To share a tot was very much akin to becoming a blood brother; it was a great loss.

CHAPTER 8
HMS INTREPID

After a highly successful period in the naval barracks at Devonport came an appointment to HMS INTREPID, a large landing ship with a large flight deck and the huge capacity to put a very large number of troops and their equipment, and their vehicles and tanks and other armour ashore in very short time. Unfortunately, for me, it was to be the nadir of my naval career, and nearly ended it. I was the Captain's Secretary, responsible for all the paperwork and administrative stuff of the ship. The first captain went on to become an admiral and commander in chief. He was a jolly good chap, and although the going was tough because of all the administrative changes we had to cope with, all went reasonably well. The next captain also became an admiral and a commander in chief, but he was a completely different kettle of fish. As an exercise in management, it was interesting to compare the two: the former took everyone with him and succeeded as a team leader. The latter was an egomaniac; competent and a chancer - everyone knew he was going places so those who wished to sucked up to him. In fact, it was a paradox that not only did he suffer to the Nth degree from proctoheliosis but at the same time revelled in it; he actually used to wear a Royal Marines' officer's cap with a Royal Navy badge on it.

I joined the ship in Singapore in 1971. This time, I flew out by VC10; back in 1967 I had flown out on an old piston-engined aircraft and it took twenty-eight hours to get there! I hadn't been on board more than a few days when my first captain was delegated to take the Autumn Midshipmen's Board (exam). My job was to gather together all the paperwork, check its accuracy and present it to the board. All was going well, although neither the paperwork from one little minesweeper nor the man himself had arrived, even by the morning of the Board. Then at 10.30, the said little minesweeper hove into the basin, back from armed conflict, still charred and a bit bloody (literally), didn't even tie up alongside, chucked off a Midshipman and his gear, and left again immediately to go back to the fray. The Mid. was given quarters, and I got his paperwork. It was all correct, but to my horror I saw that his Captain, a fairly junior officer, in his final comments, had written "sound, rather plodding, probably only suitable to be a Gunnery Officer". My Captain, President of the Board, was a gunnery officer, and a very, very senior one. But we all survived. I don't know what happened to the minesweeper's commanding officer. Never heard of him again. Don't know why.

While we were in Singapore dockyard we hosted the Commonwealth Heads of Government Conference, a prestigious group of people holding a prestigious meeting. Several of them had death threats hanging over them, of course, and so a British warship was deemed to be a very safe place to hold the meeting. We went into auto. Ted Heath was the British Prime Minister and therefore host, and he laid down very precisely what he wanted. The conference facilities were easy - a large space and lots of pencils and paper - but the social side of it (which is actually what it's all about) went into autodrive. A very British menu, they said. Roast beef, pheasant, and so on. Commonwealth wines. And Hine brandy. Ted Heath liked Hine brandy - at twenty quid a bottle in 1972. Fortunately, it all went swimmingly, and we were allowed to keep the remains of the Hine brandy - and the wines.

When all this admin. stuff was over we reverted to our military duties. We had to take a detachment of Royal Marines down to Australia for a joint exercise with Antipodean forces. Our first port of call was Perth in Western Australia - what a lovely place. Just like Scotland but a bit warmer. Indeed, there was a Highland Games going on while we were there and so I entered in the piping competition. Because I had never won a trophy there before, they put me in the beginners' section, and so I became one of the Australian bagpipe champions (1972), a title which, of course, I still hold.

We enjoyed our visit enormously and the locals were extremely hospitable. Just as I was lent a motor scooter in

Australind when I was in Ajax, here I was lent a car, and enjoyed myself widely. I went with another guy to a wonderful beach restaurant on a headland overlooking the Indian Ocean - the most spectacular view you could imagine. I ordered a large steak, medium rare, and chose a rather nice bottle of red Australian wine to go with it. When it was delivered, I found that the wine was chilled - very chilled indeed - and so I asked if I could have a red at room temperature. The waiter complied, but scratched his head a lot. It was all excellent, and we thoroughly enjoyed. I'll come back to this, as I did to the restaurant.

We sailed a couple of days later, and went round to Melbourne, where I had the most wonderful experiences: my expat host in Perth, who with his family had wined and dined me for several days, had a brother in Melbourne to whom he sent instructions to continue the hospitality. We steamed into the port of Melbourne and tied up alongside. I was immediately met by the brother, who left an invitation to dinner and the keys to a large Holden car. It stood on the jetty next to the official car allocated for my commanding officer, and dwarfed it. He never forgave me for that, either. I offered the usual on-board hospitality: English tea, then a tour of the ship, then cocktails, then dinner. In return, one always received equally good hospitality: trips out to see the area, swimming pool, dinner, car (which I'd already got in this case) and the companionship of a daughter, very often. We had several days in Melbourne, and exchanged hospitality on every day (which is what the visit was all about). Then on the Saturday, I was invited out to a nightclub. Now, nightclubs are not really my scene - I don't like all the noise and the inevitable pop music, This one was very different, as I was to discover.

My host and his wife picked me up from the ship, and we went to the club at about 7 p.m., which I thought was a bit early, but we were being given a restaurant dinner, and it wasn't going to be hurried. We had a lovely table and were served a delicious meal of four courses by very attentive waiters and waitresses. Then the fun started: the tables were cleared, coffees and drinks were brought, and then the staff disappeared. And the lighting changed. The tabled area was darkened, and lights shone on the huge end wall, which was covered with huge curtains - which opened to reveal a stage, complete with compére and backing music. All the waiting staff then appeared, singly or in groups, performing acts and singing songs, in very traditional style. Then a darkening of the lights and the opening of a spotlight on the compere, who announced in his best Australian, "Les'n Gem. As you know we proide ourselves on international acts here and tonoight we have a special act all the way from Scotland." I remember thinking "I wonder who it is, and what he's going to do. Chic Murray, perhaps, or Stanley Baxter or Billy Connolly." But the compere then said "And, Les'n Gem, he's actually in the audience and although he doesn't know it yet he's going to play the bagpoipes for us. I have great pleasure in introducing...............Alan Pearce!" and at this a box was brought onto the stage and handed to the compére, which I immediately recognised as my bagpipe case! Everybody clapped and cheered like hell, and I had no option but to get up and go on stage. I wasn't going meekly though - I had to put on a swagger, so I announced into the microphone in sombre tones that I had been sent by Her Britannic Majesty's government brackets Scottish Department close brackets to bring some culture to the heathen antipodes in general and Australia in particular, which is in great need of culture of any sort whatsoever. There was a huge approbation - in terms of equal cheering and booing and people throwing things. It was a wonderful sight to behold. So I got out my pipes - still wondering what the hell they were doing there in the first place - and played Scotland the Brave, which of course brought about much stamping of feet and clapping in time (and some yelling of things like "Hoots mon" and "Och aye") and controlled pandemonium. It was great. Then I played Skye Boat Song, the Cradle Song, My Home and Dark Island, and lots of people started crying uncontrollably. I was unashamedly proud of the performance, because it had given enormous pleasure to a great many people. I retired to my table, and discovered from my host, whom I put under severe interrogation, that he had found my steward on board the ship and bribed him £10 to "borrow" my bagpipes in their box and deliver it to the nightclub ready for the evening's show. But it had all been worth it, and no hard feelings were held.

We had a splendid visit to Melbourne, and everybody was pleased. We sailed away down the harbour with great pomp and ceremony, all of us lining the guardrails in ceremonial uniform. It all got to be too much for one seventeen year old sailor who had fallen in love for the first time with an Australian girl (work it out for yourself) and who simply jumped over the side and started to swim for the shore and was picked up immediately by the Australian coastguard who had been warned in advance that it was likely to happen. Technically, he had deserted, but at the subsequent Captain's onboard trial he was bound over to keep the peace, fined £5 and taken away for a lesson on the facts of life by a senior Petty Officer.

We sailed to our next destination via Perth again and had a few days R&R. I decided to go back to the restaurant with the spectacular Indian Ocean view, with some other officers. This time, just as a treat, we decided to have the lobster, and asked for a bottle of the local white wine to go with it. Unfortunately, the waiter recognised me, strode to the sommelier's hatch, and shouted through "It's that Pom again! Have you got a bottle of warm whoite wine for him?" Something about Australians, culture and yoghurt comes to mind. Or "moind", as they would say.

After a few days in which we replenished food and fuel and water, we sailed for Japan, where we were to carry out what amounted to a "friendship and forgiveness exercise".

It was somewhat different from my previous visit. The initial onboard cocktail party for Japanese dignitaries was very similar, but then in return the local Mayor invited twenty officers to dinner at a mountain hotel, for which transport was provided. The hotel was very typically Japanese - highly painted wooden walls and eaves which swept down nearly to ground level and then curved up again. Inside, all the walls were made of paper, with bedrooms round the periphery and one huge central hall, which is where we were to eat. There were neither tables nor chairs. We were bidden to sit in a large circle, with alternating Japanese host and Royal Naval Officer. "Sit" is a misnomer – we had to get into the closest thing we could to the famous Lotus Position, which was uncomfortable to start with, painful after a while, and excruciating after a couple of hours. But it had to be done. Protocol.

The author, 3rd from Rt, crosslegged,
at Mayor of Yokosuka's dinner

Then out came the geisha girls – one between three of us, and they knelt in front of us, facing outwards as we knelt in a circle facing inwards.

My first recollection is of the food, which must have been the very best the Mayor and Mayorate could provide. It was disgusting. One lifted one's spoon to one's mouth and it was following by a string of sludge with lumps adhering to it. It tasted like what I imagine silage laced with rotting seaweed must taste like, if you threw in a few rotten bits of fish and stale cheese. But it had to be eaten. Protocol. So I quickly learned to pick up my saki glass with one hand, shove a bit of food in with the other and then down the saki as quickly as possible to mask the dreadful taste. Unfortunately, the geisha girls were instructed - tradition - to top up glasses again as soon as even a sip had been taken. So it was a race to get the disgusting food down before falling over from excess of saki. Fortunately, saki is not as strong as you might think, and none of us had a problem.

Geisha welcomes us to mountain hotel
for Mayor of Yokosuka's dinner, 1972

Until the MC got up to introduce the entertainment. All the geisha girls appeared on stage as the curtains were thrown back, and they carried out what I suppose must have been a traditional Japanese bit of theatre: it was explained to us by an interpreter that the Prince Arojimo had gone to the river to fish, but had met and fallen in love with a girl who had taken her washing to the river (she was a disguised princess) and they married and together they founded a new dynasty. All jolly good stuff, with some ying-yang music thrown in. We all applauded politely. Then, horror! The Mayor rose to his feet and invited Honourable Guests to put on a performance in return. The Commander turned to the Second-in-Command and said "Fix it", in good naval tradition. And in good naval tradition the Second-in-Command pointed to us, one by one, and said "Up on stage!" So we did that. Then.....what to do? Unaccompanied by music? Only one thing possible. "Right," said Number Two, "Swing Low Sweet Chariot, with actions, and don't pull any punches - give it all you've got." So that's what we did.

"Swing Low Sweet Chariot" sung by RN officers (author 2nd from Rt) at Mayor of Yokosuka's dinner

The affect was astonishing. The geisha girls were all trained to cry emotionally to order, and that's what they did. They were incredibly moved by our performance, the Mayor was moved, the Council members were moved and we had succeeded. Protocol had been preserved

Formal farewell reception, Yokosuka, 1973

We returned to Singapore. I was having a lot of head pains at that time, so I took the opportunity of seeing the Doc. ashore. He referred me to the British Medical Hospital (BMH) and I was admitted to have a sinusitis operation. Although it was "BMH" it was actually "AMH" - Army Medical Hospital, totally Army run. And didn't you know it. I was admitted to the Officers' Ward and given a copy of the Standing Orders to read. It started: "You will know, as an Officer, that your first duty is to become fit to return to your Unit", and it went on to lay down the law on everything under the sun. So I was given a bed and told to stay there.

Which I did. Then at 7 p.m. there was Medical Officer's Rounds. In an Army hospital you have to get out of bed and stand to attention for Rounds, if you can; if you can't, you have to lie at attention in bed. Honestly. This is neither untrue nor an exaggeration. I complied. Next morning, the same - Medical Officer's Rounds, but this time the whole brigade: Specialist - a Colonel. Senior Registrar - another Colonel. Head of Department - a Lieutenant Colonel. Matron - a Major. Sister - a

Captain. And so on. Before they got to me, they surrounded the bed next to mine, which contained a Royal Marine Officer. Sister stepped forward to his side. "Pyjama trousers down. Lie on your front." She said. He complied. She injected him. "What's that?" he asked. "It's called a 'pre-med'" she replied. "It's to slow down your bodily functions before your operation." "What operation?" he asked. "We're going to take out your appendix out" she replied. "You'll have a job," he said. "I had my appendix out when I was twelve". Much shuffling of paper and consultation. Eventually: "You are Lieutenant Green, aren't you?" "No, I'm Lieutenant Brown". Sister then prophesied: "Well, you're going to feel a bit sleepy for a couple of days". And they all moved on. I myself was given some sort of procedure, and an operation, but I don't know to this day what it was, except that it was on my nose. Then they gave me fourteen days' sick leave. I informed my Captain. He was furious, almost apoplectic. "Without a Secretary for two weeks!" he exploded. "Outrageous!" Personally I was delighted, exhilarated, to be rid of him for two whole weeks.

I first went to see my friend and his family in Singapore City. The old man had saved my father's sight many years previously, which was where the introduction came from. He was an eye and piles herbalist (don't ask). I greatly enjoyed talking to the old man. We used to sit on the roof terrace of his house near the centre of Singapore, and talk philosophically. He had lost first one arm, then one leg, then the other leg. But he could see perfectly, and he didn't have piles. He used to say "I think Allah is coming to take me, bit by bit." But his son was approximately my age, and he used to extract me from these rooftop trysts and suggest we had a "spin in his new car", which was actually a banger, and an excuse for going out and looking for Guinness-stout outlets, and I would chide him for drinking alcohol, being a Moslem, and he would reply that Guinness-stout was a tonic and did not therefore technically come under the rules. The other attraction was the two girls, Abda and Zubaidah. They were both astonishingly, jaw-droppingly beautiful. Abda was about five years older than me, Zubaidah about my age. I saw them briefly, very briefly, just to say "Hello", each time I visited. That was because the menfolk (including me) talked and ate separately, and the womenfolk talked and ate separately. I have never understood the reasoning. Then one day, Abda got married. I felt privileged to be invited to the ceremony. I was warned beforehand, so I knew it was going to be a three-day affair. I attended two of the days, which were filled with happiness and mirth and eating and drinking and dancing. Orange juice. Coconut juice, Melon juice. Mango juice. Tea. I didn't even notice, I was enjoying myself so much.

The author at Abda's wedding, Singapore, 1968

I don't remember a great deal about it, except that it was all open-air. Also that I have never felt so light headed in my life, even though I hadn't touched a drop of alcohol (it was totally forbidden, of course, except that I did notice that the brother kept nipping away in his banger to bring new guests. He said.) It was simply euphoric. Unfortunately the other thing I noticed was that the astonishingly beautiful Abda had, with careful use of make up, manicure, pedicure and hair care been made to look really plain and ordinary. I was disappointed. But it didn't spoil the fun and after two days I was exhausted.

So, as I said, I had two weeks' sick leave. I had heard about the British Army Hotel in Penang and decided to go there. By train to Kuala Lumpur, then branch line down to the coast and across on the ferry. I told my host, who told his wife who declared that the food on the train was not fit to eat and she would give me some food to take for when I caught my train the following morning. Next day, she sent me off with a beautiful parcel, wrapped in crisp white linen with a bow on top, which she declared was "proper food". It was overnight to Penang, so I had a sleeper. We wound our way out of Singapore Central, across the island, across the Johore Straits and off into the bundu, with the sun setting and the lovely smell of roast dinner wafting through the carriages. "Last call for dinner" said a voice outside my sleeper. I ignored it, proudly, thinking of my "pure" food, which I eventually opened with some anticipation - to find a plastic bag full of rank-smelling cold vegetable curry. I did taste it, just a bit, and then decided to become a carnivore again, and as the sun was setting and we were chugging our way through a beautifully painted, sparkling white railway station, I hurled the whole lot out of the window and watched, to my horror, as it splattered itself on the clean white wall of an outbuilding just outside the station. I ducked down and kept quiet for a while. Then I crept along the corridor to see if there was a spare space in the dining car, just in time to see them whisking away the last of the food and serve coffee. I retired for the night, hoping the morrow would bring better fortune.

It did. We all disembarked in KL and I caught a smaller train down to the coast. The scenery became beautiful, and the sea twinkled and shone. With my single bag, I boarded the small

Ro-Ro ferry, and off we went to the island of Penang. It didn't take long to cross, and at the other end it was just a good walk to the British Army Hotel. The air was cleaner and the sky was brighter than in Singapore, and I looked forward to my spell of rest and recreation - sorry, "sick leave". I spent the next few days exploring the island, visiting interesting temples and lovely gardens. Including the temple of tortoises, which did just what it said on the packet - you couldn't move for them! And the clatter was deafening. The hotel itself was just like an Army Officers' Mess, with all the same facilities and, it seemed, all the same staff, all trained in the same way. It really was a good break. On my last evening, I went to bed with a heavy heart, knowing that on the following day I was to resume my quite unpleasant life with my quite unpleasant Captain.

The next morning I packed my one bag, breakfasted, paid my bill, and set off into the clear, quiet air on a walk down to the ferry. But the air was somehow too clear, and it was certainly too quiet. The main street down which I had to walk was usually, at almost any hour of the day, bustling with people, the shouts of street sellers pervading, others jostling, with smoke from cookers and pipes and elsewhere, with humans and chickens and ducks and dogs and cats all vying for space. That morning, there was nothing. Nothing moved. There was no noise. No animals, and no humans. Eery, it was. I carried on, pondering. Still nothing. And then the screeching of sirens.

Within a few moments I was surrounded by armed policemen, with dogs, talking on radios, asking for instructions, but all with their guns pointing at me. I declined to stick up my hands, but I did keep them where they could be seen, and I did not move. "Is there a problem, officer?" I asked. "Yes," he said, "there is a complete curfew for the time being and nobody is allowed out onto the streets. Nobody. There has been a coup against the government, and we are taking no chances."

"I can't help you there, I'm afraid" I said, cheerily. "I'm not nobody. I'm English. I'm not plotting anything and I don't even know who your government is. So, if you wouldn't mind, I've a ferry to catch."

The senior officer did mind. He minded very much. The evidence for this was an automatic rifle stuck in my ribs and an order to go back where I came from. I was informed that I would be accompanied the whole way. And I was - all the way back to the British Army hotel. I thought to myself that this would at least prolong my break, so I telephoned Singapore dockyard and got through to my Captain. "Hello, Sir," I said. "I'm afraid the whole of Malaysia is under complete curfew. I'm stuck in Penang." His reply was terse. "Your leave expires at 08.00 tomorrow morning." was all he said.

So I went to the lounge to see what was going on, knowing, of course, that I was not the only one affected. Some of the staff had got in before the curfew, and some lived on site. So we were able to have a chota peg and do some planning. Then I met a remarkable guy. He was an army Major - in the Army Catering Corps, not the most ferocious of regiments. But he had started life in the army as a cook, and had realised that there was promotion to be had, and had gone hell for leather to get it. He was an organiser, a "doer". Progressive. Active. So, ferocious in his own way. We discussed the options - he too had to return to his unit. "This hotel has an army Landrover," he said. "If we take it, and get to the ferry, we can make them take us to the mainland. Then it's just a question of scarpering. Just up the coast, a few miles or so, is RAAF Butterworth, the Australian air base. We'll be safe there," I forebore to think about the devastation which might occur between the sanctuary of the hotel and the sanctuary of a friendly air base, but we agreed to go ahead. We filled bottles with water, and had a good lunch. Then we went to the basement car park where the British army Landrover was, with our kit. I don't know where he got the key from, or how, but he did. We got in, and he started the engine. The roller door of the garage was raised, and we saw sunlight. And with much rev'ving of the engine, the Major at the wheel, off we went, like a bat out of the blue. It was easy at first. The streets were empty and we drove very fast, towards the Ro-Ro ferry, which we could see from a distance had its ramp down. Knowing the Malaysians, and seamen in general, I guessed they were having a siesta. We sped forwards. But news had spread, and the police were converging upon us. We could hear the sirens behind us. We drove straight on to the ferry, and jumped out. The Major went straight to the bridge and told the captain to sail at once. I don't know what language he used, or how he said it, or anything else, but it worked. The stern ramp was raised, and we set off, slowly at first, then gaining normal cruising speed, which wasn't much, but sufficed. It all seemed OK, but after a while there were some pinging noises from the stern ramp, which the Major assured me were nothing to worry about. "Nothing to worry about?" I thought, what happens when we get to the mainland? Well, we did, and again, at first it was all quiet. We turned left (there's only one road, running along the coast), and sped off northwards. Again, at first, all was well, but then we heard the wail of sirens behind us, and we raced along the (empty, of course) road towards our safe haven. With the sirens getting closer and the thought of more shooting, innocent though we were, we started honking the horn, then holding it down and generally making as much noise as we could as we approached the gates of RAAF Butterworth on the right, some half a mile away. It was getting hairy. Foreign bases are not sovereign territory, as embassies are, but they do have rights of non-interference, and we knew we would be safe - if they would just open the gates. We got closer and closer, and with heart stopping slowness the Australians slowly opened the gates, having recognised a Brit. Landrover. We sped into the base. There was no pinging of bullets. We were safe. From them. I can't say we were safe from the Australians because they said the only way we could get back to Singapore was on the afternoon flight in the Dakota (the Wing Commander almost apologised as he said it), an ancient World War Two veteran which really shouldn't have still been flying. But I figured that if the pilot was willing to give it a go, so was I. Thanking our hosts, we embarked and we took off. The draught round our ankles was traceable to the holes in the fuselage, and the shaking was due to the instability of the aircraft itself, but we set off for Singapore with much hope. It was beautiful to fly over the Cameron Highlands, the mountains where expats went to get a bit of cooler air, and then down to Singapore. But the wind coming in through the corroded fuselage was not greatly reassuring. "We made it!" I said into the mike as we landed. "We always make it" the pilot said. One day, I thought, you're going to be wrong. But I was eternally grateful, and said so. A bit of a thrill. A bit of a jape. Certainly an escape.

I returned on board that evening, and next morning turned up for duty with my loathsome captain, who didn't even ask how I was after a medical operation, two weeks' sick leave and an international internment. I don't want to sound girlie, but it was a dreadful example of poor personnel management.

But we had more to think about. The River Ganges had received an enormously over-the-average input of rainwater and had overflowed its banks. People who do not live there might think "So what?" but in that area it was enormously significant, because the Ganges outflows into the Indian Ocean through East Pakistan, now known as Bangladesh, where on this floodplain the highest "hill" is about five feet above sea level. So East Pakistan got flooded, in a big way. There were more than a million people who were first flooded out of their homes and then a high percentage of them drowned. We formed a Task Group and set sail from Singapore. Because of the effluent from the Ganges, the water there is very shallow indeed and we had to anchor several miles off the coast, and use our shallow-draught landing craft. We sent several different teams ashore by landing craft - a team of cooks who were experienced in creating nourishing meals using raw ingredients cooked in half-oil barrels (effectively barbecues), a team of Royal Marines to keep the peace, a team of water engineers who could ensure that people at least had a drink of clean water, and, sadly, a team of Royal Engineers with their bulldozers whose job it was to dig huge holes and bulldoze great piles of dead bodies into them; this may sound callous but the danger of typhus, typhoid fever and several other diseases associated with rotting flesh and a total epidemic was much too much for niceties.

Anchored offshore, we acted as HQ in terms of both communications and the co-ordination of aid. We sat there in the Bay of Bengal for several weeks. We took it in turn to do the mundane tasks over and above our professional duties. So each day, we had a duty officer manning the bridge, chiefly to ensure that no other maritime craft hit us and that we did not drag the anchor and shift position. I had to do it on one occasion. It was expected because I was a General List officer, supposedly capable of everything. But the captain decided to test me. He telephoned the bridge, where I was keeping my watch, and said "I want you to freshen the nip in ten minutes' time". It was an order, in effect, and it had to be obeyed. I stood there on the bridge, thinking, and I hadn't a clue what he was talking about. But I wasn't going to let him know that.

So I thought "Someone, somewhere in the ship must know what on earth "freshen the nip" means. All I have to do is find him and tell him to do it." So I got on the Main Broadcast (Tannoy, to landlubbers) which reaches every part of the ship and said "D'ye hear there" (standard opening for an important broadcast). "The nip-freshening team will be required to fall in, in five minutes' time." And I waited, with bated breath. A couple of minutes later I was telephoned by the Boatswain. "Foc's'le party falling in, Sir," he said. "Would you like us to proceed?" "Yes, please." I said (the standard reply to an obvious request). "Keep me informed." "Aye, aye, Sir." he said, which may sound comical to landlubbers but which is, in fact, very precise naval terminology to acknowledge that an instruction has been given, understood and will be complied with.

I looked out of the forr'ard bridge window to see what was happening. Scores of men appeared and started knocking the securing shackles off the anchor chain, while keeping another secondary shackle attached to another part of the chain, so that it could not fall. Then another team (of engineers) got steam on the capstan and started to haul in the anchor chain - but only a few feet. Then they stopped, and the anchor chain was double secured again. "What was that all about?" I thought. But, true to history, tradition and naval orders, the Boatswain reported to me, on the bridge, "Anchor chain secured, Sir. Nip freshened." I said "Very good", which is the naval way of saying "OK. Understood". Then, with the most enormous pleasure, even though I hadn't a clue what I was talking about, I called the captain and said "Nip freshened, Sir." "Very good." he said. And I notched up the most enormous brownie point of the year without even knowing what the bloody hell had happened.

(The explanation is simple: if a ship is at anchor for a prolonged period of time, the same part of the anchor cable rubs on the ship's cable vent all the time, and eventually it will start to wear away and damage ("nip") the cable. So you move it in a bit or out a bit so that a different part of the cable takes the abrasion. Not a lot of people know that).

However, we got on with our grisly job, and saved several hundred thousands of lives over a period of several weeks, and then let the civil authorities, such as they were, take over, to rebuild as they could. And we sailed back to Singapore. It was all a huge success, albeit a sad one. I was selected to write an account of it for Brasseys Annual, the authoritative UK journal of Defence matters. In the meanwhile, the East Pakistan government presented the ship with a solid gold casket containing a parchment of their thanks for our efforts. It was kept on a table in the Captain's cabin for a while and then we never saw it again.

We went to Hong Kong for Christmas. It was a sobering affair. Apart from Christmas Day itself, when everyone went silly, it was a bit quiet. All the welcoming British families and other Anglophiles who loved entertaining the Royal Navy shut up shop and we were left on our own. Christian charity had ended for the Christmas period. But we had an excellent lunch and then opened the presents we had all bought for each other. The only one I remember was a bow and arrow with a rubber sucker head for our Gunnery Officer, Ben Quick, who had the baldest head you've ever seen. We laid him on his back on a table at one end of the mess and fired at him from the other. It was quite astonishing how often the rubber sucker-tipped arrow stuck to his head. Such is fun.

But I got restless. We had been away from UK for several months, during which I had worked seven days a week to keep the captain happy. And I had had not a day's leave for a nearly a year.

One evening, ashore, I met a rather pleasant young guy called Terry Leary, from the Wirral in UK. He was about the most average, ordinary, grammar school middle class Englishman you could hope to meet - except for one thing: he was an Inspector in the Royal Hong Kong Police Force. And unlike so many of the others he was, beyond doubt, not corrupt. So they eventually made him Head of the RHKP anti-corruption unit, which I reckoned and still reckon gave him a relatively short life span if he wished to be successful in his job. But at that time he was chief policeman on the island of Ti O (not the port of Tai o, which is quite large; this island was tiny, and has now been re-named to I don't know what.) It was right on the Chinese border. The RHKP presence consisted of Terry (the Inspector), one Sergeant, three policemen and a pack of dogs. We had a drink together, and immediately got on as like minds. I invited Terry on board for a meal, and he invited me to stay with him on Ti O for a few days. Therein lay the problem. "Sir," I said to the captain. "I haven't had a day's leave since I joined. Please may I have five days off?" This was reluctantly granted and to the delight of the upper deck crew a RHKP police boat came alongside with great pomp to collect me and take me for my "holiday". It took nearly two hours to reach the island, but it was a triumphal arrival. All the honest islanders turned out to welcome the return of "their Inspector", who was an honest Englishman who could therefore give them honest answers and help them to solve all their problems. We disembarked and went up to the police house, which was quite well armoured and had the only police cell on the island which, Terry assured me, had never had to be used because "the families sort things out themselves". He'd obviously got the whole thing sewn up. With his Sergeant.

His Sergeant was also a remarkable man. He was not Cantonese, but Fukkien. Unlike the Cantonese, who are relatively of short stature, he was a giant of a man - just the bloke to be a police sergeant in a Cantonese area. He commanded great respect before he had either done anything or opened his mouth. He lived close to the police HQ.

Terry dwelt alone in the police HQ, together with his dogs - about six or eight of them - all fearsome mongrels, but great admirers of Terry. I can still remember two of their names, the ones with the most character: one was called "Tchombe" and the other was called "Shit Legs Effendi". Surprisingly, the former name is of African origin and the latter of Egyptian origin, nothing Chinese. But it was explained that it was important not to choose names which might be "unlucky" or "weak" or anything which might offend a local family. After we had consumed a cup of tea, with cakes, Terry told me that it was actually a sad day: his sergeant was retiring from the police service after a long and distinguished career. Would I like to attend his farewell dinner that evening? Of course I would!

At about 7 p.m. we got ready to go. The dogs were to accompany us. I got the feeling Terry didn't go anywhere without a dog or two in attendance. The Cantonese don't like dogs much. We walked to the "restaurant". I use inverted commas because it was much like all the other buildings on the island - perhaps "huts" would be a better description, although this one was larger. Unlike restaurants elsewhere in the world, it had just one table - a huge circular edifice with at least a dozen, perhaps more, chairs round it, set upon a hard mud floor. The dogs immediately settled under the table, and went quiet. We all sat down. Terry asked me "Do you like real

Chinese food - it's not like anything you get in a Chinese restaurant in UK, you know". I replied that I had a very strong stomach, and could eat anything. Terry laughed. "I bet you can't!" he said, with a twinkle in his eye. "I'll bet you a bottle of champagne in the Dragon Boat Bar of the Hong Kong Hilton that you won't eat everything that everyone else does" I thought I was on pretty safe territory, so I agreed. The bet was on.

The first course was clearly soup. Now, I have to digress to explain that in real Chinese style, the food is placed in the centre of the table and everyone has a ceramic bowl and a ceramic spoon. But it would be very impolite to take your own food from the bowl, because you would naturally take the best bits. So the rule is that you do take the best bits, but you put them in your neighbour's bowl. Everyone does the same. Wonderful egalitarian idea. So I got a bowlful of this soup, which was quite thin but had lots of little lenticular bits in it. I tasted it gingerly. Not bad, but the little bits were somewhat rubbery, in fact like shaved eraser rubber. No problem, though. No threat to my winning the bet. Terry said "It's real shark's fin soup." I didn't mind.

The next course was clearly a meat course - a casserole, probably pork to judge by its light brown colour. It wasn't. My neighbour plonked me a great splodge in my bowl, and I tasted it - just a little. It was delicious, so I tucked in. Terry admired my fortitude. "You know," he said " the Cantonese have all sorts of superstitions, one of which is that cats get wiser as they get older, and so you always eat cat meat when it is quite well aged. Dogs, on the other hand, get wicked as they get older and so you only eat them as puppies." I said "What....." and Terry said "Yes." Oh, well, it was eaten now. I kind of suspected what was coming next, and come it did. Another meat dish, this time quite dark in colour. Knowing what it was likely to be made this course more difficult, but I ate it. I was on a roll, wasn't I?
Then, out came a huge bowl with a thick creamy liquid in it. I could smell it straight away - honey, quite hot. I thought "We're

on the sweet course, the pud, I've won this bet!", and said as much. Terry just smiled and said "We're not on the puds yet." And then out came another large bowl and there, within, squirming and wriggling in the foetal juices in which they had been born or would have been born had they not been squeezed out of their mothers were a very large number of neonatal or pre-born live baby rats. As host, Terry picked one up by its tail, dipped it in the honey until it stopped squirming, and then popped it into his mouth, chewed just a little, and then swallowed."Cham hip fah chow ne gelou" said Terry "Local delicacy. Literally means "Baby rats drowned in honey". "Terry," I said, "You've just won the bet. I'm not doing that." I can honestly say it's the only dish in the world that I haven't at least tried, and that includes the liquid rubber, seaweed and sewage fish dish in Japan.

So that was that. I had kept my end up, just about, gained a good deal of respect from the throng, but at the last post had given them all a cause for laughter. I had been accepted into their midst.

The next morning, Terry asked me if I would like to do some shooting. As a keen member of a pheasant shoot and conservation society in UK I said that I would be delighted, but I wondered what we were going to shoot because, unlike just about anywhere else in the world, there is absolutely no wildlife in Hong Kong; not a bird in the air nor a snake on the ground, neither rabbits nor pigeons, nor anything else - because they've eaten them all. "Targets." said Terry, opening his vast official gun cabinet. Therein were pistols, rifles, shotguns and automatic weapons including what can only be called machineguns. "Grab what you want," he said, "and we'll go up to the butts". I did, he did, and off we went.

The butts were of a very professional standard. Stands at one end, a large bank of sand and rubble at the other, with targets at the far end. We first shot pistols (at which I am rubbish, and most of my shots seemed to go right over the top) and then rifles, at which I was better, and then submachine guns, which started off OK but then took control over my arms and started firing over the top again. It didn't seem to matter - we were miles from anywhere, I thought. Terry said "We'll just look closely at the targets before we go, and then have lunch". We strode the fifty metres to the sand and rubble and looked at the targets, and then I looked over the top of the bank. There, out at sea, was the entire Cantonese fishing fleet. And several hundred of my bullets had gone right over the top. Goodness knows where they had gone. But we never heard anything about it. Chances are they all landed in the sea.

Terry and I wandered back to the police HQ with our guns. We passed the jetty of the port where all the boats land their fish, and where the fish which aren't big enough or fresh enough to sell at market are ground up and put in large open-topped ceramic pots to be sold on the international market, including the UK market, as "Fish paste". Both Tchombe and Shit Legs Effendi lifted their legs on the pots as we went by. I made a note not to eat fish paste again. We finished the day with a simple meal and Chinese wine, and then retired for the night, ready to go to the Dragon Boat Bar of the Hilton Hotel in Victoria (correct name for central Hong Kong) on the morrow to discharge the bet.

We eventually got there at about 20.00 (8 p.m.) the following day and had a pleasant meal.

The Dragon Boat bar was at the top of the Hong Kong Hilton Building, which was one of the two skyscraper buildings in downtown Hong Kong (of course there are now hundreds of them). They were alongside each other - giving rise to the Great Naval Challenge of the time (although as I said there was another one, of minor proportions: the bicycle race in the officers' swimming pool at the officers' club, which was a hoot, and usually didn't end at all because cycling in the deep end is so difficult). The GNC was a race from the Dragon Boat Bar at the top of the HKH to the other cocktail bar at the top of the other skyscraper, the Mandarin hotel starting with a drink and ending when the other drink is downed at the other end. Huge fun. To win, you have to have a man stationed on nearly every floor of each skyscraper to ensure that no-one interferes and calls the lift; you then get in the lift at the top of one skyscraper, descend to the ground, cross the road without getting killed if you can and then go up the lift in the other and down your cocktail as fast as you can. The record is something quite extraordinary - but I can't remember now and if the truth be told I couldn't remember then either. But it was extraordinarily enjoyable. We didn't have i-pads or mobile phones in those days. We interacted with each other. And enjoyed life.

An incident occurred while we were there, and just before we departed. HK was protected by all three of our forces, and this included the Gurkhas, who are a fearsome lot, and very much respected. One of their chaps had been ashore in the outlying province of Kowloon, and had taken his pleasure of a willing Chinese woman. It was in a small, distant village, which was unwise, and the villagers killed him. The Gurkha Colonel, an Englishman, mustered his troops and said "Look, I know how you feel, and I very much sympathise. But we must not allow this to become more serious than it is and you are not, repeat not, to harm even a hair on the head, or any other part, of anyone from that village". Gurkhas always obey orders. That night, they went up to the village with their khukris and chopped down every building in the village to within six inches of the ground; but they didn't harm the hair on anyone's head or any other part of them, either. Justice was seen to be done, harsh though it was. No-one mucks about with a Gurkha.

We then returned to Singapore for some rest and recreation, and for the engineers to do a bit of repairing to their engines, or whatever they do. It was a bit of a sad time because one of our engineer officers had found himself unable to cope with the stress of his work and had locked himself in his cabin and refused to come out. It took the ministrations of the Padre to get him to come out, and he went off quietly to hospital. We never saw him again.

Then we sailed for UK. We got out into the Indian Ocean, and all was very quiet. Just two things took the quietness out of it. The first was that out at sea, miles from anywhere, we had a total domestic electrical failure. The whole ship went completely black, but the emergency lights came on, dim as they were, to allow essential things to happen in essential places. It was 16.30 and the Wardroom was just having its tea and sticky buns. No-one moved when the lights went out; there was an announcement from the bridge that normal service would be resumed as quickly as possible, so people went on drinking their tea and discussing the day's events, knowing that in due course electricity would be restored by the engineers. Cups chinked and biscuits disappeared as we all waited. But there was a noticeable lack of Chinese stewards. The Commander said to me "Alan, you're in charge of the Chinese Ratings - go and find them, will you?" (Another example of an order parcelled as a request). So off I went, first to their places of duty then to their Mess - nothing. I couldn't let the Commander know that I had lost some forty Chinamen, so I had to go on looking. Then, on intuition, I went out on to the boat deck. There, fallen in, in three ranks in proper naval fashion, were all forty Chinese cooks and stewards, dressed in their survival suits, wearing their lifejackets and standing next to the lifeboats! They had simply assumed that we were going to sink, and were taking no chances. I knew it would be difficult to persuade them otherwise, but just at that moment the generators were restarted, all the lights came back on, and they went back to their duties. I got a rosette from the Commander. Undeserved, but I didn't say so. Another escape.

It was two days later when we were still crossing the Indian Ocean that the other incident occurred - much more important, this time. It is necessary to explain something. Unlike in an aeroplane, where you simply reset your watch when you land after a long flight and throw your body rhythm out for some time, in a ship it happens more gradually. When you travel Eastwards, the clocks have to be put on (forward) at some stage, and vice versa. Because the middle watch (midnight to 04.00) is the least liked watch, when you are travelling

Eastwards this is when you put the clocks an hour forward - it shortens the time for those on watch, and those who are not on watch are generally asleep, anyway, so they hardly notice it (except for the stupid and the poor planners, who miss their breakfast!) Going Westward, of course, it's the other way round - except that the clocks going back is carried out during the shortest watch, the last (second) dogwatch - 18.00 to 20.00, which becomes an hour longer. It's controlled throughout the ship from the bridge, who make a pipe over the main broadcast (announcement over the Tannoy). It is customary to do it after the new watch have settled down, at 18.30.

On any RN ship at sea, in the Wardroom at 18.00 the bar is opened and a bowl or two of chips put on the bar. In a small ship the bar is just an open counter or even cupboard, and you help yourself, writing a "chit". But on larger ships, such as INTREPID, the bar is steward-manned, and the steward is responsible for unlocking and opening the grille at the appropriate times. On this occasion, our Chinese Petty Officer Steward, a nice but rather dim sort of chap, opened the bar at 18.00 and started serving drinks (it was usual to have a drink, and then go and shower and change for dinner). We were standing there, comparing notes at the end of the day, planning the next work to be done or planning the run ashore in the next port when over the main broadcast came, as expected "D'ye hear there! Stand by to retard clocks by one hour. Stand by..... stand by..... Now. The time is now 17.30." As we were resetting our watches, there was a great crash from behind us, and the wardroom bar shutter and grille came crashing down - with all of the chips and most of our glasses behind it. There was a great hullabaloo and the Petty Officer Steward was dragged round from behind the bar to in front of it. "What do you think you are doing?" someone said, not unvociferously. The Chinaman was unfazed. "You see, Sir," he said, with Chinese logic, "Time now 17.30. Bar not open 17.30. You come back at 18.00". Most of us stood waiting and looking at our glasses behind the grille, unbelieving, while two or three officers gave him a lesson in timekeeping, naval traditions and the facts of life. The bar was re-opened.

The Chinese crew, as I said, were in my Division, which is to say I was responsible for their HR matters (as it would now be described). I really enjoyed looking after them, because I was able to help them through difficulties of language and culture to be the true professionals which they were. They were magnificent, and much admired and respected. I think they liked having me as their Divisional Officer, although I never truly found out; they were impassive and impenetrable, mostly. But they did invite me from time to time to have tea in their mess, which was a very unusual thing to happen - it wasn't just a cup of tea in the British sense, it was almost a ceremony, which had been planned with care and executed with conscientious attention. And the tea which we sampled had cost an absolute fortune - a monetary sum now wouldn't help, because of inflation and money exchange rates, but let's say one cup of tea (no sugar, no milk, of course) might have cost the same as a pound of fillet steak. I made all the right noises, but I still couldn't see that it was worth it.

One of the things we did at that time was to have a joint exercise with the South Korean armed forces, followed by an Aus/UK/NZ landing exercise in Malaysia. All these South Koreans in uniform came on board and settled in on the messdecks and in the tank deck spaces; and we saw a copy of an order issued by their General which, translated, said "We are here to carry out a mission. The last time we were on board a Royal Naval ship, somebody stole a sailor's camera. If that happens again, we will find who it was and I will shoot him". We had no reason to doubt the veracity of this statement. We completed the exercise, disembarked the South Koreans and embarked the Gurkhas. I particularly recall one event.

The Gurkhas are very hungry, or so it would seem. I was duty office one day on the way to the exercise area and I had to attend the Junior Ratings Dining Hall just to check that all was well. It is a large dining hall, built to get as many people through in a set time as possible, so it had a long, stainless steel counter, at the starting end of which was a pile of preformed stainless steel trays, compartmentalised to hold a starter, a main course, and a pud. The counter was groaning with food, not because of the munificence of the caterer but because of the economies of scale and the ability to use leftovers. I stood and watched, astonished, as Gurkha after Gurkha came along, picked up a tray, put a starter of some sort on it, then piled up roast beef, chickenburgers, pork chop, toad in the hole, then mashed potatoes, vegetables, and then to my horror, apple pie on top, ice cream, banana split and then glory of glories: they were faced with two large aluminium jugs - one full of gravy, one full of custard. One jug in each hand. Both poured over the pile together. They were in heaven. I expect they worked it all off later.

Because we had in those days a "Far East Fleet" (which was bigger than the whole of the Royal Navy today) there were "official Chinese" and "unofficial Chinese" on board almost every ship. The "official Chinese" were the cooks and stewards, who were part of the Royal Navy, and had the full protection of Her Majesty and all that she stands for. The "unofficial Chinese" were the dhobi boys (laundrymen) and in bigger ships the "Sew Sews" (tailors - who could do almost anything with a needle and thread. Including, would you believe, taking your old suit with the shiny elbows and the frayed cuffs, unpicking the whole lot, turning the material inside out and sewing it up again so that you had a virtually new suit! (Except that your right breast had pinprick holes where the outside left breast pocket used to be before the operation was undertaken) and "Shoe Shoes" - cobblers who could do almost anything with leather. These chaps had all the protection it was humanly possible to give them, because they were so valuable, but they did not come under the Naval Discipline Act and in theory could walk off the ship any time they wanted to. They never did, because they were on to a good thing: good money, and when Number One (head of the dhobi boys) or a member of his crew was a bit heavy with the iron (which was often, because they used so much starch -

you could hear the next door officer in his cabin "unpeeling" a starched shirt!)

In the RN in those days, everyone at sea was allocated a ration allowance - an amount of money for the ship's caterer to feed you. It was ludicrously small, but when you are feeding several hundreds or thousands of people the economy of scale is enormous. (I remember a Caterer saying to me "I know we don't really want to have baked beans on toast on the dinner menu, but if even just a few people opt for it, which they will, we've got more money to spend on steak".) In UK based ships this was always done under MoD auspices and in accordance with their regulations. In the Far East Fleet it was optional: you could ask the Chief Cook or the Chief Steward if they would like a contract, and they would be given exactly the same amount of money per capita and invited to get on with it. If you got an efficient Chief, you got restaurant standard meals. If not, well..... he got the sack and you reverted to MoD rules. Ours in INTREPID was brilliant. He was the Chief Steward. He was a wonderful and economical caterer and a great inspirer of his staff - so he got the residue of the catering money and we got wonderful food. It was noticeable - not greatly but perceptibly - just, how standards changed when we were in or near Hong Kong and when we weren't; when we were in striking range of HK he could buy his meat from his brother the butcher and his vegetables and fruit from his other brother the greengrocer and his sauces from his cousin and his fish from his nephew and so on. Away from HK, he couldn't, and had to try and balance things out. Which he and scores of others generally did, with supreme aplomb.

That month, in Singapore, we had a wonderful example of how it worked to everyone's advantage. We had a semi-formal dinner. There was a theme - it may have been St George's day or the Welsh or Irish day or something. We had soup, then a fish course, then a main course, then before the sweet and the cheese was a small hors d'oeuvre. In this case, the menu said "baby snipe on toast with caper sauce" or some such. Anyway, it was a tiny bird, beautifully cooked and presented. But unlike many other diners I had been shooting in UK and abroad for many years, and I knew a thing or two about pheasants, partridges, woodcock - and snipe. So when it was put in front of me, I asked to see the Chief Steward (who, of course, was in my Division, and a much respected and loved man). "What's this, Chief?" I inquired. "Snipe, Sir." he said. "Freshly shot in highlands. Only best snipe for you". Ignoring the fact that it was unlikely that there would be "good snipe" and "inferior snipe" I said "Chief, it's not actually a snipe, is it?" He said "Oh, yes, Sir. Best snipe, beautifully cooked, with succulent sauce." I said "Chief, it is indeed beautifully cooked and served with succulent sauce, but that's not what I asked. It's not actually snipe, is it?" He replied "Oh yes, Sir". So I said "Chief, snipe have long, thin beaks. This has a short stubby beak." "Baby snipe, Sir. Beak not yet grown." I said "It's a sparrow, isn't it?" He said "no, no, no, Sir. Yes. But please don't tell the other officers. They are enjoying supper." After that, we both felt we knew each other better, and he and I enjoyed complete mutual trust and support for the rest of the commission.

And then I had to move on, and then began one of the best periods of my naval career.

CHAPTER 9
HMS COLLINGWOOD

Firstly, the name. All RN ships and all establishments ashore, if they have a commanding officer have, for administrative simplicity reasons, an "HMS" title. HMS COLLINGWOOD is in Fareham, Hampshire, a campus of several hundred acres. It is named after the naval commander under Nelson at the battle of Trafalgar. It is effectively the Royal Navy's electronic engineering university. About three thousand naval officers and ratings were there at any one time. I was to be the Admin. Secretary to the commanding officer. Not the Secretary, his executive operative and fixer, but the next one down. I had to do all the HR work, and was responsible for documentary security as well. Because there was such a large complement of people, and because all of the officers were of at least degree education or higher, there was a huge pool of talent, but it had to be controlled. For example, it had its own pig farm. Three thousand people leave behind a tremendous amount of waste food and peelings, to say the least, and our hundred or so pigs were very well fed indeed. Being "non-MoD-owned" they also had to be accounted for as a sort of private enterprise, and one of my duties was to make sure this happened. Every four months, there was an audit. The pigs had to be counted. And I always chose two young officers with a Masters degree or a PhD in maths to count the pigs. They invariably asked how to do it. I used to say, with a straight face, "Put your wellies on - it's pretty mucky in the pen. Then one of you drives the pigs from one end of the pen to the other, the other counts the legs as they go past, and divide by four". They always went away muttering something. I awaited the day that it was reported that we had 98¾ pigs on the farm, as ascertained by an officer with a PhD in mathematics.

Pig farms apart, there was a huge pool of talent in the Amateur Dramatics world, and we put on, one year, Pinero's "Dandy Dick". We didn't win the AmDram competition, but we did very well. The professional adjudicator, full of his own importance, commented that our little orchestra had played "Hearts and

Flowers" at the beginning, which hadn't been written at the time "Dandy Dick" was written, and clearly felt very smug. Our captain, in thanking him, commented that they had also played a string quintet version of the Beatles' "Yellow Submarine", which the adjudicator hadn't even noticed.

Another of my tasks was to carry out "musters" (audits) of the accommodation stores. One day I went into the Stores Block and saw a very young sailor standing outside the door of the "Returned Bedding" store. Strangely, he was still there two hours later when I had finished my muster, so I asked him what he was doing. He replied "The Chief Petty Officer sent me here to see Ordinary Seaman Staines, Sir." I just nodded, and said "I expect he will be out soon" and moved on. It could have been a "skyhook" or a "left handed hammer", I suppose. There is a naval tradition of such, and one should not interfere.

So, the work was pleasant enough, if a little mundane. But I was sitting in the office one morning when two burly men came past to see the captain, accompanying the ship's catering officer, who had actually left the previous Friday to go to a new appointment. They were burly because they were CID, and although we didn't know it at the time, they had just "busted" a huge scandal. The catering officer had been in cahoots with the wholesale supplier of provisions, and since we were dealing with meat and fish and vegetables for three thousand men, we are talking big money. He had been ordering provisions which he had certified to have arrived, but which hadn't, and had then split the monetary difference with the supplier. He had also described hundreds of kilos of pollack or inferior fish as "prawns" on the invoices, and again split the difference. The reason for the delay in "busting" the racket was that the police had been investigating for months, and the racket had spread throughout the navy, the army and air force, the hospitals, the schools and indeed the police force itself. It was huge. Those catering people involved were divided into two types: those who had simply accepted a turkey at Christmas or some such, which was not only legal but expected in non-governmental life but was prohibited by all governmental rules of conduct, and those who had criminally taken money which was effectively stolen from the government. The former were given a severe rap over the knuckles and told they would have to do better if they were to survive or prosper, and the latter, who all went to prison. Meanwhile, the scandal had extended to the fire service, the immigration service, prisons, surgeries and all other sorts of governmental organisations, and it got to be so bad that eventually a moratorium was called, miscreants were sent to prison, and further investigation stopped. This had an indirect effect on me and my career, as you will see.

During this period, I had got married to my dear wife, Pat. We had little money, but we scrimped and saved and eventually managed to buy a house in Hill Head, near Lee on Solent. We equipped it with second hand goods bought from the classified ads in the newspapers - because we had put all our money (and mortgage) into the bricks and mortar. It was a bit tough at the time, but was one of the best decisions we made. I do remember buying our first fridge from a policeman who wanted £5 for it, and I beat him down to £3. And having little furniture. And sleeping on a mattress on the floor for about six months. But it was worth it.

Our first son was born while we were at Hill Head. Pat declared imminent parturition very early in the morning (it was still dark) and I got her into first a delivery clinic and then into the main hospital in Portsmouth. I was duty officer that day, so I accompanied her in my best naval uniform, before I had to leave and go into the naval base. I was bemused how many people asked me to open doors for them, or asked for advice on all sorts of medical things. It's amazing what a uniform means to people.

By the end of my time at COLLINGWOOD I needed to move on to my next appointment. The navy had run out of catering officers (so many were in jail) that morale was suffering and I was told to go to another naval shore establishment (HMS VERNON) and sort out the catering. I protested, but was given no option. So off I went.

CHAPTER 10
HMS VERNON

HMS VERNON, a shore establishment in the centre of Portsmouth, was where naval officers and ratings were taught about anti-submarine warfare. This was (and still is, of course) a very important facet of naval warfare, so there were about a thousand people working there. And they all had to be fed. I consoled myself that although I was not now at the forefront of the navy's fighting machine I was going to get very valuable experience for my next appointment to sea, in the fleet. It was so. Unlike another officer who, during a NATO exercise in the Black Sea had to go and tell his commanding officer that he could not continue with this major exercise under the eyes of the British admiral and the NATO invigilators because the ship had completely run out of food and needed to go into port immediately - i.e. by supper time, because he had not accounted for the provisions adequately, and there was only one tin of bully beef left for two hundred and fifty crew. I was to equip myself with the most remarkable catering and accountancy knowledge which stayed with me for the rest of my career. I was very green, so I questioned everything. Why, for example, were we buying eight hundred bottles of milk every day when the recipes and beverages account suggested only five hundred were necessary? My deputy claimed that we had to be certain not to run out. The discrepancy was too large for me to believe this, so the following day I turned up for work at 05.30 and watched the milk being delivered. Then I watched as dozens of sailors, passing the galley on their way to their offices or laboratories or diving simulators or visiting minesweepers or submarines, each picked up a bottle or two from the crates outside and took them with them. It sounds easy to correct, but it wasn't. I told the dairy I wanted the milk delivered at 07.00 in future, and they said we were first on the round and they couldn't do it. I then learned to harden my heart in order to do what was right and I said we would transfer our custom to another dairy - all 292,000 bottles per annum of it, and they very soon changed their minds. And it went on like this - my challenging things and often being shot down in flames, but often coming up with the goods, too. And there were amusing aspects to it, as well. The Church of England Padre's daughter was getting married, and he engaged (privately) one of my chefs to do the wedding cake. He specified all the tiers, the figurines, the fans, the iced flowers and so on in great detail. With just two days to go, the cake was spectacular. Unfortunately, its spectacularness lay in the fact that it was iced all over - all three tiers - in bright blue and green icing. That took some sorting out. I was only the go-between, but by now I had a reputation to think of. It was only funny afterwards. It always reminds me that if you are going to buy something - new windows and doors, a sewing machine, a holiday, or whatever, you should always ask all the necessary questions and not take anything for granted or you won't get what you want - á la vicar, who just assumed his cake would be white.

The catering seemed to go all right after the initial disturbances, and I made sure the little minesweepers attached to us had adequate rations: they had no experience of home economics, and often ran out of proper food, but we managed to teach them how to manage on their ration allowance. Our own catering, of course, was excellent, and we ate food such as one would get in a top class restaurant - every day. Here I must bring in a remarkable officer called Lawrence Jay. He was an anti-submarine specialist, and therefore at home at HMS VERNON. He had an enormous flair for the spectacular, and so they had made him head of the Royal Naval Display team - those chaps who "man the mast" and do daredevil feats at enormous heights, and he re-introduced cutlass swinging to the repertoire. I remember him most for his arrangements for the Christmas Ball. The Wardroom at VERNON was a Grade 1 listed building; it had an entrance vestibule of magnificent proportions, with glass panelled trophy cabinets all along the back wall, surrounding a door which led to a wooden-floored dining hall big enough to have a military parade upon (which it had done during the War), and two wings with accommodation for several hundred officers. It had been an accommodation base during the War -

although as a result of the bombing of Portsmouth the specialist anti-submarine experts and their students - many hundreds of them - had been moved out to Roedean girls public school, which itself had been evacuated. (The sailors there were in bliss, living in the girls' dormitories, or thought they were, at first: there was a prominent sign by each dormitory bed which said "If you want a mistress during the night, ring the bell". They soon found out it no longer worked).

Back to the Wardroom at VERNON, and Lawrence Jay. He had been selected by the Wardroom Mess Committee to run the Christmas Ball. None of the paper chains or plastic reindeer or Christmas bells or tinsel, and certainly not glitter, for Lawrence. He had an acquaintance in the packaging business who could get his hands on any amount of polystyrene chippings, and extruded foam. So the whole of the glass trophy cabinets were filled with Dickensian artefacts, like old shop windows, with "frost" on the window panels and "snow" on the window frames, and several lorry loads of polystyrene foam chippings were put into the building, and ultra violet lights installed throughout - not only in the vestibule but also the dining hall which, once the tables had been cleared, would become the dance floor. with alternating classical string musicians and West Indian steel band. The Hall Porters were given real live braziers and persuaded to dress up like chestnut sellers, and actually roast their chestnuts in the entrance hall. The dinner was magnificent, dancing in the ancient wood panelled hall while swirling in white "snow" under the ultraviolet light, the ladies in their long gowns and the officers in their evening uniforms of all colours was something never to be forgotten. Goodness knows how many reasons Health and Safety would have for closing down such an event nowadays.

We used to have splendid dinners at VERNON. All very formal, which was the antithesis of what usually followed: chucking the junior officer out of the window, tug-of-war with the napkins, flight deck landings (see HMS COLLINGWOOD later on) and bawdy songs. The first time I was there, it got to be about 02.00 and everybody was hungry again. So we got the keys to the galley and raided it, cooking ourselves eggs and bacon and black pudding and anything else we could lay our hands on. It was wonderful. And then we carefully locked up again and returned the keys. Next morning the wardroom chef was not a happy man: not only did his pristine galley look as if a bomb had gone off in it, he didn't have any eggs or bacon to cook for breakfast.

Fortunately, we had a wise Commander. Any other person, certainly any civil servant, would have made a rule saying that it was prohibited to go in the galley when it was locked and threaten dire consequences for miscreants. Our wise Commander did not. He made an arrangement with the Chief Cook that several trays of eggs and bacon and some bread would be left prominently on the galley work surface, together with frying pans ready smeared with oil, and the keys handed to the next senior party-goer. So the next time, we all went and had our 02.00 eggs and bacon quite legally and the second senior partygoer made quite sure that we cleaned up afterwards - and signed chits for the payment for the eggs and bacon, chits which, port and Madeira fuelled, always came to far more than the cost of the eggs and bacon. It was a win-win situation, created by a wise man, whose name was Jacobsen. There is another Jacobsen later in this account. No relation, but equally wise.

Talking of civil servants and vicarious preventative rules: one of my outstations was on Hornsea Island, where there was a half-mile narrow lake down which torpedoes had been fired for testing purposes in the past, but which now housed the Defence Diving School. They all had to be given meals, and I had just one chef who worked there and kept them satisfied. It was overrun by rabbits and hares, and I wanted to shoot some of them. I applied properly, and was told that there was an endangered species of butterfly on the island, so shooting could not be permitted. I swore an affidavit that I would not shoot any butterflies, but the civil servants in charge of butterfly conservation would have none of it, and I was banned.

Back at VERNON, I had to do my stint of "Officer of the Day" duties as well as my own daily work, of course. We all had to. It was generally very routine, making sure that everything was in order after working hours, discipline was being upheld, everything was being kept clean and tidy, and so on. The only really serious bit was ensuring that the War Orders were up to date and we were ready to go to action stations should the balloon go up. I had to stride round the real estate, making sure that everyone knew I was there, and effectively "keeping order" - which it never amounted to. Two things in particular about being "duty" amused and educated me. The first was that I was doing evening "rounds" accompanied by the Duty Petty Officer, a grizzly old hand of - goodness me, he seemed grizzly - about thirty five years. We came around the corner into an entrance hall to a messdeck (dormitory) and there on a bench was a sailor lying on top of a Wren. "Attention for Rounds" shouted the Petty Officer. They both stood up. It was clear that the sailor was very much "standing to attention". "What are you doing, lad?" asked the Petty Officer. "Just necking, PO" said the sailor. "Well" said the PO "Just store your neck back in your trousers, if it'll go, and then go and stand by your bunk for Rounds".

The other was also edifying. As I said, HMS VERNON was in the centre of Portsmouth, and the main gate opened on to the main road which runs along the front to the dockyard and historic centre. It was to here that I was called at midnight one duty day by another Petty Officer in charge of the main gate. His name was Kinell, known affectionately by everyone by his rather Chinese sounding nickname "Fu".

"Listen, Sir," he said. I heard in the distance a voice shouting feebly "Help! Help!" We went out of the main gate on to the public road and there, lying in the gutter, was a sailor. He had the fingers of both hands on the kerb, and looked very distressed. We went over and looked down at him. He looked up at us. And then he uttered words which I can still hear more than forty years later: he said "Don't jusht shtand there. Get a ladder. Get a bloody ladder!" Needless to say, he was hauled in to safety, and given time to contemplate his behaviour.

They were magic days. We had a really good hockey team, and played a lot, and generally won because we had a young visiting Ethiopian naval officer called Tekestebrehan Kidane (funny how you remember these things) who could do a hundred yards in a few seconds and control a hockey ball with his stick rather like a juggler with his bits and pieces. He came home with us for dinner one night, to be introduced to English homes and culture (and home brew, which he liked). I never heard of him again, after he left. Hope he's OK.

As I said, during WW2 the whole of HMS VERNON - on Portsmouth harbour and very vulnerable to bombing - had been evacuated to Roedean school, near Brighton. They all carried on their training work at that location. Even after all those years, we at VERNON had still maintained that liaison with Roedean girls school; once a year we went there to play hockey against them, and always lost, (and took them all sorts of illicit things they weren't normally allowed) and once a year they came to VERNON to meet the sailors - and for their small orchestra to embark in a VERNON cutter to be rowed around the harbour by our sailors (Portsmouth Harbour) playing Handel's Water Music by lamplight as the sun went down. Magical. Then there was always a tug o' war across the basin (a flooded dry dock). Sailors on one side, schoolgirls on the other. It was traditional that the girls always won, and the sailors were all pulled over the dockside edge into the water.

While at VERNON, I had to organise the victualling for the local RNR minesweeper based there. So generous was I that when they had a trip across to the Channel Islands (five days) they asked me to accompany them. It was really good experience for the young RNR officers (navigating, and ship handling) and for the RNR ratings (seamanship and deckwork) but for me it was memorable for two other reasons - one professional and one completely bloody dangerous - we nearly set fire to the whole of St Helier. Firstly, I had got the victualling down to a fine art, and we ate extremely well:

proper meals for routine occasions, and bacon sandwiches throughout the night, and a cup of soup for anyone on watch who wanted one. But in St Helier I thought we would have a treat and I bought a load of spider crabs, which were kept alive for two days in buckets of seawater and by the time we came to eat them they had no flesh left at all. Big mistake.

But the really bad one was this: St Helier had, and still has, a huge jetty for boats of all types to moor at. Alongside the jetty are several huge tanks containing all the oil, petrol and liquid petroleum gas for the island. We were tied up alongside them. Late one evening, I was duty officer with only a skeleton crew when we were told to move fifty metres along the jetty for another vessel to move in. The Stoker assured me that he knew how to start the engines and we could put the ship in "slow ahead" and just edge along and then turn off the engines again. This is precisely what we did. One specific thing went wrong, something the young Stoker did not know about. There is a shaft brake - a sort of clamp which goes round the propeller shaft inside the ship - which had been screwed up tight by the senior engineer as soon as we berthed. Turning the shaft against this clamp caused the whole thing to heat up until, by the time I was called to look at it, it was glowing red hot. Another minute or two and we would have gone up in flames - and taken all the St Helier petrol dumps and LPG tanks with us. Fortunately, several buckets of water solved both the immediate and potential consequent problems, although the senior engineer never did forgive us for distorting his bearings (engineers never see things in context).

I learned a great deal about catering at HMS VERNON. I mentioned "don't make assumptions" above, and another incident confirmed this. We were to be visited by a politician - Life Peer - on a "fact finding mission" (they usually turn out to be "prejudice-confirming missions", although this one backfired on him.) Accompanied by the Press, he proudly announced he wasn't going to eat with the officers but with the Junior Ratings. He sat at a table with half a dozen of them and bored them silly for a bit then, to show that he was really one of the lads decided to share some potato chips with one of them - by stabbing his fork into his neighbouring AB's plate of chips. Quick as a flash, the sailor had stabbed his fork into the back of the peer's hand. It took some quick moves to divert Press attention and to smooth things over.

I also had a very sad catering experience, which fortunately I was able to minimise. We had two huge galleys feeding up to a thousand people, manned by naval chefs. The ancillary duties - cleaning, carrying things, storing things, and doing all the washing up, was done by civilians employed by the MoD. As you may imagine, their pay was of the minimum, and they were accordingly not "high flyers". But they were very loyal and very hardworking, and I like to think I gave then sufficient thanks for what they did. At that time, many of them were ex-servicemen, mostly from WW2, some quite severely injured and disabled. Such was Mr Eustace. He could only walk a few yards, and had a couple of sticks. He came to work bang on time every day, washed pans and serving dishes all day long, and then went home. I always stopped for a chat with him. He never complained, and was actually grateful for the opportunity to work - an ethos which may be starting to decline these days. I was thinking of putting him up for a BEM for his dedication. Then one day the MoD Plods (Dockyard Police) decided that they were going to conduct an "anti-theft" exercise on the gates of all naval establishments, and stopped and searched every vehicle over a period of two hours. Mr Eustace was stopped, and he had in his bag a half-dozen box of eggs which had come from the galley. He was charged, and, being a civilian, was tried at the Portsmouth Magistrates Court. I couldn't, of course, condone what he had done but I offered to speak on his behalf. Being a straightforward man, he had pleaded guilty. I decided this merited maximum support, so I dressed in my full uniform for the magistrates' hearing and put in a long impassioned plea of mitigation on his behalf. He had to be found guilty, of course, but he was just cautioned and bound over to preserve the peace. I was very pleased but I thought wryly that with his two sticks and his inability to walk more than ten metres he could hardly do anything else than keep the peace. Such is life. Such is luck.

Armed with my good experience of catering and accounting I was ready for my next appointment - to sea again, this time.

CHAPTER 11
HMS HECATE

It needs to be said straight away that HMS HECATE was a commissioned ship of the Royal Navy. She was also one of the three large hydrographic survey ships under the control of the Hydrographer of the Navy; she was painted white with a yellow funnel and while she complied with all the rules of the navy and of the Naval Discipline Act and flew the white ensign she was very largely autonomous: the Hydrographer of the Navy told her where to go and what to do and the rest of the navy didn't interfere. Her task was to chart the oceans, together with sister ships HMS HYDRA and HMS HERALD. There were also smaller "coastal survey ships" and "inshore survey ships" to cover all the requirements of the Royal Navy - and sell charts to the whole world, of course. Our charts were, and still are, the best in the world.

Having completed the "Supply Charge Course", a course in everything logistics and HR - which was nothing if not rigorous, and not only taught us how to take charge of everything, but also recorded the pitfalls of not checking things carefully illustrated by details of the courts martial that had been engendered thereby - I joined my ship as the Supply Officer in Devonport dockyard in the middle of a refit.

It was late in the year of 1975, and members of the ships company were living either at home (if they lived in the Plymouth area) or in the naval barracks at HMS DRAKE. They were living ashore because the galley had been stripped out and the electrical supply interrupted, not for the usual reasons; "Usual reasons" usually means that the ship was in a non-tidal basin, and the "heads" (toilets) could not be used because they discharged into the sea - or if you were in a non-tidal basin, the water you were floating in, which obviously wasn't on. But HECATE was built to different standards, and had a Biogest system (as do all ships nowadays) and the on-board sewage effluents were converted by bacteria in tanks to gas and water. The gas was discharged to atmosphere (it didn't smell!) and the water was discharged over the side. The dockyard officers, never having heard of Biogest, said the ships company should move ashore, and our Engineer Officer, Lieutenant David Abinett, (he of the Bahrein fly buttoned nose fame) took them to the discharge pipe (which he knew discharged pure water) and filled a glass and drank it. "We are not polluting your basin," he said, "we are actually diluting and thereby cleaning it for you". This lasted for a while, but with no power except for temporary lamps, the crew had to move off outside working hours, anyway.

But the Engineer Officer got his payback. The shore heads, alongside our berth, which we used while we were working on board the darkened ship, were Victorian, in a stone Victorian block called "Latrine Number 3". They had high level cisterns, rarely seen today. This meant when you flushed, the water came rushing down from above head height and cleared the pan very efficiently. Now, the Engineer Officer was a very regular man and used Latrine Number 3 every morning, mid-morning. I will come back to this, because the officer in question had two rather unfortunate bodily function experiences, and this was to be one of them.

As well as being the logistics officer I was also appointed as the Flight Deck Officer. HECATE had a flight deck and a hangar for a helicopter, and could sustain and maintain a full helicopter's crew indefinitely. So as well as ensuring the galley was fit for use (I had to "sign it off" at the end of the refit - i.e. certify it was fit for purpose and use) I had to make sure that we had enough stores (spare parts, mechanical and electrical) and consumables (cleaning gear and other replaceables) and victuals coming on board for a whole season's surveying. It needs to be pointed out that just as a housewife will perhaps victual for a week (and do a weekly shop, knowing how long things will keep in the fridge and the freezer, and what will only last a week, and the milk and bread which will perhaps last for less) we had to do the same, but planning for a ninemonth rather than a week. Then I had the money to think about; not only did I have to have enough to purchase all the victuals which wouldn't last nine months at sea (chiefly milk and vegetables) I also had to have enough to pay the whole ship's company fortnightly in cash, in those days, and to buy anything else we needed to keep us going. But of course the MoD wouldn't give you it all at once - you were allowed a month's worth, and then had to indent for the next month's worth - which was fine if you were a frigate operating out of a naval base but rather more difficult if you were off Tierra del Fuego then going round Cape Horn or surveying off Bear Island. So it was all a bit of a juggling act. The Flight Deck Officer (FDO) bit was not as taxing while we were without a Flight (helicopter and crew) but there were still preparations to be made. The engineers repaired the flight deck and did all the other upkeep of mechanical and electrical equipment, and then I similarly had to "sign them off" as fit and ready for use. This included the absolutely vital firefighting equipment; a ship always has an entire suite of equipment for fighting every conceivable form of fire - material, electrical, gas or other fuel - with much extra in reserve. And on the flight deck, this had to be doubly so because aircraft accidents in confined spaces (the flight deck was only about fifty feet by fifty feet) can be somewhat devastating. So we had state-of-the-art materials. It all had to be accounted for, of course.

And very early on, I discovered that a drum of "A triple F" was missing. This stands for "Anti-Fire Fighting Foam, AFFF" and it is a chemical that works by producing enormous amounts of filthy fire-extinguishing foam when it comes into contact with a small amount of catalyst and water at high pressure or speed, as through a hose. I was slightly concerned, but not unduly - it had probably been punctured and ditched (thrown away) and its absence had been routinely and correctly identified in time for it to be replaced. So no problem. Not for me or my team, anyway. Not for the ship. Not for the helicopter's crew. We got a new drum.

But here I have to return to the Engineer Officer's regular lavatorial habits. Someone who didn't like him but didn't want to actually maim him had filled up the high level lavatory cistern of his favourite "trap" (i.e. cubicle) with AFFF, and put

The author (the flight deck officer) discusses flight deck procedures with an Inspecting Officer, 1976

some catalyst in the bowl. So when his morning performance was over and he pulled the chain a whole gallon of illicit AFFF sped down the pipe from above head height and hit the water in the pan and the pan turned into pandemonium as the whole cubicle filled up with foam within just a couple of seconds. Word spread rapidly, as well as foam, as you may imagine. It took some living down.

Back to sensible things. The galley was completed to my satisfaction. The stores were all embarked. The fridges and freezers were full (we had the capacity, unusual for a Royal Naval vessel, for one hundred and twenty days without replenishment or support), all the bits that needed refurbishing had been refurbished, and we were ready to set off on the next season's work as soon as everyone had had their Christmas leave. This was done in two watches, of course – half the ships company on leave for a fortnight, and then change over for the other half. Here I came across a catering problem they hadn't taught me on the Charge Course. The Petty Officer Caterer (of rabbit and reindeer skin fame – see later) came along to ask me for a signature for a "by-pass demand", which is an indent for victuals which for some reason "by-pass" the galley and get used for some other purpose. It is quite rare. It was for one twenty-five kilogramme sack of dried milk powder. Needless to say, I enquired "Why?" and received a somewhat surprising reply; I will paraphrase it: "Because half the ship's company are on leave there isn't enough excrement going into the Biogest tank to keep the necessary critical numbers of bugs alive and they will perish before we become a viable source of vitamins for them when the rest of the ship's company return on board". His actual words were slightly different. Now, there is a history, almost a tradition, in the Royal Navy of playing tricks on people who are new to a task, and I really wondered if I was the butt of some such prank. So I openly questioned it, and watched his face as he replied. It was true. Not a lot of people know that. More trick-playing later.

Incidentally, it was here from the catering menu that I got my induction into the world of naval food: Spithead pheasant is a kipper, HITS is herrings in tomato sauce, BITS is beans in tomato sauce, train smash is tinned tomatoes, summer soup contains some of this and some of that, beef casserole surprise means that there is no beef in it, a cackleberry is a boiled egg, Swansea virgin is a welsh rarebit, shit on a raft is chopped kidneys on toast and perhaps the most evocative if you think about it is "babies' heads" - imagine opening a tin of hot steak and kidney pudding and splotting it on a plate.

I felt quite "settled in" by the time we sailed for our first hydrographic survey, which was in the Mediterranean. But before deploying, we had to have a "work-up" at Portland, the navy's specialist place for training new ships' crews before they are allowed to join the Fleet. In the case of warships, this is a really rigorous testing time, with crews deliberately put under stress, coming under fire from surface, underwater and the air, and returning fire aggressively when required. It also tests anti-nuclear, bacteriological and chemical defence, as well as the rigours of daily existence at sea. In the case of hydrographic survey ships, which can do none of these things, it is simply a complete check of all safety routines, from anchoring and manoeuvring and "man overboard" drills through firefighting and damage repair to mechanical and flight deck safety. It was still challenging, but in a different way. It was also rewarding, and on occasion, quite funny. For example, one inspecting officer stopped a three badge AB (an old hand who hadn't sought any promotion at all), pointed to a group of ship's officers on the foc's'le and said "Tell me what you would do if one of those officers fell over the side." The grizzled Able Seaman looked closely at the officers in question, turned to the inspecting officer, and said "Which one?"

Our catering services, our replenishment stores and our HR and Admin. were beyond reproach, so my team had turned their attention to coping with emergencies - such as feeding starving tsunami refugees in their devastated towns with our oildrum barbecues and emergency rations, to firefighting, and to damage control, all of which we were trained to do. Then we had an "Abandon Ship" drill. Everyone did what they had to and then we fell in on the topmost deck, ready to evacuate.

One inspecting officer noticed that I had a large canvas bag attached to my lifejacket and survival suit and enquired what it was. I said "It's the contents of the ship's main safe; I reckon if we land up on shore in hostile territory we're going to have to buy our way out of trouble. The ship's going to sink, anyway". He looked at me somewhat sideways, but put a tick in the box.

Then we were distracted by a "casualty" said to have a broken leg. Now, it must be explained that the previous year, some bright spark in the Procurement Department of MoD had procured some "inflatable splints", which theoretically are a very good idea. You place the inflatable splint around the broken limb and inflate it; this not only holds it firmly and securely, as a splint should, but also protects it from future knocks or abrasions. We were all fallen in at lifeboat stations and watched in wonderment as the "casualty" with the "broken leg" was laid on the deck and the uninflated splint wrapped around his broken limb. Then nearly a hundred sailors at lifeboat stations watched avidly as the Casualty Evacuation (Casevac) rating got down on his knees to inflate the splint. Guess where the genius at the Procurement Department had put the inflation airhole? Right at the top, between thighs and at the crotch. We watched in even more astonishment as the CasEvac rating's head went down between the casualty's legs and he proceeded to give him a long blow job. He got the most enormous cheer when it was all over.

Having passed all the tests, off we went to survey in the Mediterranean Sea. We called in at Gibraltar, where we picked up fresh milk and salad gear, and no doubt some fuel. (In those days, there was no UHT milk; after about three or four days we were on milk powder, and to make it taste like proper milk it had to be churned with unsalted butter. It was not very nice, but it sufficed). I have always found Gibraltar somewhat magical. Quite apart from its history there is a tremendous atmosphere which is with you all the time. I'll come back to this, because on the way home after the survey season we had an adventure or two.

Our survey area was the Tyrrhenian Sea and the Ligurian Sea, of which you may have heard. I hadn't. They are round Italy. I need to explain something about hydrographic surveying, In the old days, they surveyed by dropping a line over the side which had knots and other markers at regular intervals so that you could measure the depth (this is where the nickname Mark Twain came from). The Mediterranean is quite deep - it's about two thousand fathoms much of the way across. So in the old days if you put down a line and it read "12,000 feet" and then a mile away and another mile away from that it also measured 12,000 feet, (now all in metres, of course) you drew a chart and put a straight line between the markings. Nowadays, we know that there could be several seamounts in between those markings, and that they could come dangerously close to the surface - not good for supertankers. Our job was to find them.

For this, we had a thing called aside-scan sonar. Unlike depth recorders or anti-submarine sonars, it scanned purely sideways - so if you went past a seamount it would pick it up, and we could put it on a chart to warn people. We sailed for days and weeks, up and down, taking our readings. One day, however, the screen went completely blank and when we pulled the wire in it was bare and tattered at the end - with two shark's teeth embedded in the plastic coating. The sensor was about five feet long and six inches in diameter, so the shark must have felt quite full after its meal.

Then, typically, we would come into port once a fortnight to top up with comestibles and for what the Americans call "R&R". Our first port of call was Civitavecchia, the "Port of Rome". Many of us caught the train to Rome, and enjoyed the sightseeing for a couple of days. Here, one of our Supplementary List Officers (short term contract), Bob Ward, reached his time, and had to leave us. We gave him a massive farewell in a local tavern, at his request. I say "massive" because we had discovered that while wine was relatively cheap in Italy, if you bought a twenty litre bottle/flask/vat of it you could not only sup wine in company for many pleasant hours but also you had a beautiful terrarium to take home afterwards (if you could remember to). We saw Bob off at the station. We later heard that he had joined the merchant navy, being a good seaman and navigator, but later re-joined the Royal Navy.

We sailed for more surveying, and then spent a weekend in Brindisi, at the southern tip of Italy, quite close to the Italian Naval Base at Taranto, where in 1940 those twenty-one little stringbag/canvas-clad biplanes of the Fleet Air Arm attacked and mostly destroyed the might of the Italian Navy. Nobody mentioned it socially, of course. In fact, we were given the most generous, hospitable and sincere welcome by the Italian Navy authorities, who really pushed the boat out for us. A superb cocktail party in an enormous marble hall, with a string quintet playing and lovely little nibbles and the very best of wine and aperitifs. I remember John Page, our First Lieutenant - who had recently been a bit stinging about parts of my department - asking my recommendation as to what to drink at an Italian cocktail party. I advised him to ask for a large Fernet Branca, neat. He didn't enjoy it, but didn't criticise any more, either. He had had a very bitters experience.

We sailed again for more surveying, during the course of which we did something a bit naughty - committed a crime which harmed nobody, which nobody cared about, and for which the victims were actually grateful. We were sailing up the coast when we came across a host of lobster pots. We put down a boat, hauled up the pots, and extracted the lobsters for our dinner. However, into the pots, each of them, we put a bottle of whisky (which costs an absolute fortune in Italy) and at an exchange rate of one bottle per lobster everyone was happy. You don't get many win/win situations in life, but this was another of them.

We returned to Plymouth towards the end of the surveying season. The Hydrographer of the Navy wanted us to carry out a survey in the Western Approaches, a sea area off the South West coast of UK. There was evidence of subterranean oil, but before oil companies could carry out test drilling - a very expensive process indeed - they wanted us to look for anticlines to decide whether further exploration could be possible and economical; our ship had sophisticated equipment on board which could search below the ocean floor. The Royal Navy would be very well paid for this, of course.

Impromptu band welcomes a ship back to Plymouth 1978

We had a few days in Plymouth, to replenish, and then set sail in a south westerly direction. We took with us a contingent of scientists from the Royal Geological Society and also, because it was potentially such an important matter, and so newsworthy, a number of pressmen from both local and the more serious national newspapers. They were all accommodated in spare officers' cabins and given access to the Wardroom. They were all quite excited. For us, it was just a job, but one which we would pursue vigorously and to completion.

There was an interesting event on this journey, one which has broadened my historical knowledge and my understanding of others to quite a degree. After dinner one evening, all the day's work done, we were relaxing in the Wardroom, having a drink, and playing poker dice (also known as liar dice - a much better description). One of the pressmen, during a later game, said "You don't want to cross someone from the Press, because if you do, your name will be in the newspaper the following morning!" Our First Lieutenant, very quietly but both portentiously and decisively, said "You don't want to cross a Royal Naval Hydrographer because if you do your name might be in print for ever!" Sensing an interesting story, someone asked him how this could be. The answer was surprising, and I'll tell you now that you probably won't believe it, but if you don't you can either Google it or look on the current Admiralty chart of the Aegean Sea. He said: "Many years ago, in 1903, in fact, one of the Royal Navy's ships was surveying in the Mediterranean, charting coastlines and waters off the coastlines. One such was commanded by Captain Alvin Coote Corry RN, a very strict disciplinarian with a history of court martialling officers who did not come up to expectations. They were surveying off the island of Lemnos, the south coast of the island, to be exact. One of his officers, Lieutenant "Tubby" Lockyer had not had any leave for a long time, and wanted leave to have a break and go partridge shooting for a couple of days. Corry denied him any leave, and effectively said "Go on surveying - get on with it. No leave".

Something must be explained here for the understanding of the rest of the story. As a professional surveyor, if you discover something new/uncharted/unmapped you have to take three courses of action before you put them on a chart or a map, and you have to do it in this order: first, ensure it has not already got a name; secondly, find out if it has a name in the local tongue and either record this or anglicise it; thirdly, if neither of these apply, you can call it what you want, and put it on your chart or map. (This is why there are so many "McKenzie this" or "Harper's that" or Chapman's the others." Indeed, a previous captain of HMS HECATE, Geoff Hope, had named a sub-ocean feature "Hope's Deep" - and it will always be called that.) Back to the story.

"Near the south coast of Lemnos," went on our First Lieutenant, "there are four mountain peaks. These are very useful to navigators, who can take bearings of them, and so are important to put on naval charts as well as land maps. They had no names. Tubby Lockyer was responsible for this survey, and he decided to call them "Yam", "Yrroc", "Eb", and "Denmad" and wrote up his chart accordingly. Charts have to be "signed off" by the ship's captain before going to the Hydrographic Office at Taunton, and this Tubby's captain, Corry, did. The chart was sent off, approved, printed, and it still exists and is still in use. If you look at the mountain names, which cannot now be changed, they spell, backwards, "May Corry be damned". Don't upset a Royal Navy Hydrographer!

Very early the next year, after minor repairs and renovations, as is customary, we sailed for another survey. Somewhere very cold, so we would need highly insulated Eskimo type full suits and trousers, and boots. It was my job to get them before we sailed, and this I did. We were going to call at Tromsø, in Norway, well north of the Arctic circle - because a money imprest had to be made and milk and bread and other perishables had to be ordered. We sailed in accordance with directions, ready to do whatever it was that we had to do.

Up the Channel, across the North Sea, and up the coast of Norway. On the way, our Engineer Officer, Dave Abinett - again, he of the nose trouser button fame of earlier - fell sick with griping abdominal pains. It was apparent, even to amateurs, that he probably had appendicitis. Naval authorities were informed, approval was given for our Chief Artificer to assume his role temporarily, and the people ashore in Tromsø were informed. Tromsø has a hospital. We speeded up, and got there early. Dave was offloaded in an ambulance, but not before I had taken a hundred quid out of his next month's pay and given it to him in cash, for contingencies.

Another aside. Two asides, in fact. The senior cook and the senior accountant were between them responsible for providing food for the ship's company. They frequently disagreed, because the Petty Officer Cook wanted the best cuts of meat, the best of all provisions, in fact, but the Petty Officer Caterer had to make ends meet and wouldn't let him have them. I had to adjudicate, so we had a weekly "menu meeting" in my cabin, which doubled up as my office. We all agreed, eventually, a menu for the following week, which started with lunch on a Monday and ended with supper on a Sunday, and then it all started again. We knew that as the weather got colder, the sailors would eat more and more and our budget would become strained. The Petty Officer Cook said "Don't worry, I'll put on savouries. They all like savouries." The Petty Officer Accountant nodded. In my greenness, I enquired "What are savouries?" He said "You get a slice of toast, then you pipe POM (Potato Mashed) round it so it looks like a castle. Then you fill it with baked beans and put a fried egg on top". I said "They'll never eat that, not more than once, anyway!" The two experienced Petty Officers just smiled at me. I have to admit it was a huge success. Not only did lots of sailors choose it instead of a pork chop or a beef fritter or a roulade de veaux avec la sauce d'Avignon, they also clamoured for it to be put on more often. It cost the equivalent of 10p to make. Not only were we delighted, they were delighted, as well. So when the going got tough for those out on the open deck when we were up in the Arctic, we gave them a free "savoury" whenever they came back inside, at any hour of the day or night. It was a huge success.

Unlike the results of the last menu meeting before we got into the ice. It was a sheer coincidence, one that none of us thought of. For the last supper of one week, we had rabbit on the menu. By sheer chance, a week in advance and without even thinking about it we put rabbit on for the lunch of the following day's menu, so it was rabbit twice on the trot. No sooner was that lunch over than the internal papparazi got to work, putting up pictures of rabbits around the messdecks, and somebody put up a spoof "message from the commanding officer" saying how sorry he was that "there was only rabbit left in the freezer, but would you mind awfully putting up with it for the next three weeks", and somebody under the pseudonym of

"Adolph Von Rabbitburger" issued a book of recipes in which rabbit was the main, and in some cases, the sole, ingredient, and the rating in charge of recreational films put on "Watership Down" showing continuously. The Petty Officer Caterer retired to lock himself into his cabin to lick his wounds, and, as I later discovered, planned his revenge. When we got to the serious business of surveying in well-sub-zero temperatures, of course, it was all forgotten (particularly as we had put on some delicious meals in the interim) and people coming in from the cold enjoyed their day and night "savouries".

People were carefully timed to ensure they came back inside again at regular intervals. My respect for them grew and grew. This lasted for some days. Then it stopped, and we came back. One pleasant thing was that we would be able to pick up the Engineer Officer from hospital, and he would be able to continue his duties. This was, of course, from Tromsø, where we had to stop on the way home.

The sailors had eaten so much in the cold weather that the catering budget was considerably below par. So it was with the most enormous pleasure when we tied up at a different berth in Tromsø and looked over the side that we could see, many fathoms down in the crystal clear water, that the seabed was alive, moving, with little creatures which turned out to be prawns (or shrimps, or scampi, take your pick. Look at the dictionary.) So, having ascertained that we were allowed to do so, we laid large fine-meshed nets on the bottom under the ship and then the next morning pulled them up. This was not easy, there was such a weight of seafood therein. Chef and Caterer were over the moon, and the ship's company dined royally for several days thereafter, and since the remainder was in the freezer, for some weeks after that.

The Petty Officer Caterer had put a notice on the ship's company noticeboard two or three days before we got to Tromsø saying that in view of his catering contacts with commercial firms ashore he had been offered a bargain price for reindeer skins and if anyone wanted a piece of reindeer skin at the greatly reduced price of five quid would they sign their names below. Some fifty people signed up for this. Now, you will know that reindeer skins are very expensive, even in the place they come from, so he went ashore with his two hundred and fifty pounds, bought a reindeer skin for that amount, brought it back on board, cut it up into fifty pieces, and gave everyone a piece. He could not be "done" for fraud, because he didn't say what size they would be in the first place, and he had received and disbursed two hundred and fifty pounds, against receipt, and had not therefore gained a pecuniary advantage, so the authorities (the captain) could not do anything. But he had to go and lock himself into his cabin again. He made amends later, of course.

We collected the Engineer Officer from the hotel to which he had been discharged from hospital. He looked much better, but was a little sheepish. We didn't know why, or ask. Perhaps he had spent his money unwisely. We found out later. He had been admitted to hospital and was lying in his bed when the nurses came round to take temperatures and pulses. They took his pulse and then asked him to take down his pyjama trousers so they could take his temperature in the usual continental way - rectally. He expostulated "That's disgusting. I'm not doing that. I'll show you how we do it in England!" and he snatched the thermometer from the nurse and stuck it under his tongue. First with a triumphant smile, then with a grimace as he realised what he had done. The Norwegians chuckled broadly as they told us, and wished us well on our way.

After a few days in Plymouth, so that we could still recognise our wives and girlfriends and other relatives, we sailed again for the Med. We changed "Scientific Officer" at Plymouth. This title was a pseudonym for someone who wasn't able to do things himself, but was good at doing sums, and he was what we used to call an "Instructor Officer". Indeed, they had their own branch. They were universally known as "Schoolies". They did a lot of good work ashore in instructing officers and ratings in this and that, but at sea were generally superfluous -

except that several of them were also meteorologists, which in ships with helicopters and particularly in aircraft carriers - is very important indeed. Ours was a bit nominal. He was a nice chap, but gained little respect from the fact that he had joined the RN just a few weeks previously and was made an instant Lieutenant Commander. The rest of us had been required to work very hard to get to that rank. And earn it. And unfortunately, although very intelligent (why wouldn't he be?) he was also very green. His name was David Husband, and he was the butt of a few japes in the weeks to come.

We sailed through the Gibraltar straits, again, with a new Captain, Geoff Hope, and the new First Lieutenant who had joined earlier, Bill Frisken. Bill was one of the finest naval officers I have ever served with, by far the most proficient seaman, and a splendid human being as well. I am proud to have been able to regard him as a friend to the end of my days, and our wives likewise, (which end has not come yet, but I really must type more quickly).

With so many hours, days and weeks at sea, all of us had off-duty recreational interests to pursue: I made wooden castles and other toys for my children, Bill made ship models - very good ones too, in some of which (ships he had served in) he installed radio control. I also made a crib for a baby - our baby - very traditional and with a canvas "bed" surrounded by crinoline and cotton on a wooden frame with a "hood" over one end. The canvas I sewed by hand. Then on the advice of our "Buffer" (Chief Bosn's Mate) I washed it in seawater and hung it out to dry in the sun - repeatedly - which had the effect of bleaching it, and tightening all the stitches. We still have it. Bob Ward, previously mentioned, was a talented maker of things in German Silver; he made me two napkin rings which look very esoteric, very avant garde, somewhat cryptic, until you examine closely and see that one of them says "Alan" and the other "Pat". We still treasure them. Just as an aside but still on the theme of engraved metals, our second son was christened on board HMS HECATE, in the ship's bell.

Bill and I often went ashore together, sightseeing and shopping, but Bill also went ashore for more energetic purposes, like climbing great big mountains, which was not to my taste. We were ashore one afternoon in the little town of Brindisi when we saw in the central square of this little town a stage being erected, and folding wooden chairs being put out. We were at a cafe having a quiet coffee and we watched with surprise as the stage grew bigger and bigger and the rows of chairs got wider and more numerous. Wondering what was going on, we eventually found an English speaking workman and asked what they were doing. "Tonight," he said, "Opera. Il Travatore." Counting the chairs and running out of steam at about a thousand, we thought it must be going to be good if a little town this size can host such an audience, so we decided to attend. That evening, we turned up, and admired the finished article. The stage was vast, well robed with purple velvet curtains and surrounded by wooden flats, with a large orchestra pit in front. We bought tickets, and looked for seats. The only empty ones we could see near the front were actually in the front row, twelve of them, so we sat in two of them. After a while, the orchestra arrived. Then there was a huge fanfare and the Mayor and his entourage arrived - all twelve of them. We shuffled around a lot, looking I'm sure very guilty and wondering how to make a dignified exit, when a very serious gentleman said to us in perfect English "Please do not concern yourselves - please accept the seats with my compliments". So we watched the whole, huge, performance, in much awe and amazement, from the front row. It was one of those magical evenings which are given to us but rarely.

On board, we made our own recreation, such as quizzes. As an aside, at the end of each month we all got a messbill for what we had consumed. The very green David Husband got one which included "electricity consumed in cabin". He asked Dave Abinett in the next cabin if he had received one. "Of course," said Dave, "but yours will be bigger than mine because I've got a beard but you use an electric razor." David wrote a cheque - which went straight on the notice board with

"RPC" written on it: "Request the Pleasure of your Company" - at a personally paid-for drinks session! A jape, but no escape!

Making your own entertainment on board: UniHecate Challenge Bamber Pearce presides, 1976

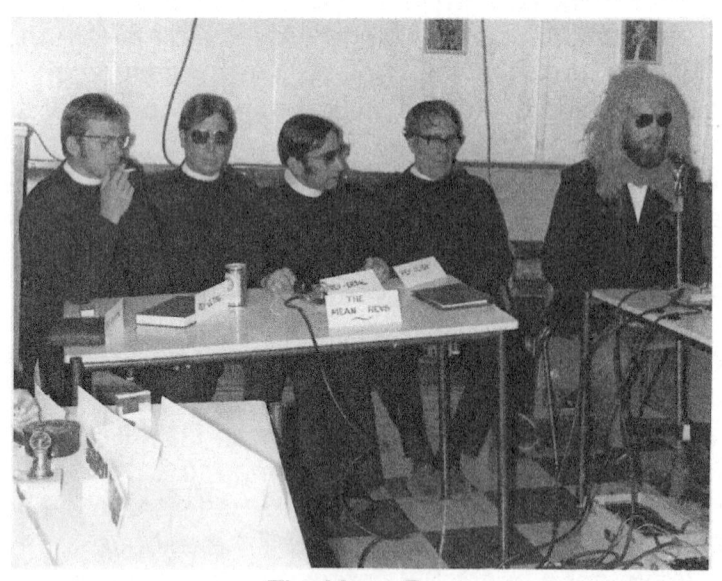

The Mean Revs

We returned to our base in Malta. While we were in the Med

we used Malta as a sort of "staging post" and every fourth or fifth weekend we put into Malta to replenish. Malta is a wonderful place if you are a tourist and like the sun and cheap booze and are prepared to accept that one-star hotels call themselves four star hotels and you're happy to stay by their pools and the food isn't terribly good, and that there is only one beach, and that it hasn't got much sand anyway. If you are interested in history, it is absolutely magical: it was the pivotal point and the point of not Custer's but the West's last stand in the Moslem/Christian battles which had gone on for centuries as the dividing line was pushed backwards and forwards across the Med and finally, after the Christian Knights had been turfed out of Rhodes, the place where they had their last stand - and succeeded against enormous odds. I am no great historian. You must read "The Great Siege: Malta 1565" by Ernle Bradford (like myself, a retired Lieutenant Commander RN and lover of the history of Malta) but be warned, if you do, that I started reading it in bed one night, couldn't put it down, and finally finished it at 03.00.

We went into and out of Malta so many times that I will condense all the Malta dits into one section.

Firstly, I was called to a much larger ship's judicial investigation because I had witnessed the activities of a swimming Royal Marine. With colleagues, he had crossed Grand Harbour, celebrated something greatly but not wisely in various bars and missed the last dghajsa (taxi-boat - pronounced "Die - so", believe it or not) and decided to swim back. Half way across he realised he wasn't going to make it, clung to a buoy and shouted for help. He was picked up by our boat. At his summary trial for "bringing the Service into disrespect" the Captain called for the senior Royal Marine officer to give mitigating circumstances and a character reference. The Royal Marine officer looked at the Captain and said "Throw the book at him, Sir". The Captain responded by saying that it was the officer's job to say good things about the man and ask for leniency. The Royal Marine officer said "Throw the book at him, Sir. A Royal Marine that can't swim across Grand Harbour deserves to have the book thrown at him." And that was that.

It was about the time that Dom Mintoff had said that his country was going to be more independent (or something like that) and at the same time the Royal Navy was withdrawing after several hundred years of very happy co-operation with the Maltese people and governments. The RN headquarters was at HMS St. Angelo, the fortress which the Knights defended against the Turks in the ancient battles which I outlined earlier. The central fort was surrounded by a defended walkway which overlooked Grand Harbour, and was by now also the home of countless jacaranda trees of various hues. We were berthed alongside, under the citadel, and in full view of Valetta. Our Maltese stewards all took leave, of course, as was their right. But it was about at that time that the RN decided that it was no longer going to have what were called "LEP's". This stood for "Locally Entered Personnel" and in the 21st century this might sound somewhat demeaning, but in fact the Goans, the Adenis, the Chinese, and the Maltese people who were not quite in but not quite out of the Royal Navy were very proud of their positions and the highly professional work that they did. And verymuch respected for it. So my Maltese team members were given the option of either leaving altogether, or of joining the Royal Navy as full members, with the same conditions of service, but losing their rights to leave when they felt like it or having the ability to take home leave to Malta when they wished. Mine decided to stay in the Royal Navy.

One of them, a Leading Cook called Vella, a sound example of dedication to the service, and quite a good cook without being outstanding, but able to get the food on the counter at the right time, had less English than most of his compatriots. But he soldiered on, and the Petty Officer and I looked after him as best we could. He got very frustrated by one particularly gobby able seaman who kept up a tirade of invective against his cooking - quite unwarranted - and we were all wondering how we could (legally) curb him when Vella precipitated the denouement himself. The gobby AB turned up at the food counter one day and said "What do you call this, you black git?" Vella had been biding his time, but now he could act. He called the Cox'n - the ship's policeman - and laid a charge.

HMS HECATE alongside at her base in Grand Harbour, Malta, 1976

Now, it has to be recorded that at that time we had a splendid RN Hydrographic Officer called Brian Dyde in command of the ship. He was exceedingly competent both as a surveyor and as a ship's captain, in his own way, which was to lead by example. He was an Acting Commander. So, back to Leading Cook Vella and the gobby AB. The latter was put on a charge of "behaving with disrespect to a senior", one down from "disobeying the lawful command of a senior" and it came up at the Captain's Table (a captain who, remember, has the authority the same as a JP in the UK). And the Captain was not going to treat lightly an able seaman who called a Leading Hand "a black git". Unusually for a simple case, I was called to the Table. "Supply Officer," said Brian, "before I find this man guilty I want you to tell me from the manual of naval law what penalties I can give him without actually sending him to prison." (This meant, of course, that the Captain would not have to apply to anybody outside the ship to impose his penalties, nor would anybody outside the ship hear about it unless the guilty man (sorry, the accused) complained to outside authority - which he wasn't going to). So I told him, and the AB got the lot. Stoppage of leave, extra duties and so on. "Also, the wearing of plain clothes (as opposed to uniform) is a privilege, not a right, and the same applies to going ashore from the ship at any time other than on annual leave". The Captain said: "Your daily leave is stopped until I say so. You are not to go ashore except for your annual leave, and when you do it will be in uniform". And that was that. There was no more trouble.

We carried out more surveys off Italy, then undertook an interesting visit to Alexandria in Egypt, then a few more weeks' surveying and then had our final long weekend alongside in Italy, in Livorno.

The author

The background to the visit to Alexandria was this: relations had been strained since the Suez Canal Crisis of 1956, a period still in living memory for many Egyptians and certainly still in that of their government. But diplomatic moves had been made behind the scenes, and while it would not have been acceptable for a Royal Navy warship to visit in order to prove friendly intentions it was deemed a good idea for an RN white painted ship with a yellow funnel (but nonetheless flying the White Ensign) to call and pay what was effectively Her Majesty's respects. This was graciously permitted by the Egyptian government

The author in Alexandria and tight shorts

We were given a good berth in the centre of this combined civilian/military complex, and allocated two Liaison Officers, who would help us take care of relations with local authorities, with interpreting, making phone calls on our behalf, and a host of other things. They were invaluably helpful, one more than the other. The first, who introduced himself as "Ben", was a bright, alert Lieutenant, Egyptian Navy, who was thoroughly enthusiastic in everything he did, polite, affable, cheery and welcoming. He laughed a lot, and we could tell that his warmth was genuine. The other, called Abdul, was the opposite. He just sat in an armchair in the wardroom, not joining in with anything. There was an air of mutual politeness with Abdul, but one could pull Ben's leg and he would pull the puller's back again.

Of course, we had some time off after all the official duties were carried out, salutes had been rendered, calls had been exchanged, mutual expressions of co-operation and friendship had been expressed, lunches had been given and attended, and a bit of calm descended. Then it was buses off to the pyramids and all the other attractions - stopping, of course at the tourist shops of "not my brother" and "not my uncle" on the way - and on the way back again. Some bought stuffed leather camels, some bought plastic pyramids; and there were also bendy crocodiles and monkeys on sticks.

Back on board, the following working day, I was discussing vegetables and fruit with the caterer. We had a chandler delivering our foodstuffs, and very good they were, too - the best salad gear I have seen anywhere, and beautiful fresh vegetables. Also fruits of many varieties - except, for some obscure reason, dates. But we also wanted some things for the Wardroom, and something different for the ship's company, and they weren't there either. (Perhaps it was a similar scenario to that which we were later to find in Denmark, where we couldn't get bacon because it had all been exported).

But anyway, dates there weren't. We were determined to get some, and some other unusual comestibles as well, and so we mounted an expeditionary party

The author on board the ship of the desert

Fortunately, we took cash. The head cook, the caterer and I hired a vehicle and set off for the market with substantial funds. We bought all the things which the contractor hadn't been able to supply us with - fresh dates by the branchful, lychees, pomegranates, mangoes, pawpaws, and at the chef's insistence, goat's meat by the hundredweight. We packed it all into the vehicle and set off back to the ship. On the way back to the ship, two singular events took place which would not have happened in UK. Firstly, as we were about to enter the dockyard, all the lights went out. I don't mean that some bulbs failed or that a circuit was broken somewhere; all the lights went out. All the street lights, all the ceremonial lights, all the mosque lights, everything. And all the cars turned off their lights, too. It was really spooky. It turned out that it was either an impending Israeli air attack or a practice for such an event. But in either case, we headed back to the dockyard in almost complete blackness. When we arrived, the guards were on edge, and very suspicious. They turfed us out of the vehicle and searched it. Needless to say, they found all our foodstuff. They wanted to know where it came from (a bit obvious, really) where it was going, and more to the point, why we wanted it. We explained quite openly, of course, and said it was for us to add to our daily rations, and we had bought it in the market for cash and no we didn't have any receipts. They obviously thought this was far more important than we did (not difficult, because we didn't think it was important at all), but there are obviously Egyptian laws about smuggling food legally bought and paid for back on to your own ship. Eventually, they made us sign a certificate saying it was for our own consumption, and, I strongly suspect, having been told from on high that this was a diplomatic visit of great importance and no shock waves were to be created, they allowed us to proceed. The quality of what we had bought was quite exceptional, and it all lasted out at sea for as long as could reasonably have been expected - especially the dates, which were gorgeous.

Then the unexpected happened. A very distraught Englishman appeared on board and asked to speak to the captain, who elected to meet him in the wardroom with other officers present. The man said "Forgive me for intruding, but I am at my wits end and I saw the White Ensign and I have come to ask for your help. I run a mining exploration company just outside the city and my deputy mining engineer has just dropped dead. Heart attack. Natural causes. No doubt. Police satisfied. Problem is, his wife's got to be told, and the British authorities have got to be told, and the coroner, and all that, but communications here are dreadful and I've been on the phone for hours and hours and got absolutely nowhere and the telegraph office say they can't get through and I'm really stuck." We gave him a drink and asked him for all the details. Then we reassured him that we had the best communications in the world and would ensure that we sent his messages to all the right people, including a radiotelephone call to whomsoever he wished, compliments of the Royal Navy, and no charge. He sat in our radio room and sorted it all out. He was very grateful, and afterwards asked if he could do anything in any way to thank us. Our captain said "Well, perhaps there is one thing. You obviously have local contacts. All my crew have come to Egypt hoping to see a belly dancer, but frankly you can only see them at the most expensive hotels, and my chaps can't afford that." The Englishman said he would fix it. And the very next day we were invited to have a party on our own flight deck, and a whole orchestra turned up complete with the most attractive and professional belly dancer you have ever seen and it's much more interesting in the flesh (pardon the pun) than it is in a film or on the television, and we were all asked to dance with her and it was a magical evening. Many thanks to whomever it was; we didn't see him again - too busy getting on with his mining, I expect.

Egyptian Belly Dancer and orchestra
HMS HECATE flight deck, in Alexandria, 1976

On the flight deck - Belly dancer with ship's company

We all did the tourist thing in our days off. Then it was time to sail. I particularly recall two things about our departure. Firstly, we called Ben and Abdul to the wardroom for a presentation. Ben was given a magnum of scotch, a huge box of chocolates, a ship's plaque and a large bouquet for his wife, and Abdul was also given a little present.

The second thing was that the contractor (chandler) came on board at 08.30 for his money. I took him to the wardroom and called for the caterer to come and sit with us. I got all the money out - cash, of course. He presented his account, which was correct in every detail and accurate down to the last ickey - but he had added on "10% harbour tax". I said "you didn't tell us about that when you told me your prices - you said that these were your prices." "Yes," he replied smoothly, "but as you know, nothing in life is certain except death and taxes." And he sat back expectantly. I said "One more thing is certain and that is that I'm going to pay you exactly what you asked for, and no more." We discussed this for quite a while, as you might imagine, and then the inevitable happened. The main broadcast burst into life and the Bosn's Mate made the usual announcement: "D'ye hear there! The ship is about to sail. The gangway will be removed in five minutes' time." "Take it or leave it," I said, pushing forward a receipt and holding out the cash. "D'ye hear there! You have two minutes to leave the ship if you are not sailing with us." He signed. I handed over the cash, exact to the last groat. He stormed out.

The departure was uneventful. We exchanged signals of gratitude with the Egyptian military authorities and the civilian authorities and it was generally deemed to have been "a successful visit". Then came the next problem. Not for the ship, not for me, but for the Stokers' Mess. On the way in, as was usual, we had money changing for the officers and sailors, and it was done mess by mess; each mess collected its sterling, brought it along to me, and I changed it for whatever ickeys were in effect. The exchange rate was decided by the MoD; I had no discretion in the matter. Everyone had changed UK currency - except for the Stokers' Mess. I had sent the Petty Officer accountant to find out why. "One of them has been here before," he said "and he knows a bloke in a backstreet who will give you far more ickeys per quid than we are doing." I said "Please go and warn them it's dangerous, and they shouldn't do it". He did, and they didn't not. Then we forgot all about it in the melée of our official departure and all the ceremonial. Until now. First day at sea was traditionally the time to exchange foreign currency back to sterling. Along came the stokers with several hundred pounds in Egyptian money, having so much left because they had exchanged enormous amounts of it at their backstreet exchange rate. "I'm sorry," I said, "The MoD can't take it back because you didn't get it from the MoD in the first place; we are not allowed to money launder." "But it's Egyptian," they said. I had to inform them that there was no way I was going to take back their Egyptian money. "But, Sir," they said "It's completely useless in UK. No bank will take it." And I had to reply "That's why the MoD won't take it, either." I felt very slightly sorry for them but they had been warned and had not taken the advice. We never had money changing problems again, and after that, they all trusted the Pusser, who was a bastard, but straight. Then it was time to sail.

It was only the following day that we received an urgent telegram from the British Embassy in Cairo: "Harbour Tax is standard practice here Stop Cannot pass on the accrual to you so have absorbed it Stop Please do not repeat Stop." We took notice of this, and the Caterer and I just looked at each other and smiled.

There is really nothing left to say about our visit to Egypt, which was a great success and very enjoyable for us - except that when we returned to the UK the customs officials in Plymouth confiscated all the ship's company's stuffed leather camels, put them in plastic bags and took them away for incineration, without option. They were all stuffed, apparently, with old, used, hospital bandages.

So, reeling a bit, we set off back to the survey ground, and then after a few weeks put in to Livorno, in Italy for the weekend.

Livorno is a typical Mediterranean port and a typical Italian port of the less industrialised type. There is very little tide in the Med, if any, and so the jetty we were tied up alongside had a height of only a foot or two. Further, we were right in the centre of the town. A street ran alongside the jetty, right next to us, and on the other side of this there was a long row of shops, mostly of the tourist type selling postcards and stamps and souvenirs and other bright things, but also a corner grocery shop and a coffee house and a flower shop and a hardware store. This street was at right angles to the main street, which of course had even more shops and bars and eateries of one standard or another. I must say I found Italy (off the tourist routes) very cute and endearing, and the people were very hospitable.

We had a wonderful, relaxing and restful visit for a long weekend, and then sailed again on the Monday morning. However, for a few weeks I had been wrestling with the accounts and amounts in the ship's welfare fund, and it was beginning to worry me. You will remember that the welfare fund is a collective, democratic club for the sailors to pay money into and take it out again when needed, as it was for all the BBQ plastic knives, forks and spoons. The trouble was that for many months there had been no fundraising, for various reasons, but there had been outgoings, and funds were dangerously low. And then I had an idea.

When warships visit foreign parts, the ship's company need to have local currency to spend ashore, as mentioned above, and it was part of my duties to arrange this, often before sailing from the UK if it was a strong currency (e.g. the US dollar) or by imprest from a local bank on arrival (booked in advance) if it was not. The rules for the ship's company are much as they would be for a tourist from UK exchanging sterling before going and changing what is left on getting back home - banks in UK will change back your foreign notes, but not coins. So it was with us. On the last night of any foreign visit, the sailors and officers would return on board and find that the Supply Officer had placed a bucket by the gangway, so that no longer useable foreign coins could be tossed in, and given to charity.

As an aside, foreign currency is classified by RN sailors as follows: it is all "ickeys", so an ice cream might cost you a couple of "ickeys" whereas a new camera could cost a hundred "ickeys" or so; high value coins were "klebs", and anything less than one "kleb" was simply "shrapnel". So the buckets largely topped up overnight by returning sailors with shrapnel, with a few klebs thrown in. Sometimes an ickey, too.

Same procedure in Livorno, although now I did have a different charity in mind; I was thinking that in this case, perhaps charity begins at home (although our sailors didn't seem to think so, judging by the balance in the welfare fund). The problem was that this money was all in foreign coins, which a bank wouldn't exchange. But I had a cunning plan in mind. The ickeys and klebs needed to be converted.

On the Monday morning of sailing, I collected the bucket of

coins and crossed the road to the tourist shop. I went in and spoke to the owner, a short, stout, dark haired, cheery looking fellow of about fifty. I pointed to his rack of postcards, shook the bucket, and said in my best Italian "Quanti costa all the cartez postalez?" He looked at the bucket and its contents, and thought for a moment. Then he grasped the rack by its central pole and thrust it towards me. "You can-a keep-a the rack" he said. "Gracias, señor," I said. "And you can-a keep-a the bucket." I sped back on board, just in time before we sailed.

There were a few sore heads that morning. It had been a very enjoyable and hospitable visit, and had cemented Anglo-Italian relations in several different ways, formally and informally, and with the word "relations" having more than one meaning, as well. But sail we did, and within a couple of hours we were back on the survey ground.

At Stand Easy that morning (11 a.m. coffee break) I got on the ship's internal loudspeaker system, with the full approval of captain and first lieutenant, and made the following announcement: "D'ye hear there! Treasurer of the ship's welfare fund speaking. I'm sure everyone had a great visit to Livorno, and enjoyed every moment they could ashore. I'm equally sure that the vast majority were far too busy to remember to send Mum or Girlfriend or perhaps anyone else a postcard. So I was thinking of you all, and I went ashore and bought a whole heap of postcards to sell on behalf of the welfare fund. They will be on sale in the dining hall at lunchtime, price - a quid each". The ship virtually heaved with a great groan as people realised that it was going to cost them a pound for every member of their nearest and dearest they had omitted to write to - and that they were going to have to stump up. To cement the picture, I pressed the transmit button again, and further announced "The captain has agreed that the helicopter will take our mail ashore this evening, and collect any remaining incoming mail from the post office." I then handed the mike to the ship's postman (honorary title and position) who said "D'ye hear there. Mail will close at 18.00, repeat 18.00. Make sure you have posted it by 18.00. That's all." The "donations" exceeded £200; our financial problem was over for the rest of the commission.

We changed First Lieutenants at some stage, I don't quite recall when, but a Lieutenant called Barry Humphreys joined us - a very popular man with an infectious smile and the ability to get people to do things, which is what both management and leadership are all about. We carried on with our survey until it was time to return to the UK - for me, for the last time in HMS HECATE. As usual, we called in at Gibraltar on the way home. This was to be a most interesting visit, for several reasons.

Gibraltar Harbour has central shore berths for warships, but not many; the main areas to tie up to are the huge moles, man-made arms sticking out into the sea, and well over a mile long if you count both North Arm, South Arm and the other little bits. We had been allocated our berth, and we entered safely through the entrance and headed for it. We noticed with pleasure that there was already alongside a large County Class DLG (destroyer/leading/guidedmissile) (I can't remember which one) and we were not far from it when we berthed. I say "with pleasure" because there is a long standing naval tradition that if a large RN vessel is in a foreign port when a smaller RN vessel comes in, then the larger Wardroom immediately sends an RPC (see "Schoolie" earlier) to the smaller Wardroom. So we tied up, got on with our various jobs of refuelling, revictualling, taking on water and stores and spares, and writing up our reports and so on, and waited for our invitation. It didn't come on the first day, as it should have, and when it hadn't come on the second morning either we began to fret about the neglect of this fine old Royal Naval Tradition. In short, we thought they must be too tight-fisted. At Stand Easy in the Wardroom, the indomitable Barry had an idea. "Right," he said, "I've got here a list of the officers in that DLG. I'll pass it round and if any of you know any of them, you're out. Second, how many of you have got a grey suit and a stiff collar?" (We all wore stiff collars on collarless shirts at that time, but some had been away at sea so long they had forgotten) "You've all got shiny-backed waistcoats because it's part of issued uniforms. So I want you all to go back to your cabins, put on your grey suits, with your waistcoats back to front underneath and put on a stiff collar back to front and then you'll all look like vicars, won't you? Back in ten minutes, please," he said. He then got a godbotherer to open the Church cupboard and get out a dozen or so bibles and prayer books and distributed them one each when we reported back to the wardroom in our grey suits and "clerical collars". As we finished our coffees, he picked up the telephone. He said "Shh" to us and then after a lot of dialling, got through to the Executive Officer of the DLG. "Ahh.. " he said, somewhat *sotto voce*, "Good morning, Admiral. I'm sorry to intrude, but I am Father Bartholomew of St. Saviours in London and we have come out to Gibraltar to visit the Sisters of the Little Convent of Mercy and Peace, but unfortunately they have all got.... Er ..... measles and we cannot be admitted, so we have a major gap in our programme but seeing your beautiful English Navy boat from the Peak in its shining British glory we wondered if it might not be too presumptuous to ask if we might have a little look round for an hour or so? We wouldn't touch anything."

The immediate response was an offer of a guided tour as Barry knew it would be, as soon as we could get there. Off we went, immediately, clutching our bibles and some prayerbooks. We practised our plan of action on the way, and soon filed up on to the deck, to be met by the duty officer, and the Midshipmen. We toured the ship, asking erudite questions such as "where do your wives sleep?" and "Don't you think it's dangerous to have so many guns on board" to "Do officers have to swab the decks every day, too?" - and our cover held. By then, of course, it was lunchtime and we were invited to the Wardroom, to be met by the Commander. He greeted "Father Bartholomew" warmly but sedately, and said "May I offer you.... I mean, I don't know if, Er, are you allowed to partake....... Er.....alcohol ...." And "Father Bartholomew" immediately said "Thank you very much, I'll have a double

Woods". Barry immediately downed his drink in one, smacked his lips and said "You know, the trouble with navy rum is that it makes one so thirsty. Do you think I might have a pint of CSB with the next one?" We all enjoyed our beers and other drinks for a while and looked set for a long session until someone made a gaffe by mentioning some technical point or another which could only be known by a naval officer, and cover was blown. They took it very well, I must say, and we all had a jolly good laugh - and then we went back to the ship and started to prepare our countermeasures against some sort of a return match.

We stored ship in double time, and the engineering departments carried out their restorations and repairs, and the hydrographers drew up their fair charts and we all got in a bit of rest and relaxation as well. Not that we didn't eat well on board, but Gib has a plethora of excellent little ethnic and cultural restaurants and bistros as well as the large touristy ones, and we all eased away the strains of having spent many weeks at sea.

Earlier, I mentioned the things that some of us did in our spare time at sea, and one of the things I did was to run a Russian "O" Level class. I had about six people in it, including one of the stewards, a pleasant if over-rotund young man called Snowball. He had joined the navy without any qualifications at all, but had got through the entrance tests, and had then grown into a most reliable and assiduous member of the Service. I never found out if he joined the class because I was his head of department or because he really wanted to achieve something, and I never asked. But he sat throughout classes, worked well, took the exam back in Plymouth - and became probably the only RN steward with no qualifications at all except for a Russian "O" Level. Everybody was very proud.

Still in Gib, we had another little event. We were minding our own business when some chap from Gibraltar radio must have looked out of his window and seen our beautiful white hull flying the white ensign and thought it would make a good programme. It did. He telephoned us and asked if we would send somebody along to be interviewed on the local Saturday evening chat show. Barry and I agreed that it should be us. We also agreed that he could become a bit technical when talking about hydrographic surveying, and I might become a bit boring if talking about logistics, so we agreed to explain each other's roles. It was a brilliant idea, and when transmitted came across very well in layman's terms that everyone could understand and empathise with. Come the day, we were both a bit nervous, so we had a stiffener at the bar before we left the ship. The taxi took us to the radio station, and we were welcomed. We were in plenty of time, so they put us in the "green room", explaining that it was standard practice while people waited to go on air, and that there was a drink for us "to calm any nerves we might have". It was a bottle of very fine Spanish sherry, along with just three glasses. By the time we went on air, we were quite relaxed.

The radio chat show was half an hour. We had been allocated half of it. The other half was allocated to a very interesting character - a Jesuit priest who had just returned from the jungle in a central American state, where he had been for three years, trying to convert natives - and who had now been granted three months' leave back in Europe. The other glass was his, and he used it well. He was small and rotund, with a cheery smile and an engaging character, and clearly a good customer for a radio station. Barry and I turned out to be good customers, too, and we soon had the interviewer rocking in his seat and laughing and drawing us out of ourselves as, of course, a good interviewer should. When it was all over, we all shook hands and the priest said how very interested he was in the work we had been doing and might he have a look round our ship? He had already decided to follow us back to the ship, and he came on board, had a cursory look round the upper deck and then asked to see the "canteen". We took him to the wardroom, where he suggested he would buy us both a round of drinks. He appeared surprised when we told him that it was all on officers' chits, and he could not therefore pay for the round. "Appeared"? After three rounds, we concluded that this was not his first time at pulling this one, but it was by now well after midnight, and time for him to go. This took quite some time to do, but with the promise of keeping the half empty bottle of scotch he had consumed, he eventually agreed, and we saluted him off the gangway in great ceremonious style - telling the Quartermaster-on-watch that on no account was he to be allowed back on board. We all had typhus, or something. But he had been an admirable companion for the evening, and we felt we had gained a greater understanding of the world thereby. I became even more convinced that Jesuits have hollow legs - especially the ones that have been banished to far distant places.

We both woke up next morning feeling a bit under the weather and perhaps a bit worried, cursing Jesuits, and wondering what the hell our broadcast had turned out like - had we been OTT? Hyper? Did anyone notice? We had breakfast, during which the signalman brought in the overnight signals, on top of which was one from the Admiral, Flag Officer Gibraltar, the local God. In trepidation, we read "Congratulations on a very good show. Highly entertaining. Good PR for the RN. Well done". We thought "Wow", and left it at that. Another Jape. Another Scrape. Another Escape.

Then we returned to UK, to Plymouth. This was to be my swan song, because we were to have our Big Inspection by the admiral, Flag Officer Plymouth. We had known about this for quite a long time, of course, and we had all made our preparations. A Big Inspection consists of a day's departmental inspection, when all a department's activities and records are examined, a "harbour inspection", when all aspects of cleanliness are examined and there is a formal turnout of all officers and ratings in their best uniforms, and a "sea inspection", when the ship sails and is asked to perform all sorts of activities. In my case, this was deploying the helicopter for a casualty evacuation, and its recovery and safe landing in operating situations. Our departmental inspection went very well, as I knew it would because we had had so much time to prepare for it, out harbour inspection went well because the Petty Officers had insisted that they inspect everybody's best uniform and advise on cleaning and pressing all the uniforms, and there was just the sea inspection to get through.

We sailed at 07.00 for our sea inspection. The Admiral's Chief of Staff, Commodore Ollie Sutton, was the senior inspecting officer and he had the whole of his staff on board with him - seamen, navigators, engineers, communicators, Fleet Air Arm specialists, and so on. It was to be, for me, a portentous day. My logistics department fed everyone throughout the evacuation exercise and the "shore support after a tsunami" exercise, and so on. Then there was an unexpected event, for real. The helicopter radio'd in and said he had a problem and had to return urgently for a recovery. This is what civilians call a "crash landing" and what we call "a precautionary landing". It was certainly for real. Fortunately, I had trained the flight deck crew for just such a thing and when I announced "Emergency Landing" each and every member of the flight deck crew knew exactly what to do: the emergency strops were prepared, the fire fighting foam (AFFF) was readied, the bridge was told to steer in the most propitious direction, the stretchers were laid out and the sick bay was informed. It all happened like clockwork, because we had practised it. And the recovery went like clockwork: the helicopter landed on our small deck with smoke coming out of his engine and once he was securely shackled to the deck and the pilot had emerged safely we put the foam on and ensured there would be no further fire, and that all personnel were safe. It was all done very calmly, without having to worry that an aircraft fire might endanger the whole ship. It demonstrated the value of preparation and training against all eventualities. And it was all observed by the Chief of Staff and his team. And the Chief of Staff immediately chose me to be his next Secretary, since I was to move on shortly, anyway. This was exactly what I had planned.

Now, during my time in HMS HECATE, I had received a bit of a shock. After the first surveying season, we had returned to

Plymouth for refit and repair, as I have mentioned. My wife was about to produce our second child, which was fortuitous as I was to be at home in Plymouth for the event. Then we got a message from MoD. The Supply Officer of HMS DANAE, a Leander class frigate on duty with STANAVFORLANT, had gone sick and had been flown back to UK. A few words of explanation. STANAVFORLANT is the acronym for the NATO STANdingNAValFORceAtLANTic, and was a group of ships from all the NATO countries which operated and exercised together on a permanent basis, individual ships being substituted for each other from time to time. It patrolled around the North Atlantic, making sure that it would be around if there were trouble - and making sure that everyone knew it was there. There was always an American ship in the group, and always a British ship, too; the others supplied ships when they could. Back to the story of my 1976 life. I was at work one day, on board the ship in dockyard hands, minding my own business and getting on with the work of ensuring that we were all prepared for the next surveying season, when this telephone call from MoD informed me that HMS DANAE, a Leander Class frigate of the force was depleted by one Supply Officer, that the NATO force had to be up to military strength at all times and that I had been selected as the man who was going to fly out there, sort the situation out, and maintain our position in STANAVFORLANT. The future of the Atlantic Alliance was at stake. They said. It was not so easy for me. I had to explain to my wife why I was going to leave her, eight months' pregnant, in fact not far from parturition, and go off to the West Indies to join another ship. It was an understandably difficult time. For both of us. But I had no option: I wore the Queen's uniform, and I had to do what I was told.

I flew out to somewhere I had never heard of before and had great difficulty finding in the atlas: Roosevelt Roads. This was a huge US naval base on the island of Puerto Rico in the Caribbean, and had been the designated place for the whole of the British Government to go to in the event of a German invasion in WW2 - to become a UK government in exile, just as the French had a De Gaulle government in exile in the UK.

The other nations would presumably have gone along with us as the whole of Europe was taken over by Nazi Germany. Although it is in the Caribbean, which conjures up beautiful pictures in holiday brochures, it was far from nice, or healthy. It was unruly, dangerous to foreigners, and somewhat insanitary. The Americans never ventured out of their base. But they rarely do, do they? (I remember when we were living in Northwood (near London) our American military family neighbours driving weekly to the US Air Force base fifty miles away where, at the "PX" (equivalent of NAAFI) they could buy all they wanted. Our US neighbour in Northwood - the wife - once said to us: "What's wrong with your milk that you have to have it delivered every day- why don't you buy it frozen like we do? And your meat?"

Anyway, the US base was absolutely huge, and it harboured a large proportion of the US Fleet and had every possible facility for the servicemen based there, with the exception of culture. Glitzy lights, yes. Cheap burger bars, yes. Loud pop music, yes. Beach and bikinis, yes. Loud evangelical chapels, yes. Bowling alleys and other machine-based pleasures, yes. Culture, no. It was not very pleasant, really.

To my surprise, I was met from the aircraft by three HMS DANAE officers - the Navigating Officer, the Deputy Engineering Officer and a young seaman trainee. They practically threw their arms around me. This is not the usual reaction to a supply/logistics officer; it's more usually "We can do it ourselves, thank you". I sensed trouble. I was right. On the taxi drive back to the ship they asked me penetrating questions such as "Are you going to be able to reduce our messbills?" and "Will we be able to have two boiled eggs for breakfast if we want to?" My sense of trouble deepened. I was met with equal warmth at the top of the gangway by three other officers, and became more troubled. What on earth was going on?

I had time to clean myself up and compose myself after the flight, and then it was time to call on the Captain. He welcomed me warmly, too, explained that my predecessor had unfortunately had to leave and go to a local hospital, and that my duties apart from being the Supply Officer were to take charge of a somewhat dispirited flight deck team. They were dispirited, he explained, because during the last exercise the ship had turned sharply while they were loading a torpedo on to the helicopter and the said torpedo had run out of control across the deck and disappeared over the side. My predecessor had been formally logged (which for an officer is the highest form of censure below a court martial; it was, nonetheless "logged" i.e. put on the formal record). The flight deck team had all been warned to be more careful, but of course it is always the officer in charge who takes the brunt of it. "We don't want you to end up getting logged, too." he said. I got the message. No quarters.

So the next day I hit my department like a ton of bricks. I had all the CPO's and PO's in to my cabin and asked them one by one what they had achieved, what they had found difficult, what was right in their sub-departments, and what was wrong. Putting together all the responses and ruling out both the sycophancies and the "intrusion factor" the answer became very clear. The previous supply officer, a Lieutenant, had been ground into the earth by other more senior officers in their own interests - one in particular - and had eventually just given up. I felt very sorry for him (I had once almost been in a similar position) and I determined that I was going to put this right.

The first thing to do was to check facts. The second was to get my team on my side. The third, which would follow, was to inspire them to greater things so that they, too, would achieve the recognition they deserved.

So I hit the accounts of each sub-department first. I went into far more detail than would normally be required, and asked penetrating questions which tested each of my Petty Officers to the limit. When I was satisfied, I relaxed, and praised them. I then laid aside each sub-department which was working properly and just needed a bit of support, and looked at what was left. What was left was the officers' catering department.

A word of explanation. From the time of Henry VIII the sailors have been fed from the public purse - sometimes satisfactorily, sometimes unsatisfactorily. The officers have either dipped into the naval pot and augmented it, or victualled themselves completely. By the time of my service, catering standards had rocketed - so much so that naval cooks were competing in and winning salon culinaire competitions against other cooks from all walks of life. And professional catering accountancy was down to a fine art. This was called the "General Mess" because the same standards applied to officers' messes and to senior and junior ratings' messes. Or should have done. In HMS DANAE the First Lieutenant (Second in Command and President of the officers' mess) was an old fogey of the Colonel Blimp school, and probably headmaster of it. He clung to old traditions with pedantic and irascible fervour and a misguided sense of patriotism and history. He thought that "General Mess" was akin to eating with the sailors and showing a white feather to modernisation; he didn't realise that it was in fact just a different way of doing the accounts. The ingredients were still cooked in the officers' galley. So, I discovered, the officers in HMS DANAE financed and fed themselves! They received inferior standards of food, and had huge messbills to boot. Because fifteen people can't live as well on a fixed income as can three hundred and thirty. It's simple economics. I couldn't believe it. The situation was archaic. This accounted for my greeting at the airport, of course, and subsequent reports from both officers and my own ratings, but sorting it out was going to be tricky. I took the Chief Caterer (my second most senior rating) into my confidence.

"How easily can we convert the officers' mess to General Mess" I asked. "On paper," he said "Very easily. But someone is going to have to convince them". We both knew exactly what he meant. The situation would be that the officers would have the same (excellent quality) ingredients as the ratings, but they could have it cooked in their own way. And with a small supplement could have all the little extras they wanted, such as curry accompaniments, chilli sherry for the soup, candles, parmesan to sprinkle and so forth. But they could also have an extra egg for breakfast or even two without the blink of the eye: what's two eggs when you're feeding three hundred and thirty mouths? I carried out great psychological preparation, starting with younger officers and those whom I knew would listen to sense, and worked upwards until I got to the glass ceiling - the First Lieutenant. But the Mess is perhaps the only thing which in the RN is run completely democratically, and when it came to a Mess vote, I won hands down. The First Lieutenant was furious, and never forgave me. But I knew I was only on board until a permanent replacement could be found and I could return to my own ship, HMS HECATE, still in dockyard hands in Plymouth, so I was free to do what was right. With the connivance of the Chief Caterer I made absolutely sure that the standard of the officers' food rocketed immediately, even if it was being temporarily overvictualled - it could be recouped later. We had steaks. We had fresh fish. We had elaborate French and other European dishes - using exactly the same ingredients which everyone else had, in order to be fair and correct. The morale of the officers' chefs rocketed, because they were being allowed a free rein to produce restaurant quality dishes with what was already restaurant quality ingredients, which the whole ship had. And they excelled themselves, as I knew they would. The extra cost was minuscule in the context of the overall budget, but I now had a very happy ship's company on my side (they were getting more varied ingredients) and an extremely happy bunch of officers. The First Lieutenant began to hate me. I had dragged down officers' standards, in his eyes. He was living either on another planet or in a different era. He could not see the wood for the trees. I expected a backlash. And it came.

You know how in earlier days all members of a ship's company had to turn out to embark coal, including the officers; it was such a vital thing that everyone except the captain and second in command had to roll up their sleeves. So it was (almost) for storing ship when you were alongside. You had to form a chain of people from the delivery vehicles on the jetty right up the gangway and down into the store rooms; this applied to both naval stores, convenience stores such as beer and NAAFI goods, through to foodstuffs, which were in the majority - fresh, chilled and frozen. Each department is expected to contribute ten to twelve hands, from wherever they could get them. So maintenance was suspended for the duration - usually just a couple of hours or so - accounts are put on hold for a while, off duty chefs are called in, and so on. The department which can most easily provide hands is the Seamen department, because they all work on the upper deck, anyway. But when we did so in Fort Lauderdale, and the hands were called to store ship at 10.30, it was all a bit unbalanced. Technically, I was in charge, because it was all stores of one sort or another. When I went up to the upper deck at 10.25 to check that all was ready, I found three Stokers, three Electrical Engineers, the whole of my department - and one seaman! So I said to the Chief Bos'n's Mate, the rating in charge "You're clearly not ready yet. Tell me when you are, please." The First Lieutenant had no option but to send for a dozen more ratings from his own department. Which of course should have been the case in the first place.

The USA was a tremendous run ashore - the people were very kind, and we fraternised and partied with them at every level. I had dinner one evening with a charming American couple and their German next door neighbours. For some reason I cannot recall we were talking about drains and the American was bemoaning the frequent blocking of his sanitary facilities. The German said "I know ze reason. After ze second vorld var voz over...." and I began to cringe and think about Basil Fawlty; "ven it voss all over, ze Americans took all ze rocket scientists back to ze USA and left all ze plumbers in Germany". Whew. It was a jolly good evening.

One of my Senior Ratings, a very serious, highly professional, kindly and sincere man fraternised with one member of a local family rather too much; she was the wife of an American US Navy CPO (he was away on duty) who I guess must have taken a fancy to his cute British accent (we all got that) and seduced him (we didn't all get that) - I can think of no other reason why he should play away; I knew roughly which members of my department had, and who hadn't, and he hadn't. But now he had. It was a couple of months later he got a letter from her saying that she was pregnant but she thought she could conceal it from her husband because the dates were flexible and she still loved him and all that sort of stuff, but now it was goodbye for ever. He was mightily relieved until, in the Mess that evening his fellow messmates said to him "Yeah, that's OK for now, but what happens when the kid grows up and starts talking with an English accent?" He got so worked up and was so distressed he couldn't think straight and came to discuss it with me. I was able to reassure him. It was my job.

We sailed for Halifax, Nova Scotia. The day before we arrived, I saw the most remarkable thing: it had got very cold overnight as we approached land, and sleet had fallen, dripped from everything on the upper deck, and frozen again. The whole ship looked like a thousand conjoined icicles, or a scene inside an old, weary ice cave, a magical palace of ice and fire. The upper deck was treacherous to walk on, so was put out of bounds until the steam hoses had cleared it. But eventually we were all able to berth successfully, and the celebrations and the exchange of reassuring words and promises began all over again. It was also an opportunity for officers of one nation to spend a few weeks serving in a ship of another nation, to gain experience and to cement relations; it was called, rather nicely "cross pollination". However, on a personal note, it was here in Nova Scotia that I became, and still am, in theory, a hunted man.

We held the inevitable cocktail party on the evening of our arrival; we all got dressed up in our best evening uniforms and entertained the good and the righteous and the deserving and the local government hangers-on and the people who had to be impressed to an hour of pure social pomp. Do not underestimate this; it was always a successful gesture and an event with outcomes - both for the UK government and for the officers concerned in offering the hospitality. (And it was the officers who offered the hospitality; the MoD insisted that there should be cocktail parties, the officers paid for it! It was an acknowledged part of one's conditions of service). At this cocktail party I met a particularly pleasant young couple - he South African but a naturalised Canadian and serving in the Royal Canadian Navy, she English, and they invited me home for Sunday lunch the following day. It was Sunday lunch exactly as we know it, right down to the Yorkshire puddings. They were very kind. They also said that I should get out and about and see as much of Nova Scotia as I could during my short stay and because they couldn't come with me they lent me their second car (I think it was their first car, really) for the duration. It was a Corvette Stingray or a Stingray Corvette, I can't remember. It was a car that I don't want to remember, anyway. Don't get me wrong - I was extremely grateful to them for lending it to me, but as cars go, it was all mouth and no trousers. It was a "super sports car" - a huge over-glitzy flashy imitation of a Ferrari or Maserati, but so cheaply built that its lack of quality could be seen with just a glance, and it was quite astonishingly underpowered - it could have been out-accelerated by a Ford Fiesta. But it looked good, if you didn't look too closely. On my next day off, I drove it out on to the Trans-Canada Highway, so as to see more of Nova Scotia. At that time, perhaps still, I don't know, the speed limit for vehicles on North American roads was 55 mph. So what was the point of those fantastically powered (and in this case underpowered) automobiles - and what still is - the point of them? Nevertheless, I got onto the TCH and out of town reached a straight three double lane highway which stretched as far as one could see into the distance, a long shallow dip down and an equally long shallow rise to the horizon. Nothing around. Literally not one single other vehicle of any sort on the road. "I wonder," I thought to myself, "if this car could eventually get to 100 mph?" So I checked all around again, and then put my foot down. I was nearly up to 90 mph when there was a great noise from overhead, a great shadow, and then a helicopter swept forward along the road and landed a mile in front of me. Two policemen got out. I stopped, of course. I was charged and bailed on the spot to appear at RCMP (Royal Canadian Mounted Police, or "Mounties", as they have always been called) offices in Halifax the following day.

Being a (fairly) law-abiding citizen, and not wishing to cause a diplomatic incident, I turned up at the RCMP office the following morning, to be charged and told to appear in court the following Thursday. I said "Of course - but actually, we're sailing on Wednesday, so I can't be there." And the kind RCMP desk sergeant said "Well, we won't be able to find you guilty and fine you then, will we?" And I said "Thank you. Am I free to go, now?" and he uttered a statement which I have never forgotten: "Yes you are, Sir. But just remember - the Mounties always get their man". I carried those words with me for many years and I have to confess that when we went to Canada for a Rockie Mountain trip some thirty years later I was still a little apprehensive as we went through immigration. But they had either forgotten or forgiven. God bless the Canuks.

We then sailed across the North Atlantic to go to Portugal to show solidarity with the new government, but we called in at Gibraltar on the way, which was logical. Now, the previously mentioned "cross pollination" of officers had resulted in our having a German officer on board. He spoke exceptionally good English (albeit with a strong guttural accent) and was very competent. He served temporarily on board HMS DANAE as First Lieutenant's Assistant and Deputy NBCDO. (The RN is ruled by acronyms, as we had found out at Dartmouth as Cadets doing EMA and ABR) and NBCDO stood for "Nuclear, Biological and Chemical Defence Officer". The function of NBCD is to ensure that in any future conflict the ship could remain safe from the effects of attacks of such a kind, and was often tested.

All naval personnel have a respirator, commonly known as a gas mask, which they have with them (or in reach) at all times. They have to be tested once a year. To test it you have to put it on and be subjected to tear gas for five minutes. This is done in a Nissen hut somewhere. You go in one end and come out the other. If it is successful you are safe for another year. If it is not successful your eyes stream and your nose streams and you are very uncomfortable for a few hours and then you have to have a new respirator. There was such a Nissen hut in Gibraltar dockyard, used solely for respirator checks and tucked away at the far end of the dockyard. We were all to be tested. The Nissen hut was about a mile and a half or so from our intended berth.

The German Deputy NBCDO who, as I said, was very competent, had arranged the respirator checks for the whole ship's company. Because the Nissen hut was distant he had arranged for a bus to take us there, in batches of fifty. But because if the bus waited for everyone to be tested and then brought those fifty back again in order to take the next batch, it would take all day and waste three hundred men's working time. So he arranged for the bus to take us there in batches of fifty, not wait, come back, pick up another fifty and so on; we were all capable of walking back a mile and a bit in a quarter of an hour. Good, logical, Teutonic, thinking.

As HMS DANAE slid across the quiet water of Gibraltar dockyard basin our German officer got on the Main Broadcast to announce how the respirator checks would take place. His guttural voice rang out throughout the ship and across the upper deck and indeed across the whole of Gibraltar harbour and quite a way into the town. He said: "D'ye hear there? Transportation for the gas chamber will commence in an hour, at 10.30 exactly. Do not be late." And then, slowly: "Zere vill be no return transport."

We fuelled and stored. And then we sailed. We were joined by a small ship of the Portuguese navy, to show solidarity. We did a short exercise out at sea for a few days, manoeuvring and simulating defence against air attack, and then we put into Lisbon. This was an interesting visit. I remember it partly because they used to sell on the street a delicacy called "sparrow on a stick". It reminded me of Hong Kong. It really was a sparrow. But much more I remember it because of our reception by the British Embassy.

The Embassy had arranged well in advance and in great detail how we were to be used as a vehicle to impress and entertain all the local civil and military dignitaries, local Anglophiles, local entrepreneurs with British interests and generally anyone else they wished to have influence over. We were used to this. What we were not used to was the fact that they hadn't actually done anything in return. I mentioned previously that one had to order stores, fuel, water and cash in advance, and that they would be waiting on the jetty or nearby. They weren't. So the Engineer Officer had to get on a phone and get things organised, the Communications Officer had to get permanent shore telephone lines fixed, and I was left with the worst problem of all: two hundred and fifty sailors who wanted to go ashore immediately after lunch and enjoy themselves - they had the afternoon off - but I had no escudos to exchange for them. Neither could I buy any local produce for the same reason. I would have to go to a bank and get some, PDQ.

Fortunately, the British Embassy Third Secretary or Eighteenth Secretary or some important person had come straight away to visit our Captain and brought with him the "Naval Attaché", a dapper little man in a grey suit with a club tie. They all went into the Captain's suite/office to talk and, as is customary, to drink sherry. I needed the Naval Attaché's signature on a Bank Imprest, which I could take to the bank with me and draw out about a quarter of a million pounds, so I got the Captain's steward to get the man to come to the door and sign. He was on his second sherry, and a bit annoyed. But then, as he signed, I recognised him! From way back! He wasn't a Naval Officer at all - he was a Chief Petty Officer, doing the job and wearing plain clothes so that no-one on board would know that he was actually ersatz. So I just said "I'll be off to the bank, Chief, but I want a word with you later." Armed with my Bank Imprest I hurried to the gangway to join my little team of money collectors. MoD rules are specific and strict, and have stood the test of time since colonial days: "when you draw out money locally abroad, the senior supply officer shall take with him an NCO of the supply staff and two Royal Marines armed with sticks. All shall be in uniform." So we got down on to the jetty, hailed a cab, and set off for the bank. We had no trouble on the way in to central Lisbon; we halted the taxi outside the bank and told him to wait, went in, collected the money, put it in the holdall, and went outside to the taxi. It wasn't there - it had been moved on by the traffic police. This wouldn't have been bad in itself except for one thing: almost exactly one year previously to the day there had been an armed uprising in Portugal, and although things had quietened down there was still bitter resentment on both sides. And guess what one side wore as a symbol of its solidarity in arms: a green beret. And what were my two Royal Marine guards wearing? Green berets, of course, being commando qualified. So there we were, standing on the street, carrying a huge amount of money and an obvious target for the other side, whoever they were. I felt a bit vulnerable and was already preparing my defence for the forthcoming court martial. Just then a large taxi/bus went past and was promptly stopped by my two green beret guards and the driver of the said vehicle must have been on that side in the civil war because he welcomed us into his vehicle and we sped on back to the ship. I don't think I have ever been so relieved in my life. Another scrape! Another escape!

We exchanged money for the ship's company, and they all went off ashore, oblivious of the drama which had just been avoided. I "asked" the Chief Petty Officer to come and see me in private. I said to him that we wanted a stream of forty-two seater coaches to every heritage site, coastal resort, beach and place of tourist interest within one day's travelling time, and that the ship's company wished to visit all the local museums, public buildings, theatres, music halls, dance places and so on etc. etc. in the city, with a shuttle bus back and forth to the ship, and we didn't intend to pay for it. It was all done within a few hours, and our visit improved. The ship's company will always remember their wonderful, interesting visit to Lisbon, and how cheap it all was. I can't stand hypocracy.

So my short time in HMS DANAE was shortly coming to an end. It had not been smooth, but I had restored the confidence of my department, who were all good guys, and was happy to turn it over to a permanent custodian for him to fashion in his own way. After three months of turmoil, I began to relax a bit. Plymouth was in sight.

Then there was the dropping of a huge bombshell. It was after dinner one evening at sea crossing the Bay of Biscay when there was a knock on my cabin door. It was the Chief Stoker. To say that I was surprised would be a great understatement. What on earth could the Chief Stoker want with me? Had he wrecked the fridges and freezers and left us without eatable food? Not within the last twenty-four hours when I had visited the said temperature controlled store rooms. Had he filled a naval store with some noxious engineering fluid or gas? I didn't know. The reason, and everything that followed on from it, was a gruesome, twisted epitome of naval history, tradition and discipline. It was so much a tale of coincidences and bizarre happenings that you may not believe what you are about to read. But it is true. The court martial transcript is on public record.

I gave him a seat and first of all asked him why he hadn't gone to see the Engineer Officer, his superior. "I need legal help, Sir," he said. "Fine," I said, "But I'll have to let your own superior officer know that you have been to see me." "It's OK, Sir, he'll be happy" he said. I asked him to explain. When he did, I knew full well why the Engineer Officer would be happy. He'd offloaded it onto me.

We have to go back quite a few months. The ship had sailed from UK with a generally very content crew. They had "worked up" at Portland and passed with flying colours. They had deployed and become part of the fleet in optimism. They had joined the Standing Naval Force Atlantic and shown themselves to be worthy combatants. On board was our Chief

Petty Officer Stoker; he was on board because he was coming up to the end of his twenty-two years in the Royal Navy and had specifically requested that his last draft before "going outside" was to a ship which was going to visit New Orleans. For twenty years, he had wanted to go to New Orleans. He was a jazz fan. In a big way. His whole life was devoted to jazz - listening to it, enthusing others to it, promoting it, and hoping to go, one day, to Basin Street. And now, in his heyday years, he had succeeded in joining a ship which was going to New Orleans.

Also on board was a Junior Stoker (the official title is Junior Marine Engineering Mechanic) whose name I don't recall. He had joined the Royal Navy to escape his family. His mother had agreed, but now wanted him back again.

So it was that when I joined the ship at Roosevelt Roads they were all still recovering from the wonderful hospitality they had received in New Orleans. Then the mail arrived. A bombshell from the mother: "Dear Captain, I now know that there is homosexuality on board your ship and my son has been kissed by another more senior member of the crew and I want you to investigate it and I want my son safe home with me."

The Captain caused an investigation to take place. There was no doubt that the Junior Stoker had been kissed by the Chief Stoker. It was weird. What on earth had happened? The story unravelled thus.

The ship had arrived alongside in New Orleans at 09.00 and the usual ceremonies, rituals, and practical activities such as storing, taking on fuel and so on were over by lunchtime. The Supply Officer had persuaded the First Lieutenant to grant general leave from 12.00 so that the majority would go ashore straight away, have lunch in the city, and relieve his food budget. This happened. It was a sort of reward for the fact that when RN ships are at sea, they work a seven day week, or at least a six and a half day week. Most people went ashore in groups, to take in the sights and enjoy the local food, but the Chief Stoker went ashore on his own, oblivious, to St Louis

Street and to Basin Street to listen to his beloved jazz. He spent twelve hours or more in ecstasy, and then started to wend his way back to the ship. It was well after midnight, and although he had of the drink taken he was as upright and proper as the situation demanded.

We now have to take a step back in time. The ship had been exercising in the North Atlantic. It was quite cold. It was going into New Orleans the following morning, and the ship's company had been reminded that the following day they would be wearing "whites" - white cotton uniform in all forms from working uniform through to the most formal - all white cotton.

In the Senior Chiefs' Mess there was an "up channel night", which was a traditional party before entry into port - but usually a home port, which involved sailing up the English Channel. Nonetheless, it was a good party, held within the confines of the Mess, and all enjoyed their rum and beer. Before they all turned in, in their bunks, they put their blue uniforms away at the back of their lockers, ready to dress in white the following morn. The Chief Elec. who slept in the bunk below the Chief Stoker, put his uniform away but left his "steaming bats" (his work boots) alongside his bunk. Now the weirdity starts. The Chief Stoker, in the top bunk, had a full set of dentures, top and bottom. During the night, he had a coughing fit, during which both top and bottom false teeth flew out, fell, and landed in the Chief Elec's boots. Next morning, the Chief Elec. was up first and was just about to get dressed and put his boots on when he remembered that it was "whites" that day, and put his boots, containing the Chief Stokers dentures, at the back of his locker. The mystified Chief Stoker, on arising, wandered round the Mess saying "Habanybobby peen my peef?" or words to that effect. Nobody had, so all got dressed in whites and lined the side of the ship for ceremonial entry into New Orleans. Then at, or rather just before, lunchtime, everyone not on duty changed into plain clothes to go ashore to see the sights and experience the experiences, and whatever sailors do.

So the Chief enjoyed his jazz without his teeth. This is significant. Because as he was wending his way back to the ship along one side of St Bernard Avenue he saw all his young Stokers on the other side of the road, and they hailed him and invited him to share a "goodnighter" with them In the adjacent Gunga Din Bar. He did so. During the course of this partying, the junior Stoker, bemused by the fact that the Chief Stoker (who was a very popular, if quite strict, man) was speaking strangely and on hearing that he had no teeth said "I wonder what a woman feels like being kissed by a man with no teeth?" and the Chief Stoker, in jest, said "I'll show you" and he leaned forward in mock amour. As he did so, the front leg of his chair broke, and he landed on top of the youngster in a heap on the floor. Everyone had a jolly good laugh, and no-one thought any more about it. Until the letter arrived. The one about homosexuality. It all had to be investigated. Properly and formally. The Chief Stoker was charged with "conduct prejudicial to good order and naval discipline", from which there is no avenue of escape, and as a Senior Rating as was his right he had opted for trial by court martial, rather than on-board trial. He had come to me to ask me to defend him at the court martial.

Realising the severity of the situation, I tried to get him to engage a civilian barrister, but he would not hear of it. "You see," he said, "I know I'm going to get done. I haven't got a chance. But I don't want some poncy barrister mincing words and trying to get me off and failing - I just want a good honest naval officer to tell the court that it was all a big jest that went wrong and make sure nobody thinks I'm a homosexual." That was it. It was his right. I had to do what I could.

The court convened in all seriousness and pomp in the naval barracks in Devonport and the charge was read out. He pleaded "Not Guilty" on my advice - simply so that witnesses would have to be called and the whole story would come out as a jest, not as a homosexual attack.

One by one, I called the young Stokers as witnesses. It went as follows:

"What time did you go ashore on... (the day)?

"12.00, Sir."

"Did you have lunch before you went?"

"No, Sir. We wanted to get ashore as quick as we could."

"So, you hadn't eaten?"

"No, Sir."

"Where did you go first?"

"There was a bar at the end of the jetty, so we all stopped there before going into town."

"What did you have to drink?"

"Harvey Wallbangers, Sir"

"Please tell the court what a Harvey Wallbanger is."

"Vodka, Galliano and orange juice."

"How many did you have?"

"Three or four."

"Then you went into town? Where was your first stop?" (an amateur form of questioning, but allowed by the court)

"Into the first bar on the main street."

"What did you have to drink?"

"Well, we all liked these Harvey Wallbangers and we'd been at sea for three weeks so we had lots of money in our pockets, so we stuck to that."

"Did you eat at all?"

"Just peanuts from the bar."

"What time did you stop drinking Harvey Wallbangers?"

"About 21.00, Sir. We'd had maybe ten of them, but we ain't no drunkards."

"And had they had any effect on you?"

"No, Sir. Well, not exactly. We all got very thirsty."

"So what did you do?"

"We changed over to beer."

"Halves, or pints?"

"No, Sir."

"What do you mean - No? What were you drinking?"

"Beer from silver buckets, Sir."

"And this didn't affect you at all, not having had anything to eat, either?"

"No, Sir."

"So you were quite able to recall everything that happened and put it down in your sworn statement as the truth and nothing but the truth?"

"Yes, Sir."

"And can you tell he court why your sworn statement is exactly the same as the sworn statements of every other member of your Mess who was present at the time, down to the very last detail, all of you having drunk at least ten Harvey Wallbangers on empty stomachs followed up for the rest of the evening by buckets of beer?"

"Because that's what happened, Sir."

"You remember it clearly?"

"Yes, Sir."

Then I called the Master at Arms, the ship's most senior rating, and the person responsible for upholding the law, and keeping detailed records thereof.

"Master at Arms, looking at your records, has there been any change whatsoever in the good order and naval discipline of the ship's company over the past six months?"

"No, Sir."

I had done all I could. Cross examination was by the prosecuting officer, a qualified naval barrister, Michael Higham.

"Chief Petty Officer are you aware of Section 1 of Chapter 18 of the Naval Discipline Act (I may have my figures wrong) which says "It is the responsibility of every ..... (senior person).... to uphold good order and naval discipline?"

"Yes, Sir."

"And do you consider rolling around the floor with a Junior Stoker in your arms being good order or exhibiting naval discipline?"

"No, Sir."

"No more questions."

That was that. The Chief was disrated to Petty Officer, as was required, and lost all his Good Conduct Badges. But the court saw fit to make sure that the timing of his disrating was such that he was able in the months left to him to regain his Chief Petty Officer's rank just before he was due to retire, and so he retired with a CPO's pension. That is the conflation of discipline and justice.

My time in HMS DANAE was over.

I had a few days' leave and then rejoined HMS HECATE. There were only a few months left of the surveying season and then we were due to return to Plymouth. I had some time previously acquired a new cook - a man by the name of Davis. His kit was immaculate; we were to find out the reason why. Although young, he made an instant impact - he joined in with the cooking of all the popular dishes - the pies and pasties, the casseroles, the roasts and the veg. But given a speciality dish he was off like a rocket, flashing his Larousse Gastronomique, preparing his delicate sauces and fussing over his presentation. However, at the end of the year when Character and Efficiency awards had to be made, I hit a snag. His efficiency was quite clearly "Exceptional", but when I came to assess Character (you're given a choice of five appellations) I remembered that he had come to the ship from Detention Quarters - a heavy sentence for disobedience of a Chief Petty Officer - and could only be awarded "Poor Character". So he was "Exceptional/Poor", which must have been a first. It turned out that in his last galley he had wanted to make a bechamel sauce from scratch but the CPO had ordered him to use a packet sauce, and he had refused.

We had nearly lost him. In Italy. He was cooking the Captain's special lunch for visiting civic dignitaries and senior officers when he put his Soufflé Exceptionelle in the dumb waiter and a blast of cold air flattened it. He was distraught and we feared for his sanity. Maybe his life.

But back to reality. The end of my time in the ship was coming up, and it was a tradition that officers were dined out in Plymouth, if possible, at a Ladies' Night with their wives, if possible. I had arranged many during my time, but because it was to be my own "dining out" I asked the First Lieutenant to select the menu. He replied that (a) I knew far more about it than he did and (b) that he would probably get it wrong and (c) that he trusted me implicitly, so would I mind just getting on with it. I immediately sought the Senior Cook's approval to put Davis in charge of the cooking - under his supervision, of course - protocol is important - but that is effectively how it was. I chose the menu: lobster bisque, a game and seafood main course, and a maritime-themed pud. And some specially selected wines accordingly.

The event was spectacular. It had all the tradition of Royal Naval dinners and we sat down for the meal, fully booted and spurred, with great expectations. The bisque was superb. The main course was exceptional - from somewhere Davis had got hold of the most enormous silver platters and the gamebirds and fish and crustaceans faced each other over a rocky shore of pebbles, oysters and seaweed and it looked just astonishing. But even this was all overshadowed by the pud. Davis had another silver platter on to which he had made a sandy seabed of honeycomb or some such, with angelica seaweed fronds and almond mollusc shards. And on top of this was a Davy Jones sea chest nearly two feet long made of chocolate, studded with pearls of citrus and bound by "brass bands" of edible gold leaf, with the lid propped open and filled with a mixture of ice cream and tutti frutti jewels overflowing on to the "sea bed". The Senior Steward bore it in and put it in front of the Mess President for him to be served the first portion. The spoon and fork were raised. We gasped. The Senior Steward froze: "I can't do it, Sir" he said. "Neither can I" said the First Lieutenant. No-one could bring themselves to cut into this masterpiece. In the end, we had to send for Cook Davis, who appeared, having hastily donned uniform, and was told that if he wanted us to eat this magnificent offering he was going to have to serve it to us himself. Quite untraditional and unprecedented. Normally, the cooks receive a polite ovation. This time the Mess went wild with approbation, and Davis was carried out shoulder high having been given an enormous glass or two of the very finest Armagnac we could muster and some beers to take home with him. The cheers followed him all the way back to his own Mess. What an event!

But that was the end. I had to return to real life, and took up my next appointment after a fortnight's leave.

CHAPTER 12
On the staff of Flag Officer Plymouth

The naval service is divided into two - the seagoing assets and the shore assets. The former is under the command of the Commander in Chief, Fleet, and the latter under the Commander in Chief, Home. Both are subdivided so as to allow major decisions to be made at the highest level, and minor decisions at the lowest possible level. The overlap occurs, of course, in the dockyards and naval bases, which "belong" to Home Command, but service the Fleet Command. Plymouth was the base for all seagoing activity in the southern part of the Atlantic, the northern part being controlled from Rosyth, in Scotland. So we had half the navy to look after. Additionally, however, because we are part of NATO, each Commander also has a NATO responsibility, and Flag Officer Plymouth (national) was also COMEASTLANT (Commander, NATO Forces Eastern Atlantic). It worked very well as long as you could remember which hat you had on at the time. But it was real, live, action stuff, and barely a week went by without some major activity of naval action and significance. For example, within weeks of my starting work there, the SS Torrey Canyon carrying 120,000 tons of oil hit a reef in the English Channel and there was an enormous kerfuffle because all the oil was leaking. At first it was thought that it could be sunk by RAF bombing, but it didn't work, sitting target though it was, and it looked as if all this oil was going to wash up in Devon and Cornwall. Then the wind changed to the West, the oil blew away and my Chief of Staff was able to signal Admiralty adding that, as he put it, "obviously God is an Englishman".

Then, not long afterwards, the brash Commanding Officer of one of our first Type 21 frigates (the first to be powered by gas turbines and possessed of great power, speed and acceleration) decided that he would flash past the shore at Kingsand, his home town, and impress all his friends and neighbours. He certainly did that. The wash from his ship hit the beach at thirty knots and overturned all sorts of fishing boats and leisure craft and it was a devil of a job to sort out all the compensation. His court martial was quiet by comparison.

Then the two corvettes built in Plymouth over a period of more than a year for a middle Eastern navy were finally completed, and they set off back to their own country. What had not been reckoned upon was that the crew had nearly all taken English "wives" for the duration, and that took some diplomatic and political sorting out when they left, too. As if that wasn't bad enough, they fired a farewell salute on leaving Plymouth Sound, but didn't look where they were shooting, and sank a fishing vessel, fortunately without death or injury – but another diplomatic incident to cope with.

There was also a fairly regular occurrence of WW2 mines and other explosive armaments washing up here there and everywhere, which required immediate action.

And the first Northerly winds of the summer months always heralded the start of the Great Cross-Channel Lilo Race, which usually required action from us, or from the RNLI.

Not to mention the RN ship (HMS BLAKE, I think) which accidentally fired its gun while alongside in the dockyard, demolishing a married quarter on the other side of the water – fortunately unoccupied at the time. It was at about that time that one other Plymouth married quarter has its occupancy increased by one, however, with the happy birth of our daughter.

Then there was the absolutely ludicrous incident where the CO of a small minesweeper decided to sail up the Hamoaze (the stretch of water from Plymouth Sound up to the dockyard) backwards. Going astern. They saluted as they did so. Flag Officer Plymouth was apoplectic at the ridiculous spectacle. The CO thought it was rather a jolly jape. He was disabused of this opinion by the Admiral. Should you wonder who this hapless CO was - it was the same, self-opinionated Charles whom we came across in Chapter 5 (HMS AJAX), one Charles now in prison for several years for something else, who didn't listen to advice.

We also had a poignant incident involving the Soviets. We monitored them, of course, just as they monitored us. They had many "fishing trawlers" in NATO and European waters that had never caught a fish in their lives - they were crammed bow to stern with radio and other electronic equipment designed to intercept any of our transmissions. They didn't even bother to hide their aerials - everybody knew exactly what they were. And one of them was heading towards Plymouth ostensibly to refuel and offload their fish (which they must have bought in Brixham or somewhere on the way round). They had to be stopped, using minimum force and preferably without a diplomatic incident. The Commanding Officer of HMS WOODLARK, a little inshore survey ship, was ordered to go out and meet them and tell them that they couldn't come into Plymouth - if their intent was genuine, they had to go to Falmouth. Tell them? How? With a loud hailer, of course. The CO came to see me and said "Alan, you speak Russian - what do I say to them?" So I wrote it down - Russian words, English transliterated script, and off he went. He met the Soviets five miles out at sea, and broadcast my message to them over a powerful loudhailer - and the Soviets immediately turned to port and sped off to Falmouth at a speed which was strictly faster than a fishing trawler should have been able to do. WOODLARK's CO came to see me afterwards. "Thank you, Alan", he said, "It certainly worked!" I said "Yes, I thought it would - but actually, you don't know what you said to them, do you?" He pondered for a while, shuddered, and then concluded that it didn't matter what he had said - it worked. To this day, only the Soviets and I know what it was that had such an immediate effect on them. Such is life. And (Cold) War.

So when someone jokingly tells you "worse things happen at sea" you'd better believe them. They do.

The bread and butter stuff was more prosaic. I had an

administrative office and staff to run. It was relatively humdrum. My Chief of Staff succeeded in livening things up by gathering together anyone who could play a musical instrument and going out on his ceremonial barge to greet every ship returning from a long deployment with a tune or two, and playing stirring marches to ships going away for a long time to remind them to come back safely. It was all jolly good fun.

As in any organisation, there was a variety of people with different views on life; human beings are all different, whatever their profession or position. And we had our fair share. Mary Magdalene, a Wren Officer who had a cold Dettol bath every morning for some reason or another and was quite good at her job. "Louis" Armstrong, the legal adviser, who organised cricket matches in strange venues, including Widecombe heath on Dartmoor, amid the gorse bushes, "Tank" Sherman, who had been accidentally promoted in the heat of Far East battle in mistake for someone else, and a droll Captain who wouldn't let a draft letter from a junior past him without changing it - he once deleted a single-word epistle which said "Concur" with a ditto which said "Agree". (Unfortunately for him he was such an unpopular man that one day someone finding his car unlocked in the car park put a shoe box on the back seat and locked the vehicle (this was before electronic locking devices) and called the bomb squad - who, using a robot called "Wheelbarrow", blew the door off in a controlled explosion). There was also the overpromoted (to Sub-Lieutenant!) officer who couldn't actually be entrusted with anything so was put in charge of the Mess catering. He had almost run the Mess out of funds when he put on a formal Mess Dinner and bought some "cheap" oysters, which were already open, from Plymouth market to make "angels on horseback" as a sign of his prowess. I was away in Scotland for three days at the time, and missed the event. I got back the morning after the dinner, and wondered where everyone was. It was eerie. The headquarters was devoid of officers. The staff were also all wondering where the officers were. They had all been poisoned. I had to take over, I was told, an account with precious little money in it and a distinct lack of brotherly faith. It all worked out well in the end; it's amazing what a good chef, taken into your confidence, can do with a bit of slow-cooked meat and some flour, and a few veg. and a bit of fruit and some ice cream - and make it look spectacular.

We also had a very self-opinionated young ADC who served the Admiral sententiously and with little regard for the feelings of others. So one day, I hailed him as he went along the corridor past my office and said "Julian, can you help me with a bit of grammar. Should I say 'the yolk of an egg *are* white, or the yolk of an egg *is* white?" He replied "Well, it's obvious, isn't it? The yolk of an egg *is* white." I asked "Are you sure?" and he snapped "Yes, of course!" and he proceeded along the corridor repeating out loud "The yolk of an egg *is* white!" much to the surprise of all the people in adjacent offices all along the corridor, who came out to see if he was all right.

The Admiral, John (later Sir John) Forbes was a serious, humourless officer, but of course very competent. He had the most delightful young - brand new - Wren PA called Penny Stinchcombe. She was adorable. Everyone loved her, and would do anything for her. Thus it was that when the Admiral went on a fortnight's leave and asked her to look after his daughter's goldfish she complied with alacrity. But one morning she came into my office and said "Beaky's dead!" I had no idea what this meant, but coaxed it out of her. She was nearly in tears. The goldfish were called Dave Dee, Dozy, Beaky, Mick, and Titch, after a pop group. She held out a tissue with a dead fish on it. Beaky was indeed dead. "What am I going to do?" she asked. "Don't worry," I said, "I'll sort it out." I took the fish and the tissue. On the way home through the centre of Plymouth, at the bottom of Royal Parade - you may know it - there is a huge pet shop which specialises in fish. I went in and asked for a goldfish "exactly like this one" Not a problem - they had hundreds if not thousands of them. I presented Penny the next morning with a live-goldfish-bearing plastic bag. She was over the moon. Unfortunately, just two days later, it was "Titch is dead!" this time in distraught tears.

Procedure - ditto. Then, two days before the Admiral and his family were due to return, it was another tissue, another dead fish, and a flood of tears: "It's Dave Dee!" "Don't worry," I said. "But", said Penny, "Look. Dave Dee's got a huge fantail with a big split along the middle of it. You'll never find one like that!" I did find one, with a huge fantail - but no split. A bit of judicious work with a pair of sterilised scissors soon had the ersatz Dave Dee looking just like the original, and no more needed to be said. Result.

I've always made it my mission to help other people.

I got the necessary brownie points at Plymouth to enrol on the Russian Interpreter's course, and off we went to the Naval College.

CHAPTER 13
The Russian Interpreters Course

The Russian Interpreters Course and the RNR Special Branch of Russian Speakers have existed since the Cold War started and some bright spark realised that if we ever had to ask questions of a Russian person it was probably no good doing it in English. The training was based in several obscure places before being centralised at the HQ of the Royal Army Education Corps (which, incidentally, had a large sign at the side of the road just inside the main gate which read "Royal Army Education Corps Centre. DRIVE SLOW"). However, the naval representative on this combined staff realised that all the naval people were being taught the language of redoubt and defile, of Advance in Review Order and mountain battle tactics, which hardly served them to navigate a Russian ship into harbour or ask a Russian sailor about his activities. So the RN section was moved. To Dartmouth. Where it wasn't wanted - it was an excrescence, and was relegated to a couple of offices at the back of D Block. We had a classroom, but no study space. I was eventually allowed to use the Drake Division spare bedding store, and kindly given a table and chair. But at least we learned naval terminology, not Pongo stuff.

It was a very intensive course. We were in the classroom and the language lab. five and a half days a week. But a large proportion of the work was actually done at home (and in the spare bedding store). We had a weekly test on a Saturday morning, and if you failed it you got a warning; a second failure meant you were off the course and returned to general duties. I actually worked six and a half days a week, just ensuring I had a half day a week and some mealtimes for the family. But we coped, and had a lot of fun, too.

We lived on the married patch in Blackawton village, and the children went to school there. I drove to work daily on a moped, with all my books strapped to the back. One Christmas I bought a sack of potatoes from a farm on the way home, and was persuaded to buy a Christmas tree at a good price, and put them with my books on the back. I'd never have made a Loading Officer: on the way home I went over a hump back bridge and the moped went up and over, backwards, leaving us all (me, spuds, tree, books) on the road. Lesson learned. I remember, too, that I was inveigled into being Father Christmas in the village hall and my own children sat on my knee and didn't suspect a thing. And the next year's Christmas tree was too big to fit in the living room, so I sawed the top foot and a half off and wedged the tree up against the ceiling and when next door's son came in and demanded to know if the tree was growing through the ceiling I got the spare foot and a half and went upstairs and held it in place on the floor while he marvelled at the "hole in the ceiling" and then went home and told his parents "Mr. Pearce has cut a hole in his ceiling for the Christmas tree to go through!"

Back to our Russian course. It was divided into three sections: Colloquial exam after six months, Linguist exam after twelve months, and then the Civil Service Interpreters exam after eighteen months. It is interesting how the course came to be eighteen months, and was therefore so concentrated: when there was still National Service after WW2 it was decided that it did not make sense, and indeed would probably be counterproductive, to have the brightest and best just marching up and down for two years, or doing some menial job. So they were siphoned off, given just six months' naval/military style training, and then trained to take the CSI exam in the eighteen months left. This just simply remained the status quo. (These excellent chaps kept in touch after their rigorous Russian training, and formed the prestigious albeit little-known "Frinton" Society - nothing to do with Frinton-on-Sea, it's the Former Russian INTerpreters Of the Navy. I am proud still to be a member of this wonderful little group).

The course started from scratch. We had three tutors: Alex Rutherford, course leader, a retired Lieutenant Commander and himself a qualified interpreter. Then David Wanstall, an Oxbridge graduate of perhaps fifty - sixty years of age, who had been a language teacher at Dartmouth since it had been a public school in the 1950's. Then there was Robert Avery. Robert was something else. Brand new and specially selected, he was not long out of Oxford and an absolute breath of academic fresh air. It didn't take anyone long to realise he lived on a different intellectual plane from most of the rest of us. Tall, refreshingly youthful but already with an academic stoop, he was a natural tutor for adults - he understood when people were finding things difficult and he knew the precise moment to drop the academic pressure and lighten the atmosphere - usually with a genuine Soviet joke. From Oxford, he had been to the Soviet Union with a group of about thirty other university undergraduates, the vast majority with left-leaning political views, and studied at MGU, the Moscow University. His stories of their time behind the Iron Curtain were entertaining, usually hilarious, apt, penetrating, and always with some reference to what we happened to be studying at the time. His summary that "thirty young left wingers had gone to the Soviet Union to see how Socialism at home would work in practice, and thirty staunch capitalists had come back those months later" quite tickled us.

The three tutors were a good balance for us: one phonetic dogmatist, one grammar disciplinarian, and Robert with his feet on the ground, from whom we got everything else. The first six months was groundwork, and moved at a hectic pace - we passed "O" Level standard after about six weeks, and forged on. There were high and lows. For me, the main high was the realisation that putting English into Russian was actually easier than putting Russian into English - for some months we had got by, by having an educated guess at Russian words; but after a while, when you knew what you wanted to say you could find a variety of ways of saying it, using known and trusted vocabulary and grammar. The lows could be long and gloomy or short and spectacular. I remember my fellow student, Derek Weaving, coming into the study room one morning looking very glum. When Alex asked what the matter was, he replied "I worked until ten last night on Chapter 28 questions, and couldn't do them. So I got up at six this morning and tried again, and still couldn't do them." Alex said "I'm not surprised. You were supposed to be doing Chapter 27 questions - we haven't done Chapter 28 work yet." Derek went visibly stiff and visibly red. Then, shaking, he picked up his pile of grammar books, translation books, grammar books and dictionaries - a big pile - strode to the window and threw them out. We were on the third floor. You can imagine the result. The marching Cadets on the road below were somewhat shaken, but did not break step, to their credit.

We all passed the Colloquial exam, but one of our number was told he had only just scraped through and could not hope to go any further. We were sad to say goodbye - he was a sterling chap called Charles Stirling.

Then the Linguist stage. Obviously, this was much harder and we were expected to be able to take just about any non-technical topic thrown at us for interpretation. Success was a great satisfaction; failure was a real fatigue. During this stage, we went to Meudon for a month. This was the most enormous eye-opener, and actually the turning point for the whole course.

At Meudon, a fashionable suburb of Paris, there was a Jesuit college. Apart from serving their God, they existed to (a) produce and sell icons to earn money for their existence and (b) to take in Russians fleeing the Soviet Union and educate them in how to live in the West. (This may seem facile; it is not. Soviet citizens were so unused to coping with money that if anything became available in the Government-run shops they would simply spend all their money buying it and sort out the problem of buying food later. They received money; they spent it. No concept of saving, or banking). The motto of people in the Soviet Union could have been (and was, among many, many groups of people) "They pretend to pay us, and we pretend to work." For example, I once met a man outside an almost empty shop in Moscow carrying a spear gun of the fishing variety. "What's that?" I asked him, in a friendly sort of way. He became very cagey. "It's secret," he said. Then, "I mean, it's private." It was perfectly obvious that he hadn't a clue what it was - but he had bought it because it was there. At Meudon escapees were given shelter, food and security, and a small weekly allowance. They then learned not to go straight to the local shop and spend it in case the shop ran out of goods. (At first they had difficulty in believing that the shop wouldn't run out.)

In return for this, these émigrés would help teach us Russian language, as did most of the Jesuit priests, too. So we had an eclectic lot of teaching available to us.

However, I must take a short step back in time to record how I got to Meudon. It was a "business trip" of course, so the MoD paid for the travel. But there was a rule that if you could make your own way to your destination by a cheaper means you would be reimbursed for doing so. One of my off-duty relaxations for the past year had been converting a Commer Cob people carrier into a motor caravan; I had stripped its interior, fitted furniture and bunks, sink and water tank and so on. I had even cut a large rectangular hole in the top and fitted a lifting roof together with two more bunks. I elected to drive to Meudon, and was permitted to do so: ferry fare plus mileage came to less than the cost of a flight.

I set off from Blackawton. It was summer. It was warm. I crossed from Plymouth to Roscoff on the ferry and then set off for a four day drive to Paris. I wasn't hurrying. Each evening, to economise, I stopped at council-run campsites, more basic than private campsites, but all that I needed. I never had to buy food for four days. Here's why. The previous Autumn, I had bought 56lb. bags of parsnips and carrots, to peel, blanche and put in the freezer for family use throughout the next months. The peelings and the blanching water I had put in a large fermenting tub together with some proper white wine yeast, and made five gallons of parsnip wine and ditto of carrot wine - which may sound awful but which is actually extremely tasty. Using the correct yeast, it had fermented out to about 14 or 15%. I took the five gallons of parsnip with me to France. Each evening, I would park in a campsite, put up the lifting roof, make up my bunk, and then set up a table and some folding chairs by the side of the motorhome, with the five gallon keg on the table, and some glasses of the half pint variety, and waited. It was never long before some passing Monsieur would stop and say "What are you drinking?" and I would say "Parsnip wine." And they would say "Ohn, Ohn, you cannot make ze wine wiz ze parsnips. Ho Ho." And I would say "Try some" and proffer a half pint glass half full, and they would drink it and declare it "Not bad," - but they always asked for a refill. Then they would go and get their wife and come back with baguettes and cheese and salad and ham and sausage - by which time another Monsieur had joined the group. And so on. Each evening, I went to bed replete, and with armfuls of good food for the following day - and usually a sleeping, often snoring, semicircle of French people on the grass around my vehicle. I got to Meudon without a hitch.

Who says priests are poor? They should go and look at the Jesuit college in the very expensive suburb of Meudon. The "college" was an old country house complete with a huge patio and beautiful gardens in an exclusive part of southern Paris. Downstairs, it had many rooms converted to classrooms, a common room and a large refectory, with upstairs rooms converted to dormitories. On our course there were some thirty or so students, just over a third French, just over a third Italian, and just under a third from various parts of the rest of Europe; there were three Brits - we two from Dartmouth, and Count Nick Tolstoy (shortly afterwards to become famous for invoking the biggest libel damages award in history for his tract about the treatment of displaced Cossacks).

It was a "total immersion" course, and it didn't take us long to find out what that meant: not a single word other than in Russian, at any time, ever. If you couldn't say at the dinner table "Please pass the salt", you didn't have salt with your meal; if you couldn't say "I've got a headache" you didn't get an aspirin. The tutors were all emigrés and had their own rooms; we all associated during the day, but in the evenings the students were left to get on with their own things. But not speaking together in their own languages - just Russian.

Each day, we breakfasted together in the refectory. Mealtimes were one of the most valuable learning times because in the absence of tutors we were completely free to make all the mistakes available to students of the Russian language, and corrected ourselves without retribution. Coming from an all-male environment at Dartmouth, for example, I had never heard the feminine use of the verb and I strongly remember the first time I heard one young woman say to another *"Ya khorosho spala"* and thinking that my grammar experience had been lacking. But it didn't take long to catch up.

Then lessons all morning. The tutors were all intellectuals and a great pleasure to be with. It was quite difficult for us, because we were not even at "Linguist" level, and a lot went over our heads. But we soldiered on. Learning about the previous lives of the tutors was incredibly interesting, and inspired us to use and listen carefully to the Russian language being offered.

Lunchtime in the refectory was a hoot. Big long wooden tables, with food served in large dishes, and bottles of table wine and Brittany cider all over the place. The French contingent (for reasons of national pride) spent the whole lunchtime complaining about the quality of the food, the Italians (for xenophobic reasons) spent the whole lunchtime complaining about the quality of the French wine, and we Brits wined and dined with equanimity.

Lessons again all afternoon, tea, more lessons, then supper - another 2-Nil gastronomic win for the Brits. Perhaps the most interesting, sometimes exciting and certainly valuable time, however, was the evenings. It was a balmy summer, and we spent many, many hours on the patio, talking, reminiscing, supping a bit, and often singing: there was a Roumanian lass with a guitar and a very deep, very fruity, romantic voice who would have had even a misogynist licking the floorboards and did have us joining in all sorts of gypsy songs. We all had to do a turn. I had discovered that the Pushkin poem *"Ya vas lyubil"* fitted perfectly with the old English tune "The lark rising in the morning air" and did many a duet with "my Roumanian gypsy". I have to admit that we Brits also tried "Swing low, sweet chariot", with actions, but it took so long to explain in Russian that the humour had gone by the time we were ready to perform it, and we gave up.

One abiding memory of our time in Meudon is that after these evening events we always seemed to be going off to bed just about the same time as the Jesuit priests were getting up for their morning prayers. You have to admire that. However, we were all of carnal age, and it was quite astonishing how often one had to climb over interlocked bodies to get to one's bedroom. These continental people really enjoy their off duty activities, don't they? But then, who but a prude, or an English person, could tut-tut? I preferred to think "It's not my business".

The head of the organisation was Father Alexei. Deeply spiritual, or superstitious, according to your views, intense, spare of limb and word, he was clearly and fully in command. What I do remember about him is that he was writing a book about Russian prepositional usage, and we spent the best part of a whole day discussing the differences between going "on a bus", "in a bus" and "by bus". I can imagine Monty Python doing an amusing sketch on the subject, but at the time it was excruciating.

Uncle Kolya was a different kettle of fish. Small, stumpy, very old, perpetually jolly, with silver hair and almost a Private Godfrey lookalike, he had the most amazing stories to tell. He was an accomplished cellist, and as a very young man he had been in the Leningrad Symphony Orchestra after the Revolution. He told us that in 1919 there had been a people's meeting, and that conductors were deemed a symbol of revanchism and elitist superior power and were therefore done away with. For several years, members of the new socialist orchestra took turns to stand up and shout "One, Two, Three, Go!" and then the orchestra would play whatever was on the programme. He chuckled as he told us that they all knew it wouldn't work, but no-one dared to say so. I learned a lot from him.

Aunty Meridiem (I can't remember her real name, just this nickname) was in many physical respects Uncle Kolya's female double. About the same size, shape, and colouring, she too was a classical musician – a contralto, or whatever is lower than that. In the mornings, mostly, (hence the nickname) she would be heard opening her lungs at some unknown part of the building and making the whole ground floor shake and then reverberate again to some operatic aria. I had never heard a trained voice close up before, and it was quite an education to realise just how many decibels such a voice can produce. I can't remember if she ever taught me any Russian, however.

Schur was a true academician, and didn't let anyone forget it. Very serious, sonorous, and proud, he had a distinct Jewish accent and style which led us to admire not only his precise use and explanation of the Russian language but also the conditions from whence it had arisen. I learned a lot from him, too. Including how to do a Jewish accent in Russian.

Sasha was the artist, in two senses of the word. His real job was painting icons, for sale, but he also taught us Russian drama. We put on a cameo production from Pushkin's Boris Godunov, the scene where the two Officers arrive to read out the Tsar's decree that a runaway must be arrested. In one of the funniest interludes in dramatic history, the decree reader, realising that his illiteracy completely prevents him from reading what is in effect an arrest warrant, utters the immortal line "Can anybody read?" and the runaway reads out his own arrest warrant with considerable changes to the physical characteristics of the wanted person. True to form, the dress rehearsal was a shambles and therefore, true to tradition, it was jolly good on the night. I was "Father Varlaam", and had to sing a (not terribly good) bass solo, the words and music of which I remember to this day. It is now one of my party pieces.

Meudon was a turning point in our Russian language learning. What had previously been an intellectual struggle became a pleasure as we realised we could really do it. We discovered, for instance, that interpreting is a matter of "meaning" not of "words". For example interpreting literally "My French is rusty" would generally result in a blank stare - no noun, and incomprehension about ferric oxide. And if you interpreted literally "I broke my arm last year" into many other languages you would immediately be labelled as a masochistic psychopath.

As an aside, "translating meaning" was proved to me later in my career (but still in the Soviet-thought era) when I accompanied a senior Brit politician to a laboratory where he was told "This is comrade scientist Ivanov, who received the Lenin award for physics twelve years ago" and Ivanov said (I paraphrase) *"Da, no erto litsomernost, smeshnoy, pokhazookha......".* The Russians' own interpreter said "He says this has not given me an unfair advantage over other comrade scientists". I was able to tell my Principal later that what he actually said was "And a fat lot of effing good it's done me!" Same thing, really, but somehow different.

In other senses, the exposure to real, live, freshly liberated Russians gave us a portfolio of information for further study and use. In my case, Uncle Kolya in particular and inter alia served to provide a host of anecdotes and much psychoethnocentric background for the 1983 NATO Oberammergau lecture which I was invited to give, entitled "The influence of the Russian psyche on Soviet military thinking". I do wish people in the West had paid more attention to it, because it presaged much of what has happened since. Ethnocentricity is a very dangerous tenet to hold and is now displacing logical thought in the assessment of world affairs.

After this wonderful Meudon experience, we returned to the

Royal Naval College, Dartmouth, to complete our studies and take the final exams.

For me, for the first time in my career, I had only one aim, one thing to do - to pass the final exam. But, Dartmouth being Dartmouth, this was not to be. All officers have to belong to a Division (a sub-college grouping). It didn't mean much, except that when the students had a mess dinner (which was a form of training for them) we were expected to attend, to teach them the correct way to do things. It wasn't a bad idea, and we didn't object helping out in this way. Until Princess Anne came to a dinner and we were "uninvited" so that other people who so far had done nothing were invited so as to dance pretty attendance on her in our absence. As I said, we didn't count.

Some of the social life, however, was very enjoyable - especially private events on the small married patch. Once we gave a "Pheasant and Claret" party, for which I had shot the pheasants, but the claret was actually rather good apple and beetroot wine, which all enjoyed. The dentist, Trevor King, over-enjoyed it, and for some reason decided to challenge the upright vacuum cleaner to a fight and ended up rolling round the floor with his tie and the front of his shirt wrapped around its rotating head because someone who was on the side of the vacuum cleaner had plugged it in and switched it on.

And we had "offered" to be a host for visiting foreign ships' officers, so that we could show appropriate British hospitality, in return for the tremendous hospitality which RN ships always receive - all around the globe. The event which we remember most vividly was the visit by the German sail training ship, the "Gorch Fock", which was used to train young officers. She came into the River Dart and anchored. Many of us issued invitations to both Training Officers and trainees. We invited four trainees to come to our home in Blackawton for "typical English Sunday lunch, and then a tour of Dartmoor in our motor caravan". The day arrived. The hour arrived. No German Cadets. So I telephoned the ship and asked where they were. There was a long pause, and then I was told "Zey are just leaving in ze transport, right now". They arrived. We gave them a welcoming drink. We chatted. We sat down to Sunday lunch - roast beef, roast potatoes, vegetables, and then apple pie and custard. We were rather surprised that they didn't eat very much, but we finished, had coffee and a liqueur, and then set off in the old Commer Cob for a tour of Dartmoor, with the particular aim of seeing Widecombe. A Commer Cob is a wide vehicle with a somewhat narrow axle and wheels, and it rolls a lot at the best of times. One the narrow, winding roads of Dartmoor, it rolled quite a lot, and I noticed that our passengers were looking quite peaky, and not talking much. I slowed down (ostensibly to let them see more of the sights, but actually because I could see that something was wrong) and we eventually arrived back at the jetty in Dartmouth and deposited them on their launch back out to the Gorch Fock. We had done our social duty. It was only later that I learned that there had been a hiccup in their programme, that our lunch invitation had been overlooked, and that in order to save face the Training Officer on the Gorch Fock had ordered four Cadets to go to Sunday lunch at Blackawton with us - despite the fact that they had just had their Sunday lunch on board the Gorch Fock.

We completed the course. We went to Beaconsfield for the final Interpreter exam. The written work was relatively commonplace, and neither of us found much difficulty with it. The oral examination consisted of questions about military superiority in attacking a redoubt under fire, and the necessity of building trenches so as to be able to attack under artillery cover. The Army officers did rather better in the exam than the Naval officers. I thought that I had wasted eighteen months in engaging in an unequal battle, and complained formally. I was told to shut up, because "Interpreters are supposed to be able to interpret anything". Such is life.

I had spent the whole of this time preparing myself and my family for an appointment to the Soviet Union as an Assistant Naval Attaché. But it was not to be, and instead I was appointed to the Fleet Headquarters in Northwood, which entailed another house move.

CHAPTER 14
NORTHWOOD: C-in-C FLEET'S Headquarters

Commander in Chief, Fleet is a very important man. When the Prime Minister, on behalf of the Government of the United Kingdom, says "go to war." it is him who takes the Royal Navy to war. On the First Sea Lord's behalf, of course. He has a large staff at Northwood, comprising experts at every level from all branches of the navy. The day to day running of things is in the hands of his deputy, the Chief of Staff. The Chief of Staff's immediate deputies are the Assistant Chiefs of Staff - A/Cos Operations, A/Cos Administration, A/Cos Engineering and the submarine branch.

I was to be Secretary to the Engineering Admiral. Responsible for all his personal paperwork and all the general administration. It should have been a quiet, straightforward albeit highly professional task, but it was not to be.

At first, everything went smoothly. The Fleet was being serviced by its engineers to the very highest standards, and was ready for anything. Fortunately.

We all had our own specialisations, and adhered to them during the working day. Then, out of hours, during peacetime, we all took turns at being "Duty Officer" down in the underground headquarters. Very little happened out of working hours - that is to say, nothing of major importance which couldn't be logged and kept for the morrow for the necessary specialist officer to deal with. Nothing to bother the Admirals or politicians with. Not until 1st April 1982, that is. I was Duty Officer that evening. Nothing had happened, and nothing was expected to happen. Some idiot might trespass into the Married Quarters patch, or there might be an incident out at sea, or the cricket pitch might be intruded by drunks or druggies, but that sort of thing could all be dealt with locally. Unfortunately for over nine hundred people, there was an intrusion of a different sort.

I was in the underground Ops Room. It was about 21.00. There was a signal saying that a large force of ships had left port in Argentina and was heading towards the Falkland Islands. I tried to contact the senior Warfare Officers - but the Assistant Chief of Staff (Operations) was reappointed from the headquarters that very day and was being "dined out" at a local restaurant by all the other Warfare Officers - including the Chief of Staff, Rear Admiral Halifax. I had to contact them- "But Fast", as the Sub-Lieutenant would have said at Dartmouth back in 1963. There were no mobile phones in those days, of course. And the restaurant in question had a telephone land line which for some reason was out of action. Why do these things always happen like that? I sent a car as fast as I could, but also wanted to speak personally to the Chief of Staff to impress upon him how urgent it was. I ended up ringing a telephone box on the pavement outside the restaurant and asking a passing dog-walker if she wouldn't mind going into the restaurant and telling a "Mr. Halifax" that "the office wanted to speak to him as soon as humanly possible and despite all other considerations, whatever the cost. Come to the 'phone". Within an hour, we had gone to war.

It was an astonishing interlude, and the facts are well documented, so I won't repeat them, just my own experiences and feelings. The Royal Navy is a relatively small organisation, and many of us knew people who were serving in the ships and air squadrons which were involved, which brought the action pretty close to home. Indeed, we had a Petty Officer serving at Headquarters whose wife was Argentinian. The whole thing was a tragedy, because we had always got on well with "the Argies". They had even bought two ships of our prestigious class of destroyers, and we had worked closely with them in the transfer of these ships to the South Atlantic. They were now going to be used against us - all for the political survival of the Argentinian leader, General Galtieri, who wished to divert interest from the disgraceful situation in his own country and the concomitant political unrest - by carrying out a diversion in the shape of a "foreign incursion".

The Armed Services went into operation like a well-oiled machine. The politicians decided what was to be done, and instructed the Commanders-in-Chief (Army and Navy) accordingly. Our Commander-in-Chief decided how it was to be done, and instructed his sea area commanders accordingly. The sea area commanders told the ships what was to be achieved, and the afloat commanders themselves decided how to go about it.

The Task Force sailed. We re-took South Georgia - a foregone conclusion because, as Galtieri said, the invaders were only scrap merchants. Then it got serious. Our professionalism was undoubted, but some bad things happened. First to affect me was that we received a message on 4th May that HMS SHEFFIELD had been hit by an Exocet missile. This was about mid-afternoon. I was helping at my quite humble level to prioritise all the signal traffic which ensued, when the Commander-in-Chief, himself, Admiral Sir John Fieldhouse, appeared in my little office, looking grave. "Alan," he said, "You live on the married patch at Valency Close, don't you?" I replied in the affirmative. He said "The SHEFFIELD's First Lieutenant lives on the married patch, near you; we don't know who has survived and who hasn't, but we do know that the Argentine Government are crowing about it and it will appear on the 9 o'clock news tonight. I would like you to go round to the family home to ensure that his wife knows about it before it appears in the news." What a very thoughtful officer, what a very human gesture of kindness in the midst of a huge battle - and what an awful task for me because we simply didn't know who was dead and who was alive and I could not give any reassurances. My wife came round to their house with me, we broke the news, she understandably broke down with emotion and we had an incredibly difficult few hours, always remembering that the utmost emotional difficulty lay with her, not with us - and there was so little we could do. It was soul destroying, and there was seemingly no way out of it. We sat and waited amid the tears.

Then, suddenly, mid-evening, as we sat there, in another flash of Admiratorial kindness and humanity, there was a knock on the door and a messenger from the Ops Room arrived personally with the news that a report confirmed without doubt that the First Lieutenant - our neighbour's husband - was alive and uninjured. I have never been a deflating balloon, but at that moment as all the tension dissipated, I know what such a balloon feels like. It was quite astonishing, and although I didn't know it at the time it was to be of great value to me several years later when I was in charge of casualty reporting and family liaison during the Gulf War. I was a much more understanding and caring person, through being better informed and experienced.

It was during this period that the Fleet Medical Officer contacted all the ships reminding them that warfare rations, food at Action Stations, combined with less physical activity could be a problem and that ensuing potential bowel problems could be avoided by the addition of bran to foods "to keep ships' companies regular". One Commanding Officer replied from his patrol off the Falklands coast: "We are currently experiencing an average of four air attacks by Argentine aircraft every day. We do not need bran to keep our bowels open and keep us regular, thank you".

But at last it was all over. We returned to normal.

At that time I was the Social Secretary of the Officers' Mess. It was called an "Officers' Mess" because it was tri-service and could not therefore be properly called a "Wardroom". In among other things, before we were engaged in the Falklands Conflict, I had contacted all the major London orchestras and said "Look, I act on behalf of a group of very senior European, US and Canadian executives and in our spare time we would like to come to classical music concerts. What price free tickets?" They all replied in the negative, except for the LSO who said "We can give you up to fifty free tickets for any concert once a month". Thus armed, and with a small budget behind me, I was able to hire coaches and offer everyone "Free classical music concert by the LSO, free travel, no parking problems in central London". I was overwhelmed with applications, the event took off in a big way, and people avidly scanned the monthly programme thereafter to see what else was on offer. Another foible I cashed in on was that we had some six or seven different nationalities at Northwood, all living in NATO harmony and peace. For the foreigners, it was a two, three or even four year appointment, so they had been able to bring their families (whose children, incidentally, all joined Northwood schools without a word of English and left at the end of it able to speak English perfectly - even the Americans). There was little international rivalry, but I decided to arouse some. I announced a "National foods evening, with international entertainment" and hired a West Indian steel band and also a group of interactive limbo dancers all paid for because I knew I wouldn't have to pay for the food: I requested the husbands and wives from each NATO country (people were married in those days) to get together and bring along to the banquet a Starter, or a Main, or a Pudding of their own nationality, knowing that there would be plenty of food - which the catering staff would lay out on the vast tables in an enticing and extravagant way. The admission fees would be relatively small - just enough to cover the cost of the wines.

As I expected, the families (I have to say the wives) all produced the most lavish and exciting European and North American panoplies of catering and hospitality extravaganza that you have ever seen. They even seemed to vie for supremacy in presentation and garnishing. It was the most spectacular display of hot and cold buffet meals. Then afterwards we had a West Indian steel band performance, followed by a display of limbo dancing (which was astonishing) and a participation (by us) display which was even more astonishing because it was so excruciating.

Another huge success. As was the canal boat midnight dinner/dance from Uxbridge into the centre of London I could go on but we were settled, children at school, making friends and so on. We integrated into the local community. The local village hall, for example, was having a "Bring and Buy" sale, announced well in advance. I wanted to buy a lawnmower but thought it a forlorn hope. We were personally asked to contribute, and couldn't, really. Then I had an idea. A few months earlier I had made twenty litres of homebrew red wine but the vinegar fly had got in and I now had twenty litres of clear, pure red wine vinegar on my hands. So I went to the mess and to local pubs and restaurants and collected some hundred or more empty fruit juice bottles, washed them out, steamed the labels off and replaced them with pretty labels saying "red wine vinegar, Northwood", and a date, and filled them with my home made vinegar. It raised nearly a hundred pounds for the village fund!

As an aside, as I started carrying more than a hundred bottles into the hall a Rolls Royce drew up outside (the hall wasn't open to the public yet) and a man in a morning suit got out of the driver's seat and a man in tweeds and boots got out of the passenger seat. The latter lifted something in canvas out of the boot (I don't know if you call it a "boot" in a Rolls Royce?) and the former said "Where may I put this?" I asked what it was. He replied "It is a floating lawnmower. My Master bought it on a whim. George here says it's completely unsuitable and my Master has instructed me to get rid of it for whatever we can get for charity." I said "Five pounds?" He said "Certainly, Sir". And I got a brand new Flymo Hovermower for a five quid donation to charity. Charity begins at home, they say. They also say "Fortune favours the brave" but then they also say "Only the good die young". Hm...

Domestic life was also quite interesting. We all entertained, very regularly. My personal triumph was a visit to the Watford fish market five minutes before it closed and buying a huge sunfish for a quid which we were (just) able to cook on the outdoor grill to serve as a meal for eight people at an indoor dinner party. "My" Admiral's claim to fame (apart from the fact that he gave excellent dinner parties as long as the steward managed to keep his beagle out of the dining room during and after the meal) was that, as a submariner, he used to attend the annual "City and Serving" lunch for submariners in London.

He was a very careful and moderate man, but "City and Serving" lunches did use to go on until the evening, and one day I got a (very) late evening 'phone call from the Admiral's wife saying "Peter isn't home yet. Do you know where he might be?" I tried to reassure her by saying that these events did tend to go on a bit and that I would try and find out. I actually had no idea whatsoever, but she needed reassurance. I scratched my head for a while. Then, after midnight, I had a call from a callbox: "Alan, I'm in Penzance, what should I do?" I soberly advised "Sir, just find a policeman, show him your naval ID, and he'll find something for you." My confidence in the constabulary was rewarded, I was able to reassure Mrs Admiral, and he returned on the first train next morning. He had simply got on the wrong train in London, fallen asleep, and gone to Penzance (two hundred and eighty-six miles) instead of to Northwood (twenty miles). Understandable in the circumstances.

It vied for the record in problematic rail transport situations with another friend of mine who had been to a similar C & S lunch who telephoned his wife from London before he left, asked her to pick him up at Petersfield, the stop before Portsmouth, fell asleep, overshot and woke up at Portsmouth, rang his wife to apologise and said he would get the next train back to Petersfield, fell asleep again and woke up again back in London). Such is life. Worse things happen at sea.

CHAPTER 15
Denmark

I was then offered the opportunity of serving in NATO, at the combined NATO Headquarters at Karup, in Denmark. On Jutland, that is. There are three Denmarks - Sjaelland (Copenhagen Island), Fyn (where Odense of Hans Christian Andersen fame is), and Jylland (which is Jutland - foreigners never could spell their own names properly; I see they now even spell Bombay with a capital "M"). Karup is right in the centre of Jutland.

The joint headquarters was situated on a Danish Air Force base, which was also allocated to NATO use. The HQ itself was a self-contained large office block. The war HQ was in the huge German World War 2 Bunker, of which more later.

We had bought an old caravan with which we intended to tour Europe during holidays and we towed it all the way to Harwich and then crossed the North Sea to go to Esbjerg on the West coast of Jutland so that we would be on time for an arrival at Viborg, where our rented house was, at tea time that day. "Best laid plans of mice and men......" etc; just after we sailed we were told that the weather at Esbjerg was so bad that the ship would have to berth at Hamburg, in Germany. It was February and it was very cold. After disembarkation, we turned North for Denmark and drove along the autobahn through the little townships until we reached the border. It began to snow. "Hello" to Denmark. We drove Northward. It snowed more heavily. And then all the little townships and their lights disappeared and we were surrounded by farming land - or so I assumed, because we couldn't see much in the dark and the snow. Mile after mile of empty road. More and more snow. It got later and later, and darker and darker. No traffic. No houses. Nothing. Just the headlights and the snow. It must be, I thought, like being on the other side of the moon.

And then, at about midnight, we saw the lights of Viborg. Bliss. Salvation. And a cessation of the snow. And there to meet us at the hotel was the guy from whom I was to take over. We got the children settled, and then slept the sleep of children ourselves.

Next day was husband to work, wife to facilities, children to school. No hanging around.

We moved into our new, rented house just a few days later. It was a bungalow on an estate. Very Danish style: medium size kitchen, huge utility room, huge single living room, no dining room, and all other rooms as tiny as they could be made. We had nice next door neighbours - Ilse and Peter, and a nice lawn and nice flower beds and no garage; in common with all other modern Danish properties, there was an ample "carport", with electrics. I was told very early on by Danes that you either plug in an engine warmer under the vehicle overnight, or you take the battery out and take it into the house overnight. Woe betide anyone not listening to local knowledge.

As personified by our later British neighbours - an RAF officer and his wife. After they had settled in with the help of their mentor we visited them and noticed in their kitchen some tins with a happy family picture on the label - parents, two children and a dog going for a walk and lots of Danish writing. "I didn't know you had a dog?" I said. "We haven't", she replied, "It's minced steak. It's very nice." Read the label, I thought. Or ask someone to read it for you.

Having finally escaped the snow on the way up from Hamburg, we were to experience the inevitable Danish winter after that short intercession. I spoke to Peter next door about it when the forecast said it was going to snow. "Don't worry" he said, "Danish drivers are used to the snow". I felt reassured. Obviously they would know how to drive in the snow. We went shopping to the town centre supermarket late that Saturday morning. While we were there, it began to snow. Now, your Scandinavian snow is not like our usually tiny flakes; it came down like great big 50p pieces, came down hard, and by the time we came out of the supermarket there was about four inches of snow everywhere. The road back to our house, which was only a mile away, was an urban dual carriageway without barriers and it swept majestically Northwards out of the city centre down to the lake, across the lake and then in a long but gentle incline up the other side. (I say "gentle" because Denmark is very flat; the highest point of the whole place is only about one hundred and forty metres above sea level, and that's a bit of a dimple. The rest is pretty much flat). The snow had stopped, and the crest of the hill could be seen, about a mile away. On the broad dual carriageway between us and the top of the rise were several jacknifed articulated lorries across both lanes on both sides, a bus sideways on to the traffic, at least a dozen cars half on and half off the road, and several more stuck on the central reservation. It was (static) chaos. We skirted the whole thing right round the lake, and I went to see Peter. "I thought you said...." I started. "Ya," he replied "Except for the first day, when it's always like this. By tomorrow, people will have remembered." And do you know, he was right. We never saw another weather related accident. Until the first snow of the next year, that is...........

By Danish standards it was quite a mild winter and it only went down to about minus ten or so. The children loved it. Strangely, looking back, with one exception, I cannot remember being cold. As they say, "There's no such thing as bad weather, only bad preparedness." And so it was. We dressed accordingly, and hardly even noticed it.

As we Brits (nearly) all lived in Viborg and worked in Karup, there was a coach routine a.m. and p.m. to take us to work and back. It was a long, wide coach, and had no trouble coping with the roads. (The Danish rule seemed to be: have an exceptionally alert and well-informed road gritting service and grit and salt all the main roads immediately before problems arise; but let the snow and ice pack down on minor roads and let people drive carefully.) The personal rule was: know your limits and don't exceed them. We were caught out just once; we went to a kro (country inn, tavern) for supper one night, and it snowed again. When we came out there was a carpet of snow as far as the eye could see in the moonlight - which was a very long way, because not only is Denmark very flat there are (apart from government plantations) no natural trees, and no hedges at all. Animals are kept in by electric fences, and arable products stay where they were put quite naturally. So there we were. One building behind us, a few other cars, and a carpet of white. The problem was not one which confronts UK motorists, no matter how deep the snow: where was the road? We had a babysitter to go back to, so taking bull by horns we set off in what we thought was the direction of town. It soon became apparent that something was wrong when the car started rhythmically bumping up and down, up and down. Then it dawned. We were going horizontally across a ploughed field. We persevered, and eventually the motion became even and we were on a road. By now we could also see lights, so we reckoned that was probably the direction in which the road led. Fortunately we were right. We got home quite late, however. Babysitter, lovely girl of about sixteen, lived on the other side of town. I said "Jump in the car and I'll drive you home". "No, thank you," she said "it's quite all right. I'll walk. It will be nice at this time of the night." Nothing would dissuade her. I wondered if she thought my driving might be unsteady, but no, she really wanted to walk. Through a town centre, alone, at nearly midnight. Feeling responsible, I followed at a very discreet distance to make sure she got home OK. She did. Looking back, it was probably me who stood the better chance of not getting home that night; a stalker would surely spend the night in a cell. But they hadn't ever had one of those. What a lovely, safe country. What a lovely people.

During the two plus years we were there, there was only one crime on Jutland - proper crime, that is. There was a bank robbery in Odense. It does not take much planning or much luck or much bravery or any cunning at all to commit a bank robbery in Denmark; the banks don't have a counter, and you don't queue. They just have desks around the place with tellers sitting at them and you go and sit down and say what you want and they give you the information you want or take the money you want out of their drawer and give it to you. Then you shake hands and leave. The Danes were aghast. A bank robbery! In Denmark! They were mightily relieved and national pride was restored when it turned out that the two crooks had come up from Germany to do the job. And had got caught by the excellent, kind, but not-experienced-in-solving-bank-robberies Danish police, who nevertheless did so on this occasion.

Technically, Odense is on Fyn, not Jutland. For the record.

Not long after arrival we met the egg man. The egg man was Juttish. "Not Danish" he said, or would have said if he could have spoken Danish or English, which he couldn't. Each Saturday, he would pile those grey cardboard trays holding thirty eggs on the back of his moped, often twenty high, and drive around the housing estates - targeting NATO personnel for the sale of his eggs - with very good reason. One would buy a tray of eggs and he would take the money and then just stand there. No conversation, because even those of us who had learned a few words of Danish couldn't communicate with him (Juttish is a strange language; there is even one sentence: "A e oo ee ay ø o ay å" - "I am out on an island in a river" is about as close as I can get, a sentence which has no consonants at all in it) and it was only after talking to old hands that we learned that he was waiting for a snaps (not schnapps, that's German, but the same thing) and he knew NATO people had a duty free allowance. Which is possibly why he sold his eggs at such a reasonable price. So the second week, I gave him a tot. He grinned, and spoke his only five English words: "One for the other leg?" Simple arithmetic made one wonder how on earth he got home again, but we saw him regularly weekly for two years.

Other surprises regarding people coming to see us included the fact that if you weren't available and didn't respond to the doorbell they would let themselves in and leave you a note - we learned not to be surprised to come in from gardening and find the gas man or the new butcher or the man from the

Council in the kitchen. The most charming of all was the chap who rang the front door bell which I answered to find a dapper, dark suited fellow in a top hat standing on the doorstep holding a business card; Danish chimney sweeps all wear a top hat, and a dark suit to accompany it. And the postmen were exceedingly proud of their uniforms and headwear, and looked thoroughly dedicated and professional. We have thought UK postmen exceedingly scruffy ever since.

But back to the Nato HQ. It was there to protect that flank of the free countries from attack. It was not offensive because it had no forces. But it played its part in Nato paper and real ships exercises which took place in the North Sea and East Atlantic. Located on the Danish Karup Air Base were the NATO BALTAP (NATO Baltic Approaches) i.e. military HQ, NAVBALTAP (the Naval Nato HQ) and AIRBALTAP, the NATO Air Force equivalent. They worked in harmony. Mostly.

I was in NAVBALTAP. The Commander was alternately (every three years) a German or a Dane. The Deputy alternated at the same time and was either a Dane or a German. The other officers could be interchanged, but mostly the head of Operations was a German Captain, the Head of Logistics was an American, and the Head of Amphibious Operations was a Canadian. By common consent, the Head of administration was a Brit. Me. The Commander could bring his own PA. When I first arrived the Commander was Danish. He didn't do much and left it to his deputy, a German Commodore called Hans Meisner, who had served at sea in the Second World War and knew a thing or two. Very shortly afterwards it changed, and we got a German Admiral and a Danish Second-in-Command, or Chief of Staff. The German Commander was Admiral H.H.H. Kampe, one of the most remarkably good commanding officers I have ever served under. He had a photographic memory and could remember where every ship of the fleet was, or should have been, or could be if he so ordained it, without even looking at a chart. Even during the heat of battle. But he was seemingly a heartless man. German officers called to his office would openly display symptoms of fear and become shivering wrecks if they had not performed immaculately; it was not nice to see. Of course, being a political appointment, he treated officers of the other nationalities quite differently and seemed to put up with what he must have seen as their "imperfections". Nonetheless, he was a quite remarkable man, and very definitely someone to have on your side.

We had exercises throughout the year. "Paper exercises" were scenarios in which the enemy were attacking NATO and we responded by saying on paper what we would have done and moving around our naval, land and air forces accordingly (nowadays, of course, it would all be on computer) and then assessing the effectiveness of what we had done. "Real exercises" involved real ships sailing and real aeroplanes flying, and real tanks and troops moving, and so on. Much more expensive, and more effective. But we had to do both.

For the rest of the time we just sat in our offices and considered, and planned for the possible future. And did the administration. And carried out social functions which in civilian life would have been called "bonding". Such as the annual "Families Sports Day". This deserves a chapter to itself. It was to be a grand affair, involving all NATO personnel of all nationalities, and their families. A few hundred people.

The very concept of a "Families Sports Day" means different things to different nations. To the Germans, it means an opportunity for all members of the family to show their supremacy over all others in all fields of endeavour. To the Brits, it means an afternoon of jolly fun when one can engage in a little bit of healthy competition and have a pleasant social engagement with the family and other families over a convivial meal. To the Danes, it means an opportunity to drink other people's booze at a far more realistic price that the horrendously taxed stuff which they are allowed by an oppressively taxing government. To the Americans it means just another barbecue and perhaps the chance of their kids doing something different for a while without using an electronics games machine. As the Command Administrative Secretary, it fell to me to organise the whole thing. I had very good advice from my predecessor.

"Whatever you do," he said, "Don't let the Germans organise the sports, don't let the Danes organise the bar, and don't get the Brits to organise the BBQ. Otherwise The Fun Day will come to resemble the 1936 Olympics, everything on the bar will disappear, and you'll have to put up with burgers and sausages that you could write on a wall with. You must get the Americans to organise the BBQ because they are allowed to import meat whatever Brussels says, and the Germans to run the bar, because not a drop will be lost. Get the Brits to organise the games, with Canadian help, because then it will actually happen".

This is what I did. We had hired a field and several marquees for the event. I had arranged for a whole pig to be roasted, and learned the secret of it - how not to have burnt on the outside and uncooked in the middle. You have to start at 4 a.m. and do it very slowly. The butcher who sold the pig did the roasting. It was really excellent - a great hit. The Americans did the rest of the catering, and it was a huge success. To describe the operation of the bar, I have to go back a couple of months. When I announced the Fun Day and dished out the tasks, two things of interest happened, both involving our German colleagues: firstly, they went into training, and had PT and running once a week after work. (How this was going to help them in the Welly Wanging and the Dwile Flonking which I had arranged, I don't know. Perhaps they were unaware what "Welly Wanging" and "Dwile Flonking" are. Or perhaps I neglected to announce that these activities were to take place. Anyway, there were two competitions we were going to win, however much they trained). The other was that the O-i-C of the Bar (one Klaus Gräff, who with his family became great friends of ours, and exchanged visits for several years afterwards) came to see me and asked how many bottles of whisky and brandy he should order. I said vaguely "I don't know. I would think about half a dozen of each" and off he went. Then a few days later, another visitation: "How many bottles of beer should I get?" he asked. "Say two each, on average, especially if it's a hot day" I said. Then after that, it was soft drinks, and then finally "How many ice cubes do you think we shall need?" and the penny dropped - he was offloading this facet of the decision making on to me in case it went wrong and the German Admiral found out. He could then say that he had done what he had been advised to do by Herr Pearce. So I said "Four thousand two hundred." And let him get on with it.

There was to be a third interesting thing involving the bar, on the day itself. I was in the field, now beautifully marked out and tented, and at 09.50 for a 10.00 set-up (another decision I had to make) the bar and the drinks still hadn't arrived. My deputy began to fret. "Don't worry," I said. "They'll be here". At 09.59 there was the sound of diesel engines at the end of the lane which led up to the field and three Merc. estate cars drove on to the site, followed by a van carrying trestles and benches. "Blimey," said my Petty Officer, "they must have been waiting at the end of the lane!" I replied that they probably had, but whatever - we had a bar, on time.

The first race was a "proper" race - the 1,000 metres. They all set off. As they passed the beer tent the two Danes peeled off. As they passed the barbecue the two Americans peeled off. Having done their duty, the two Brits peeled off, leaving a German Captain and a German Sergeant struggling to win. By the time they finished there was, unfortunately, nobody interested enough to cheer them, except for their immediate families. The welly wanging went splendidly, with the Canadian winning but with the last placed American landing his on the barbecue. The Dwile Flonking was a disaster, because nobody but the Brits could understand what was going on, so we won without praise. The various stands took quite a bit of money for the cause - a jewellery stand, a toffee and fudge stand, the "plastic duck on a stick" stand, but my biggest hopes for a successful return of cash for next year's event were dashed. One "Paff" Grant, a lovely man, a Royal

Navy Fleet Air Arm Navigator, had been instructed how to run a "Bunco Booth", in which people hope to win money but don't. The system was simple and relied purely on statistics. Two packs of cards are shuffled and laid face down side by side. The Operator (Paff) says he is going to turn over the top cards of each pack simultaneously, and then the next ones in each pack, simultaneously, and so on until, perhaps, exactly the same two cards appear at exactly the same position in each pack and are exposed simultaneously. "I say it will happen. What odds will you give me against?" cries the Operator. Now, the maths is counter-intuitive, and people were saying 5/1, 10/1 and even 100/1, but Paff was instructed not to take lollipops off children and not accept more than 10/1 or more than 10 Kroner bets. The maths is relatively simple, and compounded by the two facts that you don't say which pair of cards and you don't say whereabouts in the pack, so the odds of it not happening are 51/52 to the power of 52, which is 0.3643, so the chances of it happening are 63.57% of the time. So the dealer wins, most of the time. Unless, of course, the Operator has too much to drink and can't remember what the hell he did last, in which case the punters win everything and the Bunco Booth, which was to have supplied a cash float for next year, gets cleaned out and you make no profit at all. But that's life.

Overall, however, everyone enjoyed the event very much, people from all nations competed amicably against each other, sat and chatted with each other, ate together, drank together, and had a jolly good time, which is what it was all about.

But it wasn't all about having fun. I had to go to the NATO Staff Officers' College at Oberammergau in Germany to do a NATO Staff Course. It was a two week course. There were temporary married quarters for families, so you were encouraged to take kin, if not kith. We drove there, in our new duty free Volvo. It was a trip of a thousand miles, but we stopped several times on the way down, overnight. We had been advised by German friends that "Gasthof mit Schlagterai" meant B&B with own butcher, and so we complied and were very grateful for the advice - we stayed at some delightful places, and ate the most delicious foods. We eventually arrived at the NATO HQ in Oberammergau and booked in to our quarters - a quite lovely flat overlooking the town and not far from the Conference and Training Centre.

Danish dancers at the Families Day

Each day at a very reasonable time I put on my uniform and went in to the Centre. We had lectures, most of the time. They were all held in the semi-circular lecture hall, and each seat was wide and comfortable and had a pull-out set of headphones in the arm-rest. The reason for this was simple, but understanding the cost implications less so: although the universal language of NATO is English, and although the French were not part of the military structure of NATO, the price to pay for having them agree to have anything to do with it at all was that all lectures, all conferences, all documents would have to be translated into French as well. So there was a French interpreter in the interpreter's booth at the back who translated every word of everything said for the whole fortnight into French - even though there were no Frenchmen present and everybody else could speak English. I will leave you to cogitate upon that now that, even as I write, the UK is continuing its three year struggle to achieve Brexit. How on earth Concorde ever managed to get built and to fly, I do not know. But I am quite sure that if there had been no agreement to have an "e" on the end of the word "Concord" it certainly wouldn't have been built. No chance. Words are important.

Back to Oberammergau. There were many interesting lectures, all designed to edify us. But more was the aim to get us to circulate, to communicate, to socialise, and to bond. Not a bad idea. I'm not knocking it. It worked.

Each NATO nation had been offered the opportunity to give a lecture on an appropriate subject, and this is what they did. One was outstanding: a Colonel Kleftodimos of the Turkish Army gave a lecture on something or another which was clearly quite interesting, but his accent was so awful I could only understand about one word in every five - which didn't make for much understanding. Then I had a bright idea. My French isn't awfully good, but I knew I could understand more than one word in every five. So I got out the headphones and listened in French. When the talk was over, the US Major on my left said "You know, that's what I admire about you Europeans - you can all speak each other's languages." I just shrugged non-committedly. I wasn't going to get drawn into that one. After coffee, we had a talk from a US Colonel who came from the deep south and had such strong, drawling, vowel distorted troglodytic speech that I couldn't understand him, either. So out with the headphones again. When it was over, the Major on my left accused: "Whaddya do dat for. Can't you speak goddammed English?" I deigned not to reply at all, this time.

There was a slot for "visiting officers' talks". We had all been advised some weeks before the course that it would be appreciated if any visiting officer(s) would like to give a talk on a specialist subject of their interest. I offered to give a lecture on "The Influence of the Russian Psyche on Soviet Military Thinking". I spent ages working on it, developing it, researching it, making it interesting with anecdotes and generally polishing it until I was satisfied. I was giving it to several hundred experts in military matters, so I knew it had to be of the best. I knew it was good, but the reception it got was absolutely outstanding, and such comments as "opened my eyes" and "never seen it from that perspective" were abounding, especially from across the Atlantic. There was just one slight glytch, which I didn't foresee. At one stage, I put a Vu-graph on the overhead projector and took it off a little too early. There were shouts of protest. To ameliorate the situation and lighten the atmosphere I said "I'm sorry, Ladies and Gentlemen. I should have remembered the Vu-graph rule: leave it on until the Marines' lips stop moving." I knew there were no Royal Marines in the audience. There was a cheer and much laughing. But I had forgotten that there are other kinds of Marines, and when there was quiet again a booming voice from a US Marine Corps Colonel at the back of the Hall said "I'll level with you later, Lootenant Commander Pearce". He tried, but I lived to tell the tale.

My script was requested by officers from several other nations, and taken back by them for further study, which was complimentary and gratifying.

We came back from Oberammergau, the whole family, in the middle of a heatwave. English heatwaves are quite warm, but European heatwaves are something else; the "continental effect" means that warms are warmer and colds are colder. This was hot. We set off in the Volvo estate - which although it was a "luxury vehicle" still didn't have aircon in those days - to drive back to Denmark, and by noon it was very uncomfortable. During the afternoon it got so hot that I parked in a layby, took off all my clothes, wrapped a towel round my waist and got going again. By evening, we were exhausted. But we decided that we had got more than half way and we weren't going to go through this again the following day, and we would drive on. We got home in the late early hours of the morning. Relieved. Never experienced anything like it, not even in the Far East. All relative, I suppose.

Back in Denmark, it was soon time to plan for the Christmas festivities. It was, after all, August. It was the Brits' turn to put on an event, and another officer (Major Donald Campbell, Parachute Regiment, of whom more later) and I decided that it just wasn't good enough to have a cocktail party or a Rumtopftevening or a McDonalds dining experience or a smorgasbord - we were going to do something different. And we had plenty of time to plan it.

We decided that to be quintessentially British, it had to be an Old Time Music Hall. There were one or two problems: we didn't have a hall, we didn't have an orchestra, and of all the Brits living in Denmark only one (me) had ever been on the stage before, and only one (Mrs David Benson) could play a musical instrument of any value to a song and dance routine. Fortunately, it was the piano, so we had a start. The hall we hired at Løvel, a village not far away; it had a spacious room and a beautiful stage. We had a pianist, and by devious means we got hold of a drummer from an army camp in Germany; he was really good, and because he was so good he only needed one rehearsal. Donald was in charge of all acts, and Mary Benson was in charge of all music, scenas and Players Choruses, including the final "Bull and Bush". Both of them were absolutely brilliant.

They rehearsed separately and then it all came together at the end. Some thirty people all joined in; we had a Players Chorus of nine, which is quite sufficient for a small show, we had a very able stage crew, we had lots of keen - if completely inexperienced - actors, and then we hit a truly remarkable contributor: Paff Grant of the Bunco Booth celebrity. It turned out that he could paint. Pictures, I mean. And we wanted a Victorian/Edwardian type backcloth for all the scenas - a street scene such as may have existed in Oliver Twist's time. And Paff did it! He bought rolls of pure white wallpaper and stuck them together and made a twenty foot by ten foot street scene such as you have never seen, except perhaps in the musical "Oliver". The effect was gobsmacking. And the opening and closing scenes were guaranteed to astonish everybody. We were in awe of it, and looked after it very carefully.

The Brits' Old Time Music Hall, Denmark 1985

So we were ready to go. We announced the event many weeks ahead so that people would all be able to put it in their diaries and attend. We laid emphasis on the "Old Time" aspect of it and invited everyone to attend in the costume of the late 1800's. Most people understood, and made costume plans accordingly. But one day, I was sitting in my office when the German General from Baltap came round - a most unusual experience because we were the naval wing and he wasn't. But he was the senior German in the whole place. He stepped into my office and closed the door behind him. For a German, he looked sheepish "Herr Pearce," he started, "Thank you for your invitation. My wife and I shall certainly attend your Old Time Music Hall. But I am a senior officer of the German Army and I would not wish to look foolish by putting on a fancy dress costume in front of all these other people. I do not wish to stand out. Therefore I shall wear a grey suit." I waited a moment. Then I said "Sir, of course I respect your wishes. Therefore I am obliged to tell you that everyone else in the audience will be wearing Edwardian or Victorian costume and if you attend in a grey suit you will certainly stand out, I'm afraid." I knew the effect my statement would have. I knew he would go away and get someone down the chain to check on the facts. He did, and they did, and I found out later that he had sent an urgent request to the German National Military Museum to provide him and his whole team with full (Prussian?) turn-of-the-century uniforms for them all to wear - including those spiked helmets, curved swords and spurs!

Donald and I had between us organised several skits: an "opera company" who had lost their musicians and had to say their words instead of singing them, a knife thrower who specialised in throwing invisible knives into balloons which were popped from behind the wall, a sand dance routine, a magician who could declaim random telephone numbers from anywhere in Denmark (while someone behind the curtain looked them up and whispered them to him), a boxer in a half exposed ring who got flattened by a little girl, and an escapologist who couldn't escape - he hopped around the stage, handcuffed and inside a mail sack while there was a spotlight and a drum roll and then - nothing. Except a bloke handcuffed inside a mailsack hopping around shouting "Help!" The stage manager dragged him to one side, dropped him off the stage, and then bowed ceremoniously.

But we needed a "first half closer". Those with experience of these things will know how important a first half closer is. Late one evening at my house, Donald and I came up with a plan. It was nearly the same trick that Angel had used many years previously in AJAX. We had a senior British officer who was actually a bit of a pompous idiot, full of his own importance because he was the "senior British officer" but actually an RAF Engineer Officer Group Captain, quite handy with a maintenance manual but useless as a manager of people. (He had actually banned RAF wives in the Players Chorus from sitting on the knee of anyone who was not their husband, and Mary had to rewrite one scena completely!) He was fair game, as long as we didn't go over the top. After a warning that "this trick sometimes doesn't work", his watch was switched, ostensibly smashed to bits and the parts poured into his hands with "sorry, it didn't work this time, either." And then close the curtains while the piano tinkled some half time music, as he looked astonishedly at all the smashed bits in his hands with no help coming from anywhere. While everyone else went to the sumptuous buffet and/or the bar.

(With several months to spare, we had carried out reconnaissance on his left wrist, taking surreptitious photographs of his wristwatch as necessary. By the end of November, we knew the exact make and model and even the serial number of his expensive watch. Then we went to a watchmaker and asked him if he had an old broken watch of exactly that make. Fortunately, he had. It was well broken, and he gave it to us for nothing. We smashed it up even more, but ensuring that the maker's name was still readable on the watch face, and then we were all ready to go. It went like clockwork (sorry). We didn't explain. Or give him his watch back until the following day.)

The whole show went splendidly, and the accolades were outstanding. Every member of the audience had dressed up and the ambience was superb. A never-to-be-forgotten event.

Quite early on in my time in Denmark I had joined the NATO Hunting Club. "Hunting" is what we call "shooting" and "shooting" is what other nations call firing at targets, and "La Chasse" is what we call "hunting". So the NATO HC shot laid-down birds, principally, of course, pheasants. It was a minority sport, and short of funds to pay for e.g. hunting area rights, but in the winter of 1981/1982 there had been an event which changed all that. There were huge storms in the North Sea, and tremendous winds ravaged Jutland, which, as I said, is very low-lying. They flattened a lot of what was the only forested areas in the whole of the land - the pine tree plantations. Pine is very important for the Danish furniture industry, but there were limited amounts of it - and all in these plantations. Vast swathes of damage were done by the storms. What is not well known is that pine/deal/fir wood can lie on the ground after felling for a certain number of days and then for reasons which I don't know it becomes useless. If trees had been flattened, they could only be of commercial use if you could "harvest" them within that number of days. But what had been flattened, and what hadn't? It was difficult to tell from the ground, and accurate charting from a civilian aircraft would be problematic and probably inaccurate. But the NATO Hunting Club persuaded the NATO Air Force units that it would be a good idea to do an aerial reconnaissance over the whole of Jutland, and photograph it (for the military record, of course) and this was done within the day. The whole of Jutland. The photographs were not classified material, so copies were given to the Danish Forestry Commission, who got to work with a recovery plan within the day, and less than twenty-four hours later had been able to decide in what order to recover all this valuable timber before it became unusable. They were eternally grateful. It was not a coincidence that all the valuable shooting land, all the drives, all the game crops and all the stands lay in and around the forestry plantations. They gave us virtually carte blanche after that to shoot wherever we wished.

Danish shooting was highly regulated, quite properly. But it was also highly self-regulated, with more rules than even we have. I shot several Saturdays and although the bags were never big, they were very satisfying: you are allowed to shoot all sorts of game - both flying and ground game - within the allocated seasons, which are very strict; there are, for example, different seasons for cock pheasants and hen pheasants. Rule No.1, I was told: You have to wear a hat. It would be disrespectful to shoot a living thing without being properly attired. Fortunately, I have always had a deerstalker, which drew approval. Rule No.2: do what the Group Leader says. That's common all over, for safety reasons as much as anything else. Soon it was my first shoot; we set off from the "base camp", a hunting cabin in the forest, at about 09.00. The sun was only just up, and it was very cold. I did not know, but an hour or so later the Huntsman's wife would light the large woodburning stove in the centre of the hunting lodge, ready for our return for lunch. Lunch was highly convivial, mostly cold foods but with plenty of hot soups and drinks and several glasses (tiny glasses) of snaps. Then off for the afternoon's drives.

Almost my first shoot brought a problem at lunchtime. The Danes, as we all do, had a variety of hunting dogs, and they were allowed into the hunting lodge at lunchtime, although not fed there. One of them, a delightful little Dachshund, sat on the bench next to me. I absent mindedly patted it on the head, in the way that one does, and it sank its teeth into my hand. Hand and feelings both hurt, I looked down: the dachshund had been in conflict with a fox, and the fox's teeth had opened up a gash across the top of its head - which I had patted. My anguish subsided; I felt very sorry for the dog, which had done its best.

Then off we went for the afternoon. The Danes embrace the German concept of "Klapjagt" (I hope that's correct), literally "clap hunting". Which means that you stand with your back to the drive and then the beaters come through the rides, clapping, and you shoot the game as it goes away from you. Not an English concept, but that's what they do and if you tried to do it any other way you would be shooting shooters or beaters, not shooting game. Very disciplined people, hunters. We had only moderate success, although one good Danish shot brought down a deer, making the day's total two, and there were a couple of hares and a few rabbits as well as the pheasants and some pigeons. Not good, but not bad. And of course, it was all going to be eaten (In common with nearly all other shooters, my chief rule was that I would only kill that which I was going to eat). Before the (early) dark we got back to the hunting lodge where, to my surprise, the Huntsman's wife had laid out a long, thin carpet of pine fronds and the game was laid out on this in strict seniority order: bucks, does, hares, rabbits, cock pheasants, hen pheasants and then last of all pigeons. Then I learned why we had to wear hats: we were lined up alongside the laid-out game and at a sign a bugler played the Last Post and we ceremonially took off our headgear, bowed our heads and paid homage to the fallen creatures. Then it was all divvied up and we went home as darkness fell.

Living in a foreign country is a lesson. I learned a lot from the HQ Civilian Admin. chief, Jens Petersen. (Incidentally, another aside: "Petersen" is a very common name in Scandinavia, as is "Jacobsen", for obvious reasons which equate with "...son" in English and "Mac..." in Scottish, "O'" in Irish, and "Ap..." in Welsh and so on. But I was astonished to find that whatever rank, Danish military people, for all the informality and personal sincerity of the Danes, called each other by their surnames. I first heard it when a Petty Officer shouted "Hey, Jacobsen..." along a corridor and a four-stripe Captain leaned out of his office and called "Ja?" It was also of interest that Captain Jacobsen pronounced his own name "Jackson", and that is how he was known.)

Back to Jens. In a relatively "ordinary" job in Admin., he was nevertheless quite remarkable in many ways. He interested me linguistically in that - and this is extraordinarily uncommon - you could not tell by his words, his accent or his demeanour that he was not English. Second language speakers, in my experience, no matter how good, will always be detected at some stage. But not Jens, if he didn't want to be. Even his sense of humour was very English, although this in itself was not unusual, for Danish sense of humour is very similar to our own: while we were there, for example, "Not the Nine O'Clock News" was repeated on TV in every episode, several times over, and the joke which ends "Lady Ponsonby? Let me look in my diary. No, I see I didn't like it either" is quintessentially English. He had spent winters in Greenland in the days when there was little communication and the relief ships could only get through in the summer; I asked him where they got Vitamin C from in those circumstances, and he said they had to eat raw seals' liver. "One man wouldn't do it, and he died" he commented laconically. He smoked a pipe. He had a house overlooking the lake, with a garden sauna, to which he invited all the Brit officers on Sunday evenings. There was a small clique of us. The sauna would be heated to exactly 100 degrees C by the time we arrived, and if this seems excessive it should be pointed out that the sauna experience works because the body is so hot that it longs for cold and jumping into a lake with floating ice is positively lovely. They were very pleasant evenings, remarkably convivial with wonderful hospitality, but paradoxically, to us, we were never invited into the house. In fact, in the whole of our time in Denmark we were only once invited into a Danish home, despite the exceedingly good and friendly relations we had with so many Danes. (It was a pig farm. Our children had been doing voluntary work. Don't ask). Just as the emotional Russian will start talking about "Douche", which doesn't translate but approximates to "the inner drivings of the soul", or the Aborigine will go on "walkabout", the Scandinavians including the Danes will unsuspectedy succumb to something now known as the Law of Jente (Danish - "Jenteloven") which also doesn't translate. Jente is an ethnocentric interpretation of something much older and much deeper and which by extension says "I will be your friend, but you may not sit round my camp fire. I do not apologise for who I am and I do not care about your approval. This is my camp fire. You have no need to sit at it."

Hmm. If you can get your head round that you're doing a lot better than me. I was being commentarial about the Danes, who are one of the most delightful peoples on earth. They have such *taste.* Their glassware is beautiful, their works in wood are beyond compare - even little things like egg cups and door stops, and their wrapping of goods purchased is a delight to see. Our first Christmas brought surprises. We were warned about the Nissemen, who live in the loft throughout the year and come down at Christmas to do mischief so it is essential to leave them a glass or two of snaps. Then advised to have a ride on the Juletog (pronounced You'll a'tow") which is a Christmas train, before buying a bird or tree.

The Juletog is a steam train which runs on a single line out of the town and into the countryside. It consists of a steam train, several old passenger carriages, and several flatbed trucks at the back. On the outward trip, you drink free "Glügg", mulled wine, which of course puts you in the mood. Mood for what? Mood to spend, of course. After nearly an hour, the train enters a cutting, and stops. There, all along the grassy banks, the locals, who are all dressed up in traditional Danish costume, have laid out their goods: Christmas trees, turkeys, geese, chickens, hams and sausages, decorations, and anything else connected with the festive season. You buy it and put it on the flatbed trucks, all labelled. Then you chug off back to town again. A magical experience.

Arriving back in town, you see something you hadn't seen before. Alone in a square in the centre stands an old hotel, looking quite Elizabethan. We were astonished. It was wrapped up like a Christmas parcel - a two metre wide red silken sash horizontally round it, a similar sash over the top, and a huge bow tied in the same red sash on the roof next to the chimney. It takes your breath away. We have some splendid memories of that day's outing.

Father Christmas and the decorated Juletog

Back at the NATO headquarters at Karup, things continued apace. Which is to say that not a lot happened. We had the usual planned exercises, some with assets, some on paper. One day after an exercise which involved real troops and ships and aircraft, a US aircraft left its carrier in the North Sea and was flying to Copenhagen for some reason or another. As he approached, we asked if he would like to call in for a refuel. The offer was declined. It shouldn't have been. Fifteen minutes later over a deserted stretch of Jutland he ran out of fuel, ejected, and the aircraft crashed - without anyone having been harmed, fortunately. We recovered the pilot by helicopter. Now, it so happened that at exactly that time the International Conference of Air Crash Investigators had just kicked off in Copenhagen and so thirty or so specialised air crash investigators embarked in a Hercules transport aircraft to fly to Karup to get some practical/exercise experience. As the US Hercules approached Karup we heard the pilot say on his R/T "That godammed landing gear warning light is playing up again." And he came in to land. But the warning light wasn't playing up - it was really working, and warning him that at least part of his landing gear had failed to deploy; so he came in on one set of wheels instead of two, tilted over so that the aircraft slid along the runway on one front wheel, one tail wheel, and one wingtip, described a beautiful arc and came to a stop facing back the way it had come. Mercifully, again, no-one was injured, but it was extremely fortunate that the aircraft and pilot had not one, but thirty, specialist air crash investigators who all got out of the aircraft and investigated their own crash. What a thorough report there must have been.

Talking of "thoroughness", it was a delight to serve alongside some very thorough (if rather blinkered - except, of course, for "HHH") German officers.

The German Chief of Staff (second in command) of AIRBALTAP (NATO Air Forces Baltic Approaches) had, however, suddenly become very ill and had been ambulanced back to Germany. His almost immediate replacement was a highly competent German Air Commodore who was training to take over the post anyway but had not completed his English language course. (English is the language of NATO - but see "Oberammergau" for a French, US and Turkish perspective). He was parachuted in, and got to work immediately. His superior, an amiable Dane with impeccable English, helped him settle in. He had been in post only a few days when his first challenge arose. Mary Benson, wife of Squadron Leader David Benson of the RAF contingent, telephoned in to say that her husband was ill and could not come in that day. The call was put through to the German Air Commodore. Thinking quickly, he realised that he would have to relay this information to his superior, in case he heard it from someone else, and so he asked for more information. "What is the matter with him?" he asked. Mary said "It's not serious - he's been sick and got diarrhoea. He'll probably be back tomorrow." The German Chief of Staff reported himself to the Danish Air Marshal. "I have to report" he said, "that Benson, Squadron Leader, will not be at work today. He is sick." "I'm sorry to hear that," said the Dane. "I hope it's nothing serious." "No," said the Chief of Staff, who had been working with his dictionary before the interview with his senior, "He is sick with gonorrhoea. I have researched it." The senior Dane did not let an eyebrow flicker. "Are you quite sure?" he asked. Said the German: "Ya, in fact it was his wife who told me."

On a very much more serious subject, it has to be recorded that the combined NATO Headquarters at Karup were contained in a conglomeration of perfectly ordinary looking offices on the air base; the War Headquarters, to which we all retired in war or for exercises, was in a Second World War bunker which the Germans had built. It was enormous, perhaps sixty metres by forty with walls five metres thick, and impressively high. All in solid reinforced concrete. Built, no doubt, by prisoners of war. In the middle of the adjacent forest. Looked very formidable. But it was outdated so a new one was to be built. Underground. Not far away. To modern standards. And the old one had to go. It was an excrescence. Plans were made.

Social plans were also made. Any excuse for a party. The date and time had been announced, and we all met with our families to watch the blowing up of the old bunker - from a safe distance, of course. We started with tea on the lawn, and then we all had canapés and a cocktail and assembled behind a concrete wall to watch, or rather to listen to and then watch, the old bunker being blown up.

The demolition teams had drilled holes in the old bunker five centimetres in diameter every metre across and up and down the whole edifice, inside and out. Thousands of holes. All packed with dynamite. It was all to go up together. There was a countdown, at the end of which there was a huge explosion and clouds of smoke and debris rose up into the sky and there was a great cheer from all of us as we peeked over the top of our protecting wall and looked at the huge pall of smoke which surrounded and raised our glasses in tribute to what we thought was the ex-bunker. When the smoke cleared, we all had to do a double take. Shaken - yes, stirred - a bit. But not broken; the bunker was still there, looking just as it always had, but with no windows and a bit smoky. They tried four more times before they gave up, and then they just planted lots more trees and inimical shrubs around it and put up signs saying "Keep Out".

While we are on the subject of loud bangs, I need to record another episode in the NATO calendar: the "Officers' Personal Weapons Test". It needs to be said that other NATO nations are not as squeamish about weapons as we Brits are; they recognise that it is not the gun which kills, it is the user of the gun. They also believe that in the protection of their home soil they need officers who are armed and ready to act at very short notice. And they recognise the need to trust those officers. So they are issued on joining the armed forces with a personal weapon (usually a pistol) which they not only keep throughout their service but also take home with them, so as to actually be "ready at all times". We live on an island, so I suppose that gives us a bit of time to get weapons out of the armoury if we need them.

However, quite sensibly, NATO officers are required annually to test their shooting skills with their "personal weapons" and one morning I got a Memorandum from the HQ security officer saying that on "such and such a date" all officers should attend the butts to practise and verify their skills. ("Butts" - a shooting range with targets at one end in front of large sand bunkers to take the bullets which had either hit or missed the target, and a distance marked range up to two hundred metres. The "targets" in question consist of a group of cardboard soldiers on wooden poles, life size, which pop up for three seconds so that you can home in on them and fire, and then go back down again into their pits).

The other Brits kept quiet, but I decided I'd have a go at it. I had taken my Brown Bess musket, the one which helped us defeat all these pesky Europeans in the first place, and I told the Security Officer it was the only personal weapon I had. It was, of course, a replica weapon, but exact. It was a muzzle loader, which means that you have to put down the barrel a gunpowder load, cover it with a wad and then put the ball or the shot in and finish off with a cardboard blank just to stop it all falling out. I reported to the butts with my "personal weapon" (which they could hardly ban, having laid such emphasis on the importance of the event). I, of course, was having a hoot. The others, particularly the Germans, laughed at my "personal weapon" and got on with their shooting, putting little holes in the cardboard targets. Meanwhile, I was filling my barrel with a double load of black powder (which I knew it would take) followed by a wad and then, in an inspired moment, a whole handful of Meccano nuts and bolts instead of ball or shot. I took my position at the firing point, fifty metres from the target. When I said "Ready" the cardboard soldier popped up for what should have been three seconds, except that I was ready for it and fired straight away. As all muzzle loaders will know, there was a short delay then a big bang and a huge cloud of smoke. When the smoke cleared, there was no soldier and no pole - I had shot the whole lot away, leaving just a smoking wooden stump. "That's the way to do it!" I announced, as I packed my bag and left. "No enemy left."

They didn't ask me again.

I alluded earlier on to Admiral HHH Kampe's brilliant understanding of situations and of people. He knew that if he asked a situation appreciation question of a German officer he would receive the "expected" reply, if he asked an American officer he would receive the US opinion of the situation, if he asked a Dane he might or might not get a reply and so he often mused about whom to ask what. So it was that one day I was sitting in my office minding my own business when Kampe himself came in and sat down. I knew something was up. "We have some information," he said. "There have been reports of some articulated tracks on the seabed in the western Baltic. We do not know what they are. But I have a script in the Russian language which I would like to be translated into English so that we can examine it." I had to say "Sir, with the greatest of respect, I am an interpreter, not a translator. There is a huge difference". He said "Can you do it?" I said "Yes, but it will take me a week, free of other duties." He said "Make it so." He had obviously been to Dartmouth at some time or another. "Make it so." is a very final instruction.

Now, I've been called an idiot in my time, I've been reprimanded for stupidity, I've been chastised. But on this occasion, I managed to do it to myself, all on my little own. I made myself look a complete fool - but fortunately only to myself; nobody else knew. Here's how it happened. The first rule of translating is: "Read the whole document through". I didn't. I just started. I got out my dictionaries and I spent day and night for a week translating this document, bit by bit, checking and re-checking each paragraph. Then I got to the very last paragraph, which said "This article is reproduced from The National Geographic Magazine Volume No. .... by kind permission of the authors." To my horror, I realised that I could have gone out and bought the appropriate copy of the National Geographic Magazine and saved myself and other people a lot of bother. I just kept quiet, and handed my script over to the admiral (having checked it against the original, of course). He was delighted. The tank tracks on the seabed in the Baltic turned out to have been a perfectly ordinary scientific exploration by a Swedish minerals company. 'Nuff said. Follow Healey's principle: "When in a hole, stop digging". I did. A scrape. Bit of an escape, really.

The Baltic is in many ways quite special. Two areas in particular surprised me, for entirely different reasons.: Travemunde and Bjornholm. Firstly, Travemunde. It was on the westerly bank of an inlet between West Germany (as then was) and East Germany (as then was, under Soviet control). We stood at the end of what was a little like a fjord and looked North into the Baltic. On the west side (Travemunde) there was a little pier, a beach, a promenade with little cafes and ice cream stalls and parasols, and little yachts at anchor, with people swimming or just enjoying the sun, and children running up and down and making sandcastles. On the East German side, there were strings of barbed wire, chain link fences, shrubbery razed to the ground so as not to restrict rifle fire and, for all we knew, land mines. You will realise what an enormous shock it came to an Englander. The West Germans had been living with it for years, of course, and were used to it. The reverse situation took place some years later when several Soviet military people were allowed to visit Portsmouth, and received a very, very big shock. This is recorded later under the account of the visit of the Soviet ship "B'yezuprech'ni".

We had, incidentally, a friendship with a German family in Viborg; Colonel Michael (I don't remember his surname) and his wife and two children who had, on hearing that the Berlin Wall was to be built and the investment of Berlin, and crossing the border stopped, simply packed their bags, left their house and everything else they owned behind them, gathered the children and got on the Underground from the East where they were living and got off again in West Germany just before all transition was prevented by the Soviets.

Bjornholm was interesting for a completely different reason although one which is just as much associated with democracy as a distinct opposite from what we had seen at Travemunde. As an adult I had always been interested in the idea of Proportional Representation (PR) as a jolly good democratic principle. What could be better than having a consensus? Well, we hadn't been living in Denmark for very long before they had elections. I talked to my neighbour over the garden fence about it. I asked him a few (neutral) questions. He replied "I don't know; I'm not going to vote." I thought this odd, in a PR country, and asked why not. "Well," he said "there are many different parties and not one of them can command a majority. So whoever comes top will have to make a compromise with one or probably more than one other parties. This means that, at the moment you cast your vote, you don't actually know what you are voting for because your candidate and his party have necessarily got to make concessions to other parties and they may have to give up the very principle that you voted for them for."

The second reason I went off the idea of PR was hearing from Danish people (they have a story about it, which may or may not be true) that in a previous election a major issue was whether NATO should be allowed to put nuclear weapons on Danish sovereign territory or not. Now, I can't recall the exact figures, but let's say that in their PR parliament there were two hundred members in favour and two hundred members against when the composition was just four hundred and one members altogether (these figures are not correct; they are illustrative). The one member who was left was a farmer on the Danish island of Bjornholm (which is closer to Sweden than to Denmark) who in common with all the other Bjornholm farmers fertilised his land with seaweed which he collected from the seashore, and who had been elected as member of parliament for Bjornholm because he had sworn to fight to get the taking of seaweed off the shores of Bjornholm by visiting Swedish farmers outlawed - seaweed thieves, as they saw it. In short, therefore, the decision as to whether to allow nuclear weapons on Danish soil in the defence of the whole western world was actually decided by a seaweed farmer from

Bjornholm, who had the casting vote in parliament. "Think on", as they say in my part of Lancashire, "Think on".

Time passed. Work progressed. It was the social side of life which was most interesting. The finale came astonishingly spectacularly. I had been working at my desk for an ordinary week. It was Friday afternoon and we were all about to pack up for the weekend. As was my wont, I toured the small HQ before leaving. HHH Kampe's PA was just locking up, too.

"Bye, Astrid," I said as I passed her office. "Have a nice weekend. Are you doing anything special?" "Ja," she said. "The Headquarters are going to Esbjerg to hear Handel's Messiah." "Oh," I said. "I didn't know. I would have liked to go to that." "You were invited," she said, "But you did not reply." I knew this was not the case because we would have joined the trip like a shot. But Astrid was one of those people who are not going to admit to ever being wrong, whatever. "Oh, well," I said. "Never mind. I hope you enjoy it. By the way, what language are they singing it in?" "Why do you ask?" she said. I replied that it could have been sung in English, or German, or, in Esbjerg, in Danish or even (unlikely) Juttish. "They are singing it in German, of course," she said. "Handel was German". I smiled, and just remarked that he had spent most of his life in England. I thought no more of it.

Not that weekend, nor on the Monday nor the Tuesday. Then on the Wednesday I suddenly realised I hadn't seen Astrid that week, which was unusual. So I popped up to her office. After the usual trivialities I asked "How was "Messiah"?" She mumbled "Very good". Sensing why she had mumbled, I said "What language did they sing it in?" And she even more mumbled, very quietly, "Nglsh." I said "Sorry, Astrid, I didn't hear you" and she said, positively, with reluctance, with the air of someone who has been rumbled "I said English. I do not know why they sang it in English. But they did." I said "That's because Handel was English. Naturalised." And left it at that.

The following day, a junior German officer "happened" to bump into me in the canteen. "I hear you have some reservations about Herr Handel, Herr Pearce?" and I replied "No, not at all. Splendid fellow. Eighteenth century composer. Born in Germany, but wrote all his good music after he had emigrated to England". There was a pause. Of a couple of days, to be exact. Then a German Air Force Officer dropped in to my office and said "Did you know that Georg Friedrich Handel was born in Halle - Saale - in Germany on the 23rd February 1685? Some people are confused about that fact." I said "I am not at all confused, because I know that he was indeed born in Germany but came to live in England when he was quite young and never went back to live in Germany again". He left.

Things were hotting up. Finally I was accosted by a German General. Straight to the point, he just said "Handel was a very German composer." And I replied "Yes indeed, but he wrote all his choral works in English." And that was that. Except that after we had left Denmark in the normal course of events to a new appointment in Portsmouth, actually many months later, I had a postcard from a German Admiral whom I had known in the lower rank of Captain in Denmark. I still have it. I treasure it. On the front there is a picture of a sitting man's crossed legs; he has on one red sock and one blue sock. In Danish, it says "Ingen er perfekt men du er Ganske taet pa...." which is "No-one is perfect, but you are pretty close...." This incident, which I had forgotten long previously, but which the German hierarchy had clearly not, ended with this postcard. And because the situation was so comical, I record the words on the postcard verbatim:

"Dear Alan, thank you for your nice story about our common favourite, G.F.Händel, and his parents. Did you know that his father, a surgeon in Halle (today in East Germany) wanted him to become a lawyer? Thus, he studied law until his father had died (in Germany). Only then he concentrated his effort on music. He was already adult and famous when he decided to go to England - where he knew that someone like him was urgently needed. This happened after he had been for about four years in Italy and after he had worked during 1710/11 in

Hannover. From there it was an easy decision for him to follow the Hannover dynasty to London where this German family had just come into power. And the Brits who could not pronounce his name Georg Friedrich Händel made him "George Frederick Handel", which he finally accepted. Nevertheless, Alan, let's enjoy his music and brotherly share his life. Best wishes, and Auf Wiedersien!".

That was it. End of engagement. Do you know what I really enjoy about a German joke? You never know whether they've told one or not.

Things went on routinely. Then it was my time to leave, and I got a report saying that my (British) relief was due to arrive on such-and-such a date, but that he was coming in his own yacht and it was a bit weather-dependent. He arrived (late) and we left. I later learned that he was actually more cantankerous that I had been, so perhaps they remember me with warmth. Whatever. The Soviets did not invade and the West was still secure. And I had done my (little) bit.

We came back to a married quarter in Portsmouth, or to be more accurate, in Hill Head, near Lee-on-Solent on the western side of Portsmouth harbour. We had no MQ problems at all. Our plan was simple: throughout our time in Denmark we had been keeping a very close eye on the UK housing market, with a view to returning and buying a property if things started to move fast. We were lucky in that things did start to move fast - but not until after we had returned to UK and bought a house in Down End, Fareham, which was very convenient for most RN appointments in the area. I was appointed to HMS COLLINGWOOD again, this time as what in civilian life would be called the Deputy Bursar.

CHAPTER 16
HMS COLLINGWOOD again

It suited me fine. It was an amiable shore establishment with vast pools of talent (including AmDram talent) with splendid sports facilities including its own swimming pool. Three thousand people to accommodate, feed, pay, allocate equipment and resources to, and to look after their HR needs.

Talking of sports facilities, I used to look forward to April, when the groundsmen started work on the cricket pitches and put up the practice nets. I used to play in the nets regularly. My Captain got to hear about this, and surprisingly coyly asked if he might join us. He did. He was an excellent batsman, despite the fact that he had suffered from polio as a child and could not run. His timing was splendid, and it was a pleasure to play with him. It was also a pleasure to play with a tiny little Indian fellow, who was a genuine wrist spinner, and an American, an oppositely huge bloke with enormous forearms and - reputedly - a formidable baseball player. He was rash enough to say he would hit any ball out of the ground. Eventually - we were taking turns at everything - it came about that the little Indian was bowling to the huge American. The latter had a huge grin on his face. The first ball came down, quite slowly - which increased the grin - and then spun viciously off the track. The American took a huge swing, missed, and his stumps were flattened. He got angry. The next ball spun the other way. Another mowing scythe. And the wicket went down again. Six balls. Six hits. The American left us, saying it was all a dirty trick (and by implication a "Commie Plot") and he never tried again.

But the cricket was good. The first summer, we played the Wardroom of HMS Sultan and we won, although we weren't expected to. The post match drinks were effusive. Late that night we wrote a letter to the MCC challenging the world touring XI (who were here instead of the banned South Africans) to a cricket game. Next morning, we found that we had actually posted it. There was a bit of a wait - then a letter from Sir Gary Sobers saying that he had carefully considered our request, but that such a match couldn't actually be programmed in to a busy test match schedule, but that this was not to be taken as a sign that they were afraid of playing us, and would have done if they could have. What a charming response!

The work was routine, but the extra-curricular activities were most interesting. I taught a Russian O-Level class, for example. As usual, I started with about thirty people most of whom thought they could do it without much effort (it always happens) and dropped out. I was left with three students, all very keen but one dyslexic, still keen and a perseverer. All three took O-Level. The dyslexic chap didn't pass, but got a commendation for his effort. The other two both got A Grades.

I myself kept up to date with my own Russian by going to RAECC Beaconsfield for a fortnight's refresher training once a year. (This went on throughout the rest of my naval career.) I met some astonishingly interesting people from all walks of life. Once we all went to Bekonscot model village where a tutor put us through a real grilling with interpreting about a Morris Dancer team with a leader who has a pig's bladder on a stick, and a list of all the fairground rides. Once we went to Amersham, where the head of the WI showed us around - including the grave of Ruth Ellis, the last hanged murderess; half of us were pretending to be Russians, the other half British Interpreters. The WI lady got it a bit wrong, and when thanked for her guided tour said in reply to our tutor: "I think they speak excellent English - they are a credit to you"!

Perhaps the most amusing one of all was when we showed a party of real Russians round RAECC. They hadn't a word of English. We visited the library. The librarian lady was exactly the model you would choose if you were making a programme about English libraries: elderly, short, straight backed, petite, grey suit, grey hair tied in a bun, lovely lady. She had, of course, not a word of Russian - why would she? The Russians asked politely "*Scolka knig ou vas yaste*?" and I interpreted

"How many books have you?" and she replied "Thirty thousand." And I interpreted "*Treedsat tuichach*" and they then asked, in Russian of course, how long you could keep books for and then "What happens if people don't return a book on time?" She said "They are fined."

Now, here started my immediate interpreting catastrophe. An interpreter knows if he has got something wrong by the blank stares, but he or she has to soldier on. You usually wake up in the middle of the night as the ghastly truth of your cockup dawns on you. Such it was for me. The Russian for "to fine someone" (e.g. for parking incorrectly or not returning a library book on time) is "rasstraffovats" but unfortunately the very similar Russian "rasstrelovats" means "to execute by firing squad". I chose the wrong one. The Russians gasped, and shouted "Niet! Niet!" and the little old librarian lady (who didn't know what I had said) nodded vigorously and said "Yes, we do. We do. We really do." We moved on. I woke up in the middle of the night. Nothing I could do about it. That's interpreting for you. Severely bad interpreting on that occasion.

But there was an amusing incident in the mess that evening. We were having a pre dinner drink and in discussion a female Lieutenant Colonel said to my colleague, a submariner: "I think women ought to be allowed to serve at sea, even in submarines." And he replied "Ma'am, are you aware that we do six week submarine patrols and it's only after three weeks that we change our underwear?" She said "What, you mean you only take two pairs of underpants with you?" And he said "No, Ma'am, we only take one pair and after three weeks we take them off, turn them inside out and put them back on again." To her credit her gin and tonic shook only slightly, but I think she may now have rethought things a bit.

Then back to my main job at HMS COLLINGWOOD, the naval shore training establishment in Fareham, near Portsmouth.

We had lots of interesting fun events. As Bursar-wallah it fell to me to be Treasurer of the annual Open Day event. This was a huge jamboree, where the public were allowed to come in and see lots of exhibits and events; but it was also a sort of oversized village fête, with ice cream wagons, sideshows, burger bars, beer tents and stalls selling all sorts of things. And all in aid of naval charities. It was a bonanza of a day, which was usually attended by quite several thousand people. It was always a great success, and made a great deal of money for charity - not least, of course, from the beer tents.

The first thing that went wrong was that I booked Corelli's ice cream van. But it was the wrong Corelli. The Corellis had come to England after the war, and made ice creams - very well, and very successfully. Then there had been a family rift. One brother Corelli had always come to this event. I booked the other one, not knowing. The other brother turned up as he always did, and there was a knife fight in the main square. We got that sorted. The rest of the day went extremely well, and at the end we were all exhausted.

Once over, we all relaxed and went back to work. Then, as the days passed, it was my task to collect in all the monies from the stalls, and produce the accounts. I worked away assiduously. Then, to my horror, I came to realise that the beer tents had not made a profit. Usually, their profit was about 40% and contributed hundreds of pounds to the overall figures. What had happened? It was most unlikely that anything had been stolen or lost. So there was an enquiry. It revealed that in all previous years, the beer tents had been run by a highly experienced, older officer who had come up through the ranks and knew all the tricks and wrinkles, and sorted them. This year, the arranging and supervision had been given to a young "Schoolie" officer, highly intelligent, well educated, well read, but incredibly green. And the first task he faced even before we started was the broken glass from the beer tents. So he arranged for plastic ones. So far so good. But he knew that people would buy beer in their thousands and chuck the plastic glasses all over the place. So he instituted a returnable 20p per plastic glass routine. Again, so far, so good. Knowing the plastic glasses shouldn't be used again, he arranged for large skips to be placed behind the beer tents for their disposal. What he hadn't bargained for was the ingenuity of the local boys, who simply repeatedly went round the back of the beer tents, retrieved piles of plastic glasses, and went to the bar saying "My Dad told me to bring all these back" and the barmen, happy that they had not been discarded on the roads and paths, gave them 20p each for them. They did it over and again as the bartenders changed. They must have had an absolute fortune by the end of the day.

The event had been a success. But by the time the bills had been paid the profits were considerably down. Mistakes noted for next time.

And talking of mistakes, I must record the doings of one Leading Cook called Bradford. Funnily enough, he came from Bradford. He was a jolly good chap. He was of West Indian ancestry, and very black. He had a good sense of humour, and sometimes it got returned with a vengeance. Like the time he prepared the packed lunches for thirty people to go yomping in the Black Mountains on an initiative test. Someone took out the hard boiled eggs from his packed lunches and put raw eggs in their place. The outcome was tumultuous. But the event I remember most, as I was actually there, was when he was serving at the sumptuous main course counter in the dining hall when a brand new class of Nigerian students came in for the first time. They looked at the heaving counter, bewildered. In particular, they didn't know if the beautiful individual pies were meat or not, and if so what kind of meat it was. Then their leader looked up and saw Bradford. A kindred spirit! So he said "Hey, man, what's in de pies?" and quick as a flash Bradford said, in his strong Yorkshire accent "It's no-one tha knows".

We had the AmDram festival again. We put on "The Lark" by Jean Anouilh, the story of Joan of Ark. I played The Inquisitor. It is a role not to be overplayed, because it was The Promoter who was the nasty bit of work, not the Inquisitor - he is there just to ensure that the iniquities of any religious trial are made to look fair, even when they aren't. We all thought that the lass who played Joan, who had been brilliant, would win "Best Actor". She didn't. I did. And for reasons I can't remember, we didn't even attend the award ceremony, so someone else had to accept the "Oscar" on my behalf. I found out the next Monday.

The author (L) addresses Joan in the play "The Lark"

As I remarked, social life was good. We had some splendid summer and Christmas balls, and several other mess dinners in between. One quite quiet mess dinner was made interesting by the after dinner games, which were many and various. One was called "Flight Deck Landings" and was required to be played by the most junior members of the mess. Mess tables are highly polished, and very long if you put one at the end of another several times. You thus have a shiny, slippery aircraft carrier landing deck. At the far end, you place two strong people with napkins knotted together into an "arrester wire", and at the other the young tyro hurls himself down the tables in a simulated deck landing, with his arms outstretched ahead of him and his hands wide open to catch the "arrester wire".

Great cheers. More beer. Then when the greenest of all does it, the two strong men just lift the "arrester wire" and the "pilot" skids off the end of the tables at speed and crashes into the wall. More cheers. But on this occasion, he split his head open. Much blood. Fellows picked him up. Stewards cleaned the wall. Chief Steward told Mess President he was dismantling our flight deck. In the corner, our grizzly old Doc. jumped up and leapt into the fray. "I may have drunk a lot," he said, in considerable understatement, "but when there's an emergency I can just snap my fingers and be in control again and take over." And he led the wounded and bleeding ex-pilot off to the sick bay (sick bays are open 24/7). To our astonishment, they were back twenty minutes later, the former to have another gin and the other to the applause of the flight deck staff, and other games were resumed. The ex-pilot had a beautiful line of stitches across his scalp, and all bleeding had stopped, so he was able to join in again. But a young visiting reservist surgeon lieutenant who had observed these goings on found a moment to take the ex-pilot to one side and said "You are to come to the surgery tomorrow at 7 a.m. before everyone else comes in, and I will sort you out." On the morrow, at 07.00, he removed all the old grizzly doctor's stitches, which had actually been sited across the young man's hair parting - thereby stretching the skin tight and stopping the bleeding - and stitched up the actual wound. Success, if late.

I was a bit sad at one of the last events I took part in at COLLINGWOOD. It was my turn to host the graduate job seekers whom the MoD had assembled and sent us to see if the Royal Navy was for them. I showed them round all the various departments - the radar section, the countermeasures section, the missile schools, the audio interception section, the communications centre, the underwater weapons group and so on and then took them back to the wardroom for tea and a question and answer session.

I called for questions. The first was "How much holiday do you get?" and I replied "Six weeks, if you can take it, but often things are too busy or you're away at sea." The next was "Do you get a company car?" to which my answer was "No." Then "Do you get membership of BUPA?" and "How much sick leave are you allowed, and do you get sick pay?" and "Do you have to take your sick leave by a particular date? "and "Do you get Bonuses?" My patience was wearing thin. "Would anybody like to ask what it feels like to be a member of an organisation which is helping defend the United Kingdom at sea against hostile attack?" No, there wasn't. "Does anybody know what "Pro Patria Mori" means?" This question not only perplexed them, but as I could see from the looks on their faces caused them to think I had gone mad. "Is anybody thrilled with the idea of travelling round the globe and visiting interesting far flung places?" I asked in desperation. I got one reply "What allowances do you get for leaving the UK, and can you come home if you don't like it?"

I gritted my teeth and said "Gentlemen, you may be interested in finding out if the Royal Navy is suitable for you, but I think you may not be suitable for it. Please stop drinking our tea and go home". And that was that.

A few months before I left this appointment, my boss's replacement had a heart attack and could not join us. I was asked to take over his responsibilities as well as my own, and this I did for several months. I got the higher rate of pay for the period, but not the higher rank, which was a shame, but it proved the point.

CHAPTER 17
CINCNAVHOME

The title tells it all. The depleted Royal Navy (when I joined, there were seven aircraft carriers) was by now divided into a Fleet Command and an Everything Else Command, known as the Home Command, so there was a Commander in Chief Fleet and a Commander in Chief, Naval Home Command. The latter's HQ was in Portsmouth. I was to join the staff as the Staff Supply Officer in charge of Reserves logistics. It was a fascinating job. I travelled all over the country, and to Gibraltar, to meet Royal Naval Reservists, to check their books, and to help them with problems. Most of them were RNR reservists because they "wanted to do their bit" or so that they could get sea trips in the mine warfare ships, or to look good on their CVs, or just for the socialising that goes with being a member of any group. I didn't mind this a bit, and if I could help them, I would.

One of the most successful RNR units was at Liverpool, from where the Battle of the Atlantic had been won. That battle has been overshadowed by the glamorous Battle of Britain, which was vital and involved flying heroism by people from many nations, of whom the British, Commonwealth airmen and the Polish were greatly numerable. But that went on for only a few weeks; the unglamorous Battle of the Atlantic, vital for all the food and fuel and everything else that comes into the country, lasted for four years, took 100,000 lives and was perhaps the single most important factor in the survival of the United Kingdom. None of us would have been here in this peaceful country had we not won the Battle of the Atlantic.

It was called HMS EAGLET, was very well run, very professional, dedicated, and a useful fighting asset. I used to go there, as to all the other RNR units, to inspect the accounts and give advice. On the first occasion, I attended a "drill night", an evening training session. During the day, I had found the accounts impeccable, as I knew I would, so the evening was a bit of a formality. "An officer has come up from Commander in

Chief's office to see you all" was how it was put to the Reservists.

At other times I went as part of my duties to several Salon Culinères (or is it Salons Culinère?) both military and civilian. It was a great pleasure to see the advances in the culinary arts, to have a laugh at some of the crackpot ideas, but also to look at new developments in industrial catering. I was introduced to these events some time previously, at HMS COLLINGWOOD, where a chef had come to me with his Petty Officer and asked if he could have 10lbs of butter on a bypass (see "HMS HECATE" for definition of "a bypass"). The Chief Cook and I both queried it, and the young chef shyly admitted that he "wanted a go at ice carvery and butter carvery". He was a good chap, so we agreed. He kept the main galley open after work on his own initiative for several days, doing whatever it was that he was doing, and locking the fruits of his labours away in a fridge overnight. Then one day he proudly asked the Chief and me to come and have a look; we were both completely stopped in our tracks - "gobsmacked" would be the modern term - at what he had to show us. It was what can only be called a statue, a carving about two feet high, in butter, of a young fox with its paw outstretched trying to unroll a hedgehog. The detail was just astonishing. He had even managed to get an expression of frustration on the fox's face and a look of relief on the face of the hedgehog (if I can say this without being too anthropomorphic, but dog owners and country people will understand what I mean.) This truly amazing piece of work gained second place in the competition. Standards were very high. Later in the year his ice carving was the head of an Indian chief in full headdress, more than two feet high and also pretty remarkable.

At the Portsmouth Naval Salon Culinère that year I was interested to see not only our own chefs in each of the disciplines but also the RN chefs from HMS TAMAR in Hong Kong, who had proudly come over to demonstrate their capabilities in the competitions. They were working away and I noticed that no-one was talking to them, so I wandered over and introduced myself and had a chat. After professional questions, I asked if they had had time to go ashore, perhaps to visit London? "Oh, no," said the leading cook. "Too much pleasure in Portsmouth!" Being a sailor myself, I thought I knew what he meant, and said "Oh, well done. That's the stuff!" and he replied "No, no - too much plessure - plessure of work in Portsmouth". "Oh, well." I thought.

There were two "call-aways" during this period, the first for just a few days, the second for several months. This was 1990, and it was clear that "Glasnost" and "Perestroika" were having their effects, and that relations between East and West were beginning to thaw. One of the best ways a country can signal its desire to improve relations with another country is to invite an informal warship visit (Remember HMS HECATE's visit to Alexandria in Egypt, the first such event after the Suez Crisis). We heard, at quite short notice, that the Soviet "Sovryemenn'y" class cruiser "B'yezuprechn'y" was going to pay a five day visit to Portsmouth. (This was particularly significant, because the last Soviet ship visit to Portsmouth was in 1956 when Khruschev and Bulganin visited the UK in the warship "Orzhonn'ykidze", during which visit Commander "Buster" Crabb, Royal Navy lost his head - literally -- and both his hands as well, reputedly diving underneath the Soviet ship to look at its propellers.)

This visit was to be quite different. All the available Russian interpreters were gathered, and we allocated ourselves tasks - interpreting at lunches and dinners, supporting sporting and social events for all ranks, and conducting visits to HMS VICTORY and other Portsmouth landmarks and attractions. This "for all ranks" really confused the Soviets, just as did their visits ashore, and for the same reason. Soviet internal propaganda had always portrayed the British upper classes (usually male, always wearing suit and bowler hat and carrying an umbrella) as treading on all the other British suborned peasants and honest workers and leaving them reeling in the gutter or hedge; by analogy, this meant that British officers would constantly be doing the same to British ratings. They were most surprised to find such officers and ratings talking amiably and easily together, and completely astonished that an officer should interpret for Russian and British senior and junior ranks in order to make proceedings easier for all. Both sides learned a very great deal during the five days - which was what it was all about, of course. I was not surprised to have to cope with difficulties of cultures between principals: a lady lunch hostess, for example, told a Russian Captain that the flowers on the table came from her garden, and asked if he himself was a gardener? He replied, in Russian of course: "Tell her that in the town where I live, a good many miles North and East of Murmansk, the permafrost relents only for a few weeks in July. No, I am not a gardener". I broke the rules and interpreted for the good lady hostess just the last six words of this, which sufficed. We also took a party of Russians up to London for the day, on the train. They stared out of the window at the passing houses and housing estates, always asking "How many families live in that building?" whatever type of house it was. (The Russian language does not have a word for house. The one used in text books is "*dom*", which actually means "block", i.e. of flats. The nearest word "*Osobnyak*" means "villa" or "residence" and the clue that it is pejorative lies in the fact that "*Osobnyakom*" means "aloof".)

But the biggest surprise, nay shock, even for me was a revelation, a stopper in the tracks event, a Road to Damascus thing and a highly emotionally charged moment - just about as electric as anything I have ever encountered.

You see, apart from the bigwig events, it was also important that the senior non-commissioned officers and others should get to know each other, and so an invitation had been sent by the Warrant Officers' Mess of HMS SULTAN (the large shore establishment which trains marine engineers and also houses the Interview Board) to all the senior NCO's of the Soviet ship. I was asked to interpret, but only when needed, because "gentlemen of the sea" can always communicate by sign language and other means - until they get stuck. So I attended, sat alone at a table with a Coke, and waited. The first thing that happened was that everyone accepted a drink and then disappeared! The Russians could not believe that the cars in the car park belonged to anything other than the oppressive upper classes with their suits and bowler hats and umbrellas, and certainly not to non-commissioned ranks of the RN. So they were all taken outside and to my amusement were allowed to drive the cars around the car park and in some cases out on to the airfield as much as they wanted. They were like little children with new bikes! It was hilarious. But that is not the point of my extremely serious story.

They came back into the bar, and proceeded to drink and converse. They all became quite jolly, and became great friends. I was occasionally called upon to interpret a word or two, but mostly they just got on with being bosom friends. And then, as I sat there, I noticed a rather older Russian chap, perhaps of about fifty years, sitting on his own at a table, perfectly still, with his head down and his arms by his sides. "Oh, dear," I thought, "He's had too much to drink. I'll check if he's all right." I couldn't have been more wrong - he hadn't and he wasn't. I moved over and sat next to him, quite silent for a few minutes, and then said "Are you all right?" There was no response. So I waited a minute or two and then quite gently said "Are you all right?" The response was electric, stunning. He slowly sat up, shook himself, and then after a moment quite suddenly and unexpectedly smashed his fist down upon the table very hard and shouted "Seventy years! Seventy years!" Not having a clue what he was talking about I sat, silent, and waited. Then, after a minute or so he suddenly smashed his first down on the table again and shouted "Seventy years!" I didn't know what to say or do, so I kept quiet and waited. The next thing that happened was that this rather older Russian Warrant Officer started to cry, quietly at first, then with great sobs, more sobs, bigger sobs until I began to worry for his breathing and ventilation. Then the noise stopped. For a moment. Then without warning his fist came crashing down upon the table again and this time he shouted "Seventy years! Seventy years they have lied to us!" and he broke down into fits of sobbing again.

If from childhood, you have been told that parents do not know as much as the State, that the grass here is very green, much greener than on the other side, that foreigners are all trying to get into your country, that news is only censored to keep children from being infected, that Capitalists succeed because they tread on the prostrate bodies of working class people who would really prefer to live here under communism, that the traitor Trotsky died when he accidentally fell and hit his head on an ice pick in Mexico, which is a very cold country, that all the empty shelves in the shops are entirely due to outside interference in the internal matters of the State, and that senior politicians drive round in big cars and live in expensive houses because they have to be protected from potential Western infiltration, then you will believe it because you have no reason not to and you will receive a very big shock when you find that it is not actually so. It would be like waking up in another world. And that was exactly what this man had done. He had woken up in another world. The real world. People in the West, in the UK, were just ordinary, quite nice people who smiled and talked to each other and seemed to have quite pleasant lives, the very antithesis of what he and all the other Soviet children and adults had been told since birth. That was what he was sobbing about. He and all his compatriots had been lied to for seventy years by the "elected" Soviet elite, who were far more autocratic and oligarchic than anything you would find in the West. He felt cheated. To put it mildly.

There wasn't really anything I could do about it, so I sat and waited and talked trivia until I judged that the situation was at least safe and then I had no option but to leave him to his own speculations. But I did wonder how many others of his comrades were starting to feel the same. All of them, perhaps, to one extent or another. But that's what "Thaw" is about.

The other call away was more spectacular and memorable by far, but for different reasons. Again, a 'phone call started it. It was the Appointer in London, who wanted to know "if I could be spared for a few weeks to do a vital job elsewhere." My boss certainly didn't think so, and said so quite firmly. I just kept my mouth shut, because I knew who was going to win. He was even more firmly overruled. I was to be a part of Operation BEACON then its commanding officer.

Now, we need a bit of historical information here. This was the beginning of a huge operation run by the EU to provide food aid to the ailing nascent country of new Russia. It was perhaps one of the great unsung milestones of post-Cold War history.

The Soviet Union/Russia/CIS (remember the CIS?) was in a period of great change. It was only a short while since the Gorbachev/Rutskoi revanchist business and not long at all since Yeltsin climbed on top of a tank outside the (other) White House. The rouble - indeed the whole economy - indeed, everything in the country - was in a state of enormous flux. Just about anything could happen in the following months and years. Civil War was highly likely. We now know, of course, what did happen but at that time "just about anything" was a truism, not a surmise.

By the end of 1991 the country had a looming food supply problem. Agitation had started. The West recognised the problem. The West also knew which cities had been the epicentres of all previous Russian explosive activity: Moscow, St Petersburg (by whatever name), Saratov, Chelyabinsk and Nizhny Novgorod. This was not a hypothetical problem; this was a real, looming, dangerous, threatening problem for Russia and for the world. Avert revolt in those centres and there is a chance that risings throughout the whole country might be averted.

Russia needed food aid. There was a certain incongruity about the world's equal-biggest nuclear arsenal and an aspirant to remaining a top world power being in need of aid from abroad but that was the situation as it was. (As Professor Alexander Kennaway pointed out in his excellent paper (E81) it was just another example of the Russian capacity for tragicomedy; Russians have always waited for gifts from above."The Tsar is far away but I know he would save me if only I could reach him".) But, as I said, this was not a hypothetical problem, it was a problem that needed solving. Urgently. The USA and the EU decided to act. The EU created a humanitarian aid programme, and the UK contribution was launched as Operation BEACON.

Beautiful begging, St Petersburg, 1992

Whatever you may think about the EU this was a brilliantly conceived and produced programme. The USA had already given considerable supplies to Russia, but as they found there is no limit to how much the Russian black market can absorb. And that is where most of it went. Paradoxically, therefore, the EU decided to "sell" its food aid to Russia.150,000 tons of food aid was "sold" to the Russian government: this was distributed (by them) to the Regional governments (+5% oncost) who distributed it to the Districts (+5%) who passed it on to town councils (+5%) who gave it to distribution centres (+5%) who sent it to shops (+5%). The Russian Government money was then converted (by the EU) into vouchers, which were given to the real needy - war pensioners, the very aged, the incapacitated, mothers of multi-children families and so on - so that they could "buy" our food aid. The three main advantages of this strategy were (a) that the really needy got the aid (b) by pricing the commodities correctly at just a few percent below the native prices (meat, sugar, butter, cooking oil and babymilk powder) we did not simply wipe out the Russian indigenous meat, sugar, butter etc. industries and (c) every time a train or a ship or a lorry was unloaded there was someone there from Central Government, the Regional Government, someone from the Oblast, the Town Council and the distribution authorities all to check it and make sure nothing of theirs disappeared. And we, the EU crew including the BEACON team, were there to monitor them. We know that we actually lost less than one half of one percent of our stuff on to the black market - a huge triumph.

Each EU country (but chiefly UK, Germany, Belgium, Holland, France and Italy) had provided serving military Russian Interpreters to the cause for a period of up to six months. So it was that on a cold day in 1992 I found myself in my (our) St Petersburg office opposite the Admiralt'yestvo overlooking the Neva and undergoing briefing with all these other European military officers. Our mission was simple: "Ensure the aid gets through to the target". We were not to know of the astonishing series of incidents and escapades that were to ensue and of the tragicomedy we were personally to witness, but we set to work with a sense of pride which had still not diminished by the end of the operation. My "patch", of course, was St Petersburg docks and container port.

We worked out of the office in the mornings, inspected throughout the day, then met daily after work, often very late, to review progress, in what became known as "the Officers' Mess" which was the night bar of the Astoria Hotel. This was fascinating, because it was also the central haunt of the high-class call girls of St. Petersburg. They were all well educated, well read, well dressed and well balanced young women who had just decided on a different occupation and way of life. They congregated in the evenings just as we were finishing work and meeting up for a drink before relaxing for the rest of the evening. They were a great pleasure to talk to, because they had a broader view of life than most, and were certainly glad to see the back of the Soviet Union. We used to chat at the bar, and there were two unwritten rules: firstly, that we would not avail ourselves of their services and secondly, that if their 'phone rang they would be off like a shot in the middle of a sentence if needs be to attend to a client. It was sheer symbiosis, and each side gained. I think we left a lot of moderate voters behind us. Certainly a lot of friends of the West.

In the evenings, in "the Mess" we exchanged details of the checks we had carried out that day and the potential pitfalls for the following days. We recorded statistics. We planned. We behaved socially very much as one did in an officers' mess (except for the call girls). We forged enduring friendships within the European nations.

The author outside the office door - St Petersburg 1992

On a personal note, I should record that we were all allowed one 'phone call home per week. (On the first mobile 'phone I had ever seen - it was the size of an attaché case! Actually, it was in an attaché case!) Also that my driver could get me tickets for the opera or St. Petersburg ballet at almost exactly

14 pence. Also that, having eschewed the cans of Finnish beer, which were very expensive, and the hotel snacks (ditto) (we were self-catering apart from breakfast), I had discovered that you could buy "Champanskoe" round the corner for much less than a quid a bottle and caviar and biscuits at the local shop for a dollar; I used to smuggle them back to my hotel room for R&R with friends on evenings off. On my second 'phone call home, I was asked what I was actually doing at that time; being an honest person, I had to say that after a very hard day down in the docks we were drinking champagne and eating caviar before going out to the ballet. You may imagine that there was a bit of a silence on the other end of the line for a while. I was "supposed to be working". So I decided that it might be misunderstood if I said that when we got back from the ballet I was going to have a stiff one with a call girl before going to bed, and said no more on the subject.

I should report upon how the delivery of food aid to Russia was actually carried out.

We (the thirty-six "Inspectors" - all military Russian interpreters from EU countries) - were living in the top three Russian city hotels and working in the bottom three Russian work environments. Now, "top three" will probably mislead you into thinking it was jolly good. It wasn't. And as for v.f.m. it was appalling. It cost $459 per day, room and breakfast. You could buy lunch and dinner too if you didn't mind paying for what was still Soviet-standard goods and service. For example, two hard boiled eggs on a plate with a dollop of mashed potato and some tinned peas was not very good cuisine, especially at about $50. Your boiled eggs at breakfast were included, but unless you were in the first tranche of people to sprint across the dining room when the hatch was opened and the bowl of boiled eggs were put out you didn't get any; after a while we set up a "buddy" system so that one of our number would get to the eggs first because others were impeding the passage of competitors. Crude, unpleasant, unfair, demeaning and lots of other adjectives, but at least we got eggs to sustain us. As for other meals, it wasn't long before I found Dom Architektora down a sidestreet: a bijou restaurant which sometimes had what you wanted - if this expression seems strange to Western ears, then my experience one day will elucidate. I picked up the browning sheet of Gestetnered foolscap paper which was the menu. "I'll have the ham, please." I said. "No ham" was the reply. "OK, what meat have you got?" "Today we have no meat." "Ah, well then, cheese and salad, if you would". "No cheese. No salad". So I said "Well what have you got?" "Today, we don't have anything." "Well, why are you open, then?" "Because if we didn't open we wouldn't get paid". But at other times we did get some nice things.

Back to our operation. I used to proclaim vehemently in the UK about "bloody Health and Safety" but since then I have not done so. If you had worked in a country with no H&S rules, you would agree with me. For example, it was generally agreed that the huge "deep freeze" built by Peter himself in St P. docks would have fallen down years ago (only solid ice is keeping it up) if it weren't that winter kept coming back again. And I'd only gone a few metres inside this huge ice cavern before I realised there wasn't an alarm button to press to get out if things went wrong. The event that shook me most, though, was my RAF colleague standing alongside a large ship moored to the jetty on the fast-flowing River Neva and calling to me: "Alan, this wire tying up this ship is actually making a loud humming sound" and my shouting "Andy - trust me - do what I say - just get out of there as fast as you can! Run!" Naval readers will understand; the wire was about to snap and lash all over the place.

Thirteen days out of fourteen we inspected the sites to which EU aid had been delivered to ensure it was getting to the people who needed it. To do this, and to cope with Soviet/Russian beaurocracy, we had to have "a document". This document had to be signed by somebody important. In the St Petersburg region at that time it was the Head of External Relations for the local government. So we went to see him. He worked in a huge forbidding Tsarist-era building with no signs to say what it was and no welcome and no joy.

The beaurocrats therein, as if to emphasise that they still held all the power, said that only one of us would be allowed an interview. So that was me. I mounted the steps completely without trepidation, for I had a diplomatic visa, and I had no axe to grind, and I had (so far as I knew) no enemies. I was led along great corridors, but to my surprise I was not told to sit and wait. I quickly worked out that this was because they all knew that this interview, and this signature, had to happen, however unpalatable it was. I was shown into this cavern of an office with a single occupant and a single desk and a single window and a single light, but two chairs - and came face to face with this astonishing fellow. What made him astonishing was that he was completely emotionless and expressionless - think about it: how many people have you met who are completely and utterly emotionless? And, I thought, probably not a very nice person. I sat before I was invited to. We faced each other. A strange, strange bloke, I thought. Glum sort of chap. Dour-faced. Incredibly staring eyes. Didn't want to see me, but had to. Obviously a political climber, although nobody, or few people, I don't know, outside Russia had heard of him at that time. Very reluctant to sign a piece of paper allowing a Westerner to go wherever he wanted to check that food aid was getting through. Loss of face, I suppose. I had thirty minutes with him, discussing things, simply because I drew it all out to try and find out what would happen. Nothing did. Eventually, he just signed. I stared at his signature for a long time, and then at him, and finally I felt constrained to say to him "Do you know - I understand why you are so grumpy, and I am so content: it's because you still believe in Marxism/Leninism and it doesn't work, while we believe in Marksism/Spencerism and it <u>does</u> work". He understood all right, but his smile was a grimace, not a real smile. I didn't see him again after that. Not personally, anyway. I see he's done quite well for himself, though

Armed with this document, we (the naval contingent (1 RN officer (me), one RAF officer (don't ask why) (Andy) along with our driver (Sasha) a retired Soviet naval Kapitan 3rd Class) drove into St P docks. The first thing we saw was a clearly man-made pile of stuff covered with grass; it was over 100 metres long by 10 metres high and quite deep. "Stop" we said "We want a photograph of that". Sasha complied, but did not understand. It was unloaded coal. Can you imagine such a thing in the West? Coal with grass growing on it? We explained. Sasha still did not understand. Difference of cultures again, I suppose.

Grass-covered coal mountain - St Petersburg docks 1992

Into the container port first. Think of Harwich, or Southampton. Enormous. We had ninety-six containers of humanitarian aid arrived the previous day and we had to check them in. Easy - at Southampton or Harwich. In St P - enormous, with all the same huge lifting equipment - not so easy. Here, the people's crane drivers had always been allowed to unload the containers on to the people's transporters whose drivers, being people, were allowed to put the containers wherever they felt like. All very well as long as they told "the centre" where they had put them. But generally, they didn't. Hey Presto - a container port with many thousands of containers largely untraceable. It all got sorted out in the end, of course. But we wanted our ninety-six now, at once.

We searched, we scoured. Nothing. Eventually we went to the huge office admin block and spoke to "The Boss". As so often (a) he had the drink taken and (b) he hadn't a clue what was going on. As we crept away down the long, whitewashed corridor, Andy stopped me in my tracks: "Look at that door. Look!" he said. On it, a sign said "Bureau Kontainer-poisk". We looked at each other. "Lost container office"? "Lost container office?" In an international container port??? We went in. A quite elderly woman sat alone amid a pile of Russian A4 equivalent paper gone brown round the edges, as it does. Now, in any Soviet organisation there was always someone, somewhere, who knows what's going on; it's never the bloke at the top and rarely anyone near the top, but this person existed. We had found her!

We explained the problem and she said she would do what she could. Come back tomorrow. We returned the following day and a Boots plastic carrier bag of Western monogrammed biros, and several bars of chocolate later we knew where all ninety-six containers were. All over the bloody place - but we knew where they were, and we called in lorries accordingly. We had won the first battle.

On the way back, we passed the coal mountain again, and then drove past a newly planted avenue of young trees, each of which was clearly holding up the two posts which had been not very successfully driven into the ground alongside them. Same ethos, I suppose

The following day we went to the other docks. The new consignment was sugar.Sugar was not so easy. Because it came in sacks. That day I was deep in the hold of a merchant ship which was unloading sacks of sugar when I noticed that for some reason the odd sack was breaking open and spilling out. I also noticed a stevedore bloke who was so fat that he couldn't get his arms down by his sides and who was clearly waiting for the "go home" whistle. I sidled towards him to check. He had large rubber bands round his wrists and ankles. He had been pouring spilt sugar down the inside of his sleeves and trouser legs with the result that he waddled around like a cartoon penguin. Not wishing to create a "them and us" situation I blew my whistle and in the silence ordered "all men dressed like penguins - report to the upper deck". Laughter in court. The penguin clearly understood the epithet because he tried to tell me that spillages were his, but once I had disabused him of this and confiscated the rubber bands there was little he could do and in any event his mates had laughed so much at him that he slunk away with his tail between his legs and we had no more trouble.

Which are our containers then?

1992 - St Petersburg (the "Penguin" is hiding!)

The cooking oil was easier to check, because it was in plastic bottles. We had no difficulty in tracing it from delivery ship through the transport centres and the retail outlets to the consumers. Unfortunately the recipients didn't seem to know what "rapeseed" oil (clearly labelled bottles) is, and we recorded not so much an increase in frying so much as an increase in cars conking out with severe engine problems because vegetable oil doesn't perform as well as specialised 15/40 Castrol.

Talking of not knowing what something is, it must be noted that at first our rump and sirloin steak ended up in sausages while people were frying skirt and chuck and blade, and moaning about it. This was because Russian butchers are adept at cleaving joints with an axe - but without discrimination. Our checking and correction of this led to one of the most bizarre experiences of our inspecting role - the surprise on the butcher's slab - of which later.

Working thirteen out of fourteen days, once a fortnight, we went off to the black market sites to see if we could buy any of our stuff back. We mostly failed (just half a percent loss) but we did learn a lesson or two. One stall was selling a pale green liquid in one-litre bottles, some full, some half full. We sniffed it. It was indubitably cheap cologne. I asked the vendor why some bottles were only half full. "Well," he said "some people can't drink a whole bottle". On an adjacent stall was a smoked sausage vendor. One "salami" had been cut in half and on the cut end was clearly a cross-section of something furry that wasn't from a cow or a pig. No-one seemed to care. But I did buy a brand new Russian dictionary set for less than a couple of dollars.

The first fifty (50) tons or so of EU food aid had arrived by air. Wonderful publicity for the politicians and the airy fairies. But just symbolic. The next one hundred and forty nine thousand, nine hundred and fifty tons (149,950 tons) arrived by ship, train and lorry. After a week or so we inspectors settled into a routine. In the early days the work consisted of monitoring the arrival of goods. This was a daytime only job in Moscow, but in St Petersburg it was a round-the-clock operation, working six or eight hour shifts. The army officers from the various EU countries stood by and supervised the inspection of the trains and lorries as they were unloaded, my colleague and I did the same for the ships arriving at St Petersburg docks, and the other air force officers did what they could.

My last stint in the docks was one of the most interesting. A merchant ship was unloading sacks of dried milk powder and I was monitoring the Russian regional inspectors who were watching the unloading operation and counting things on to their lorries. All seemed to be going smoothly as pallet after pallet was craned out of the huge hold and I was beginning to think about tea. Then there was a shout from the top of the crane: "Forty Yobbing sacks! I'm only lifting forty sacks or this yobbing crane is going to fall over and yobbing kill us all". The stevedores in the hold protested that (paraphrased) it was not always possible to get exactly forty sacks on to a pallet; translated into human this meant "the sooner we've got it all off the sooner we can go home and we're going to put as many sacks on as we can". The crane driver climbed down from his crane and pointedly sat on a bollard. The stevedores decided to get ready to go home anyway. I knew I had to act swiftly. I blew my whistle and ordered: "Crane driver and chief stevedore to the Captain's cabin. Now. Rest of you, wait there." and as I had so often found, it worked. The Captain was surprised to see us, but complied with my request to get a bottle of duty free out of his hidey-hole (in return for which I would not tell anyone that he had a hidey-hole, or where it was). He wanted his ship unloaded, and to be off. The four of us had a tot. That was enough for me, but half an hour later the Captain had got a second bottle out for the others and it was time for me to move: I said to my three new dearly beloved bosom friends "I'm going to write down the words of God Save the Queen in Cyrillic script and if you can sing it we'll all go back to work - forty sacks per pallet, please, and I'm sure the Captain will let you take home what's left in the bottle if you do. I'll hang onto it for the time being." We sang. "Khod sive are Khrashus Kveen" It was dreadful. But we all went back to work, the job was finished and we all went home.

Once initial deliveries were over, we began to chase our commodities through the delivery chain to the consumers. This was a different ball park. The Russian regional, city and other inspectors had done their jobs, and melted away. We EU inspectors were now on our own. We had this "Right of Access" document, signed at the high level I mentioned, and each day we chose to check out a different processing centre or retail outlet. Once we went to a huge dairy. Just once. The smell was dreadful, and the sight of a cat having its kittens in a pool of milk in the central yogurt processing area put us off dairy for the rest of our stay (we were already off salami, as you might imagine from the previous paragraphs). Then off to a huge bakery. As much as wanting to check that our supplies were (a) getting through and (b) being used for the purpose for which they had been donated, we wanted to settle a bet: my colleague said that Russian bread goes stale after less than a day and I said that I reckoned it's issued stale. At the bakery we were proudly offered a taste of the bread as it cooled on the racks. It tasted stale to me. Andy very nearly agreed. But he's a vegan, and has not much sense of taste. We agreed to differ. But whatever, we agreed it's less than a day.

As an aside, I did actually feel for Andy. What is there for a vegan to eat in Russia in April? The answer, apparently, was bananas and nuts. Goodness knows where he got them from, but he had made friends with some Russian vegans. There's an international vegan Jewish network, I think. Talking of making friends, I did receive what I thought then (and now know) was a genuine offer of "up-homers" from the First Officer of a Russian merchant ship. This was exceptionally enlightening for both sides. His flat was a Khruschev flat. They didn't have much, and I noticed that after the meal, during which we finished off a loaf of bread, there was nothing left in the kitchen. That illustrates how very kind Russians are to "friends"; this couple had literally shared their last loaf with me. I didn't say anything, but his wife said "there will be more tomorrow" and it was left at that. I got them some things, to say "Thank you".

I was invited to many other homes by people I had met. There were two difficulties. The first was exemplified by a typical exchange of words on the 'phone: "Alan. Come at one o'clock": "I can't come at one, I'm working until six": "Yes, I know, but come at one, anyway". They couldn't get their heads round this "work" thing getting in the way of a social invitation, and similarly me likewise in the other direction. But it always turned out OK in the end. The other was knowing what to take. In the West, it's generally a nice bottle of wine and/or a bunch of flowers, isn't it? I knew that wine would not last five minutes, nor would it touch the side of the throats so there was no point in its being "nice", or even being taken at all. So a bottle of vodka it had to be. Each time.

Once I was invited to a weekend dacha in the forest on the bank of Lake Ladoga. There were three families and me. It was large, creaky to the point of having bits falling off, and dank - but it was a dacha and it was a holiday. It was notable for many (to me) new experiences. For one, I took along the vodka. Knowing that the three husbands would drink it, I also took along a bottle of Malibu. At the first toast, the men drank their first tot of vodka and the three wives shyly and tentatively took a sip of their Malibu. The men demanded a taste of it. I explained it was "for ladies only". But they tasted it, grimaced, declared it to be the most poofy thing they had ever had, and gave the glasses back to the wives, who went on to enjoy it for the rest of the evening. Then, much later, one after another, the wives all came along to me separately and shyly and asked what it was. "Coconut liqueur" I replied. "What's coconut?" all three of them asked. Another memorable event, nearly the terminal episode, was my preventing a new-to-the-game barbecue-maker from lighting a pile of linden branches outside the dacha with a five gallon can of petrol and a burning rag on a stick.

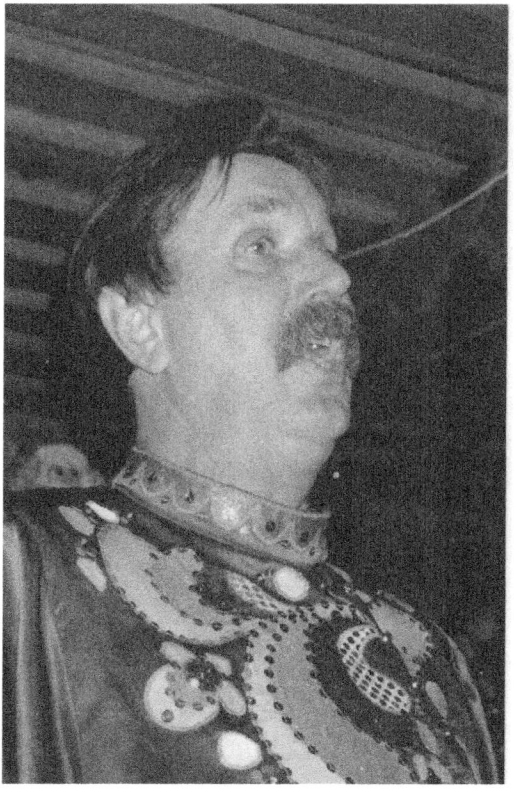

Russian bass at forest barbecue, 1992

Who's that on the left? Village dinner 1992

Monday. Back to the routine. My next target was the island of Kronstadt. As far as I knew, no-one from the West had visited this heavily guarded island since - well - probably before the 1920's. I had the certificate which entitled me to go anywhere that our food aid had been delivered - and that included bakeries and butcheries on Kronstadt. Our driver, Sasha, was sceptical. "You'll never get on to Kronstadt", he said. "Nobody gets on to Kronstadt." So off we went. We drove over the long causeway and got to the guard hut. Out came a Warrant Officer. He was inclined not to accept my documentation. So I followed Part 2 of my previously learned and rehearsed routine advice on "How to deal with Petty Beaurocrats". I engaged him in conversation, during which I pulled out a photograph of my wife and children and asked him if he had any children. He said that he had but he hadn't seen them for months and I commiserated and we chatted for a while about families and history and the soul and the world in general and the meaning of life and then before you could say "Jack Flash" he had decided that I was a genuine sort of cove and waved us through.

The author being nice, and very English. 1992

Googling, I see Tripadvisor has reviews of "the top ten restaurants on Kronstadt". Ten? Top Ten?? There was only one that we could find then, and to call it a restaurant would be something of a terminological inexactitude. Sandwich if you were lucky, and then you didn't know what was in it. What a change in twenty-five years (if Tripadvisor is to be believed). But what a place it was, at that time. Large sandstone colonial-type blocks of houses arranged in squares, with sidewalks. And all around, rusting warships. Hulks. All over the place. Unlike the impression of stepping back into mediaeval times (as was the village I visited outside Pushkin a bit later), Kronstadt was like stepping back into early Georgian Bath or Bristol – but in sandstone rather than Bath stone, obviously. Jamestown, St Helena, I recalled, seemed to be rather more up to date.

By May that year things were proceeding smoothly and it was clear that only spot-checking was required, rather than full scale, head-on invigilation. A light touch. By this time, all the Russians in the business knew what "Goom Pom" (*goomanitarnaya pomosch* - humanitarian aid) was. There were several highlights of this phase of the operation. The meat problem and the sugar problem had been solved (incidentally, as an aside, I was personally sceptical about delivering sugar - I was convinced it would all be fermented to produce "samogon", but a later visit to a look-alike medieval village taught me that in the countryside everything savoury grown in summer (tomatoes, cucumber, squash etc) goes into vast family jars of vinegar/salt (reusable annually) and everything sweet (apples, pears and all fruit) goes into vast family jars of sugar water - both for use throughout the winter. In this way is vitamin C provided throughout the year). Back to the highlights. We had been slightly worried about the baby milk powder (now euphemistically called "formula milk", I understand) which could be used for just about anything, but which was designated to succour babies. It was the one item of Humanitarian Aid ("goom pom") which was issued on a prescription, from chemists'. I was in one chemist's shop when a woman in, I guess, her mid-twenties, came in and handed over a prescription. The shop assistant started loading cans of (EU) baby milk on to the counter. When it got to eight, I felt justified in intervening, and demanded to see the prescription. "Have you got sixteen children?" I asked her. "Yes" she said. "What are their names?" I asked. After she had trotted out the most common six or eight or ten Russian forenames and several patronymics , she began to run out of inspiration, and faltered. "Come on," I said "You must remember your own childrens' names?" She began to bluster. "You've altered this prescription" I accused. "No I haven't" she said. "Well why" said I "is everything on the prescription in black ink, including the number "1" under "number of children" but the "6" is in blue ink?". "That's how we do it here," she said "you wouldn't understand, being a foreigner." Once I managed to convince her that I understood rather more about the situation than she did and that she would not be prosecuted if she told the truth she admitted that she didn't have any children at all! She had taken the prescription from her next door neighbour. We put it down to experience, but I knew the word would get around that we were continuing to check things.

About this time was an incident which exemplified the Russian proclivity for improvisation. We were driving down a highway at speed when the exhaust fell off the car, completely, and the car behind ran over it with much noise and many sparks. Sasha sped off down a side street making a noise like a dozen tractors. He then simply pulled up outside a friend's house and told him what had happened (not that the friend hadn't heard him coming). Within three minutes a pile of old tyres had been placed alongside the vehicle and it was tipped on to its side to expose the underneath (they kindly let us get out first) and a new (old) exhaust was bolted on. We were then tipped up the right way, and proceeded on our way. It took less than half an hour. No doubt money changed hands, but I didn't see it. Eat your heart out, Quickfit!

I stayed for one night at the medieval village. The house was made of wood and had been built by its owner, my host's grandfather.

First I noticed the garden. Not one square inch of it was not growing vegetables. Secondly I noticed what the Aussies would call a "dunnie", and I won't record what we would call it. It sat on top of a hole fifteen feet deep and was reputedly never emptied. There was some olfactory evidence for this. Thirdly I noticed that there was a lovely black American 1930's car outside. It was immaculate. Grandad had been driver to a Russian general in WW2 and had "exchanged" a bombed out vehicle for this "acquired" American model. At the end of the war, the general had gifted it to his driver. Naturally, there not being a US spare parts centre in the area, I asked grandad how he kept it going. "When something breaks, I make a new bit" he said. "I made a new carburettor myself, last year". "Where is your workshop?" I asked. "I just do it with my hands" he said. "I had to replace the front wings two years ago. I just got a sheet of metal and beat it into shape over a rounded tree stump. Then I painted it and bolted it on". The result was astonishingly beautiful. Motoparts couldn't have done better. But then of course it wouldn't have taken them three months.

The author with Russian Grandad and his hand-preserved car and his medals. Near Pushkin 1992

Traditional band in the forest outside Pushkin, 1992

Local wooden church near Pushkin, 1992

I returned to work the following morning to discover that Colonel Michael (German Army) had gone down with appendicitis over the weekend, had refused the air ambulance back to Germany, had been operated upon in the local hospital, had been told that regrettably they had left a swab inside him ("as happens in the West, sometimes, of course") and even more regrettably that they had now completely run out of anaesthetics. At that stage I know without any inkling of doubt what I would have done, but a German wasn't going to show any fear in front of Russians and he insisted upon being opened up again without anaesth.......................... I can't finish this sentence.

We were now pursuing our "Goom Pom" meat and other commodities further down the chain to the retail outlets. In one, meat was to be prepared to be cleaved (cloven?) into chunks on the ubiquitous cross grain tree trunk sections which have served so well for centuries. Andy and I went into this "shop" (It was still an era to put inverted commas round the word "shop"; the Russian word is "lavka" and that literally means "counter" - i.e in a collective store) and asked to see the records for meat deliveries. "The butcher is not available". "Show us the place where the meat is received". We looked at what passed for a cold store. "Show us where you cut up the meat". "In here, but it is locked". "Where is the key?" "It is lost". "We will wait while you find it. This will have to be reported". "OK, here is the key". We opened the door to find the butcher attending personally to a female colleague who just happened to be having a lie down on the butcher's tree trunk meat slab without much on but stockings and one shoe, holding a bra in one hand and a pair of panties in the other, surrounded by succulent cuts of beef and looking a bit coy. "We are only here for the meat receipt records," I said. We collected the delivery records and politely left, averting our eyes. Not our business. Another lesson in life.

I worked late that evening, doing my records. I was walking home when a huge black Zil or Zim or something pulled up and the driver said "A dollar?" I got in. We chatted. By his language I could tell that this taxi driver knew something about the sea and about military matters. It turned out to be a naval staff car, and he, its Lieutenant driver, moonlighting. We discussed whether it was better to serve in Vladivostok and not see your family for years or serve in Murmansk and have all your teeth fall out for lack of vitamin C and not see your family for years. I almost volunteered for the Black Sea fleet, the arguments were so persuasive. We exchanged more and more ditties, as only naval people can do, during a very pleasant - and very comfortable - late night trip back to the hotel.

I thought philosophically as we said farewell, "nearly the end". I know lots of Russian people were grateful for our humanitarian aid but I wonder if the Russian leadership will be grateful for what we have done to avert a crisis. Perhaps one person in particular wasn't.

The author at the farewell reception, Moscow, 1992, with..............

It all had to end, and a little while later it was time to wind it up and go home. COM EU had already left, so I found myself responsible for all thirty or so EU military officers remaining for the last phase. I sent my final weekly progress signal to the Chief of the Defence Staff, to whom I had reported directly throughout; it was optimistic, but not without a tinge of bathos. Discerning readers will understand. We all then centred on and congregated in Moscow for a final "with Jaques Delors" reception - photocalls in full uniform, the lot, and then had the most delightful meal in a Georgian restaurant as a "thank you" before preparing to depart.

Not with a bang, but with a whimper: the last couple of days in Moscow, the trip to the airport and events in the departure lounge held one or two more surprises for us. But nothing to compare with what we had already seen.

The Kremlin

On the first of our spare days before the flight home, I happened to come across a huge departmental store which was the Soviet equivalent of the NAAFI. I bought some fishing tackle, and a game bag which on reflection was a waste of money because it was made of such thick (albeit beautiful) leather that you couldn't prise it open to get anything in. But it looked good on the wall. At the same counter I bought something, not because I wanted it (was I turning into a Soviet citizen? Buying something because it was there rather that because I wanted it?) but because it was so utterly ridiculous that I knew it would be a hoot at social gatherings: have you seen a Second World War film with a pom-pom gun with a circle of concentric rings round it? This is to "offshoot" against a crossing target. In this store, I found some metal concentric rings for attachment to a shotgun; they were about eight inches across, and would have smashed off in anything but a clay pigeon shoot on a flat field with no-one around.

Then off to the clothing department. I selected a pair of Rocket Force shoulder boards in the rank of Major, and took them to the cash desk. The woman peered at me. "You can only have these if you are an officer," she said. I whipped out my RN ID card, issued to me for my use for naval purposes (to quote the charge against you if you lose it) which of course was in English script but had my photograph on it and a very impressive signature by someone who signed himself "Master at Arms, Royal Navy, HMS DRAKE". She looked at it and said "That's OK, then," and sold me the shoulder boards. She wasn't interested in the fact that I was clearly foreign, just that I was really an officer. That's class distinction for you.

Anyway, back to the black market, in a side street, where I bought a spoof KGB warrant card and stuck my own photograph in it, just like the other tourists did. But I think I looked rather more fierce.

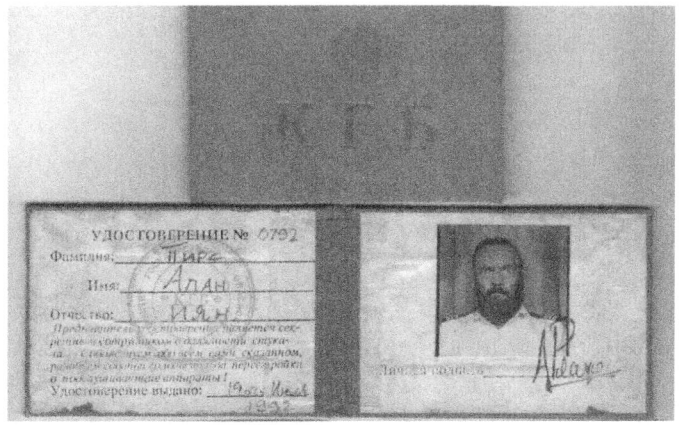

Spoof KGB ID card

A night in an hotel, packing all the stuff I had bought, including game bag and fishing rods and nets and so on, and then off to the airport. I left plenty of time, then doubled it. It was a wise decision. When I got to the queue, I found it was very long and moving forward at Soviet speed. I calculated that we were not going to make it, either before the aircraft was full, or before it took off. So I pushed to the front of the queue with all my baggage. Frankly, I pushed in, waving my diplomatic visa. An Australian voice said "You're bloody rude, you are." I said "Thank you. To be called 'rude' by an Australian is indeed a great honour". And I weaved forward on to the aircraft. I was right. They didn't all get on. But I did. The sense of relief at getting away from that dreadful place was overwhelming, but my thought was how very much worse it must have been previously under Soviet rule, when you body belonged to the state and your mind belonged to the state as well. I shuffled forward towards my British Airways seat and I couldn't help it but I got down on my knees and kissed the floor of this British territory. Then I looked up and saw a pair of nylon stockingly clad legs in front of me, and then up into the eyes of a BA air hostess. "I'm sorry," I stammered. "Please don't worry, Sir," she said. "Lots of people do that." Catharsis. I now know the true meaning of the word "catharsis".

I still had a slight problem. Because we had been required to fly out with not only the necessaries to do the job but also the accoutrements that were required for the final photocall - full uniform and all that - we had travelled first class, or whatever it's called this week. The sixteen of us had quickly discovered that "first class" meant free drinks, so we all ordered those little one quarter bottles of real champagne which we knew they had. And then refilled, and so on. Until the air hostess (or whatever they're called this week) extremely politely told us that as they couldn't top up in Russia, they had to keep back stocks of champagne for the return flights. We had made a note of this. So when we lucky ones embarked at Moscow Sheremetovo airport had got seated, champagne was demanded. And it kept coming, throughout the flight. I knew I was being picked up at Gatwick, so I didn't hold back. The problem at Gatwick was that there was a green light and a red light, according to what you had to declare. I had already decided to declare all the stuff I had bought, even though it wasn't actually worth a lot, so I set off for the red light. Unfortunately, there were two and a half of them. So I looked at the green light and there were only two of those, although they too were moving around a bit and so I bisected the two green ones and got out to what I now know is true freedom. Little Englanders, who only England know, do not know how lucky they are.

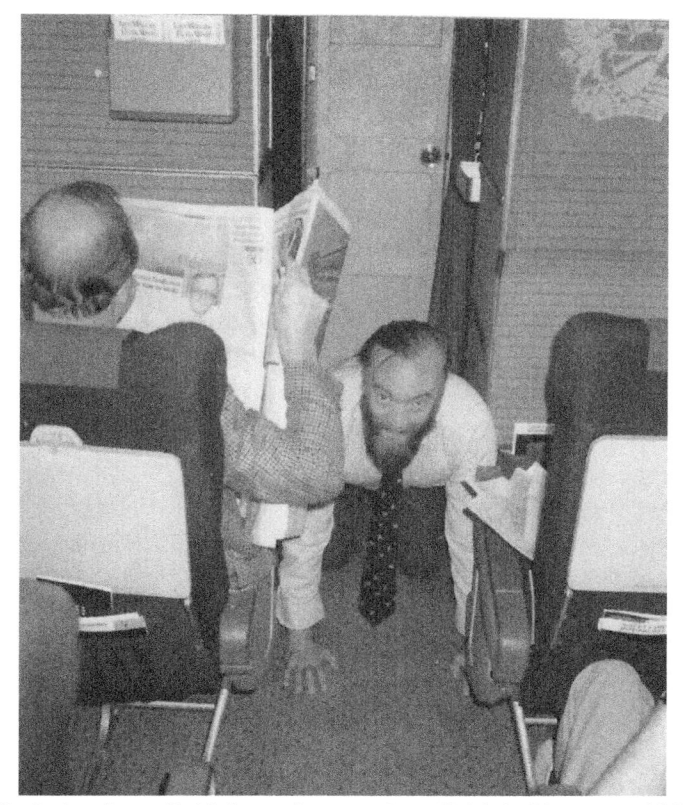

Safe back on British territory - chez British Airways, 1992

There I was, back at Portsmouth. It wasn't long before I heard that my German, Italian and Belgian counterparts had all been asked to do a tour of military and governmental establishments, giving talks on their experiences. I just came back to Portsmouth and got on with my duties.

But then it was time to move on. Not far. Another Portsmouth appointment - which of course I chose because we were settled there and because I had all the contacts to find a job in what everybody else calls "civvy street". I was appointed as the new Staff Officer responsible for the administration of the Royal Navy's social services, and head of the RN Alcohol Education Team.

This was again on the staff of the Second Sea Lord, and the title was "Senior naval deputy to CNPFS and DNPFS". Now, this will clearly take some explanation. The letters stand for, respectively Captain and Director of the Naval Families and Personal Service; this, too, needs some explanation.

Up until about ten years previously, the RN had a Welfare System. It was creaking, and it was universally disliked as the refuge of scroungers and the work shy, even though this was not entirely true. The image was wrong - and the concept was fundamentally wrong. So after a commissioned report by Lord Seebohm, it was decided to embrace the civilian model of Social Services provision. This was a deep and fundamental change; the navy, in common with the other two services, had for decades solved personal problems using the "chain of command", which is to say that your military superiors would find an answer to your problems for you. The RN introduced a civilian-modelled system, which was groundbreaking because it removed people's personal problems from the chain of command by making them private and confidential - even to commanding officers; the only stipulation, quite reasonably, was if such problems affected the fighting capability of the ship. It was a bold move, and it worked. The operatives were qualified social workers, half naval and half civilian. Instead of having the CPO or the Sergeant Major solving your problems for you, you were given all the necessary advice and guidance so that you could make up your own mind as to the way forward. The former system ensured that next time you had a problem, you went back to the CPO or the Sergeant Major; the latter empowered you to deal with it yourself if you could.

The boss (CNPFS) was a splendid fellow with his feet on the ground. But I served as the moderating influence to ensure these junior social types didn't run away with daft ideas, and as the bloke who could speak rationally to naval authorities on the subject.

My induction was fraught. Known as a bit of a "straight in your face" person, my colleagues on the staff had a huge sign printed for my new office door; it read "Welcome to the office of the Really Caring and Sharing and Lovingly Kind Lieutenant Commander Alan Pearce. Before you enter - PULL YOURSELF TOGETHER!" The other stunning factor, within a week or two of taking up the appointment, was my administration of the induction system for naval personnel who wished to serve in this service - it simply involved gathering the application forms and supporting evidence and collating them for the induction board. Applicants had to fill in a form, of course. They had to give references. And they had to write an essay saying why they wished to take on such work. I couldn't help reading them, even the ones that didn't need reading. I was stunned, shocked to the core. There was an essay by a Wren who said that she wanted to help other people in distress because since she was a seven year old she used to come home from school daily and get her mother up from the floor and give her water and try to get her to eat something and find a way to get the vodka bottle off her while getting her up to bed. And a young man whose father used to beat his wife unconscious on a regular basis. And another whose family were all on drugs and used to go out together and steal to pay for it. It was at that time that I realised how very ordinary my own life was. I nearly said "how normal my own life was", but any social worker will tell you that there is no such thing as "normal". I used not to agree. I do now.

My two predecessors in the job had, for some reason, been afraid to throw anything away, so I inherited vast cupboards of files. I spent my first days and weeks clearing out and ensuring confidential destruction of everything that was no longer relevant or of use. Then I could move, as I could see things in perspective. During the second part of my induction, I had to go to Bristol University for a two-part residential course in the philosophy and practice of social work. To say that I was again stunned would be an understatement. One revelation was an understanding of depression: it was a case of a man who had lost a button off his jacket. My earlier reaction would have been "well, sew it back on again", then followed by a more kindly "would you like me to sew it back on again for you?" both of which completely miss the point. Which is, that when someone has a problem, then it's the size of the problem as seen by them that counts, not the size of the problem as seen by you. I have carried this thought, extrapolated in many ways, for the rest of my life. I wish I had understood it earlier.

Another revelation was real life; we were discussing talking about things, and a husband and wife attending couple said they had lost a child at childbirth but that they had "put it behind them and agreed not to talk about it ever again". The professional social workers were horrified, and said "it's going to come out one day to haunt you." But they wouldn't have it. In similar scenarios all over our family worlds, I wonder how sapient that may be. We all have ghosts.

Anyway, fully trained, I settled into the job - which wasn't social work, of course, but making people aware of social work in the RN, and ensuring that the paperwork got done. My bit of it was quite mundane. But I did have to act as Divisional Officer for all these would-be naval social workers. So I used to give an introductory lecture to all the trainees, which I started most piously and in a socially inclusive style by saying "I want to share something with you all. I want you to share it with me while you are here under training and while you practise what you have learned out in the field. What I want to share with you, most sincerely, is.............. The Naval Discipline Act. You are still subject to it, whether you like it or not. Don't forget it. Any questions?" I got a lot of grimaces, but I got no problems and I think I probably saved some people from themselves.

At Portsmouth we were still based in the 1733 Old Naval

Academy, which has a plaque on the wall saying "This academy exists to teach young officers in the six necessary qualities for naval officers: Mathematicks (sic), English, French, Navigation, Fencing and Dancing". Things have changed a bit. I had my office on the top floor. It was an eclectic group of people in the ONA. The pompous Jake Francis-Jones, by now a Captain, had a new Secretary who announced that his name was Wayne. Jake interviewed him on his arrival. "I'm not having an officer called "Wayne" working for me," he said. "I shall call you Charles". And so it was. Those were the days.

Jake I knew and understood. An African white. He never gave me any trouble. I actually liked him. In fact, I unashamedly used his pomposity on one occasion: outside the ONA parking was highly restricted, and allocated to Commanders and above. But there was a short space at the end of the row and I often used to squeeze my Volvo in. One day, I came out to go home after work to find a notice under my windscreen wiper: "You should know as a Volvo driver that it is a long vehicle and you have obstructed my parking space. Do not do it again" signed by a Commander. So I took it off and tucked it under the windscreen wiper of the adjacent far-more-senior Captain Jake's Volvo. I never heard any more.

The Old Naval Academy was a charming building. It had a green in front of it, in the centre of which was a very old, very large mulberry tree. Mulberries are very soft and extremely difficult to pick, so one day in the holidays we got a net and my two boys climbed up in swimming trunks and shook the branches. We got many kilos, ate a lot in fruit salads and made wine with the rest. Delicious.

The ONA was also a wonderful setting for the Murder Mystery evening we put on. We planned for months, and went the whole hog. A member of the medical staff obtained a perfectly formed model of a human being of realistic texture and colour, a friend at the local newspaper ran off for us a whole evening edition with a "stop press" about a break-in at the Manor, police colleagues gave us identikit pictures of ourselves, passports were forged, a restaurateur provided fake menus and wine lists with hints and clues contained therein and we did an evening show for ninety-six people (we had to limit numbers, it was so popular). Then, as darkness fell, with no-one anywhere near the answer, we all trooped into the mess hall for a sumptuous meal, prepared and served by our wonderful staff. I had arranged for three things to happen during the meal, towards the end. Firstly - the electrics of this ancient building being so primitive - it was easy to throw a central switch and plunge the whole place into darkness. Secondly, we placed this very lifelike medical dummy in a heap at the bottom of the vast staircase which wound its way up to the third floor around the sides of the entrance hall. And thirdly - having held auditions - for one of the waitresses to do an enormous scream three seconds after the lights all went out. The result was astonishing. Some people froze, some darkly discussed the anomalies they had found in the menus, some went out into the hall in the dark and fell over the body, and some waited just a few more seconds before the lights came on again. There was general pandemonium. Then a policeman arrived carrying a copy of the evening paper, demanding to know what a "tontine" was, and who was involved. It required brandies all round to restore order. You will have to imagine the rest. It was one of the most successful mess entertainments ever.

But life was not all social fun. We actually worked quite hard. Twice yearly, for example, I had to run a live exercise (which means real people have to do real things, even if just "for exercise" i.e. play out a scenario) This one was a "Casualty reporting" and "family liaison" exercise - vitally important if morale of fighting people is to be maintained. In this case, the scenario was a mythical engagement in the Middle East. We received casualty reports. We informed next of kin, and so on. The Wrens were much better at it than the blokes: I remember one sailor, speaking to a somewhat deaf next of kin and having not made himself understood, shouting down the 'phone "No! No! Delta Echo Alpha Delta!" and then feeling that he had carried out his duties satisfactorily. I also learned that bad injuries can be good news. If you have been told that your NOK is missing, whereabouts not known, after a ship sinking, then "We now have a report that your ...(relative)... has been taken on board another ship with two broken legs and a broken arm" is really good news.

On a separate LIVEX we showed that it is not only junior people who make big mistakes. The exercise was set at a large naval training establishment, and the scenario was that a large British warship had been sunk. It was to test how we handle the Press, and how we deal with distraught relatives. These "distraught relatives" were specially chosen Wrens, some twenty of them, of all ranks, who had been told quite categorically to imagine that their loved ones had been serving on that ship, that they had converged on the training establishment in search of news and - crucially - that they were to behave as they thought they would in real life, that they were in a high state of emotion and tension and, particularly, that they were acting as civilians, they were not to respect anybody's rank and they would be given complete exoneration if anybody pulled rank on them. Once the exercise started, they were ushered into a large room in the wardroom mess, and given tea and sandwiches and a briefing by the Commander; it amounted to "I'm very sorry, but we haven't any information to give you; we don't know much about what has happened yet." To which one "wife" (actually a Chief Wren), said "Well you should have. It happened more than twelve hours ago, and if you can't tell us anything at all you are not doing your duty competently." At which the Commander said "Well, I'm afraid we are not able to at the moment", at which the "wife" swore violently and personally and in great detail about the Commander's parentage and legitimacy. Then all the other "wives and relatives" joined in and started shouting "Bastard! Bastard! Bastard!" which had the result that the Commander, who had certainly never been treated in this way before, fled, and then made his really big mistake: he ordered that the door be locked "to keep them under control". The exercise was stopped, and it was pointed out to him that not only had he falsely imprisoned a large number of people but also that he had done just about the utmost damage to naval public relations. Not to mention the distress and misery he had visited upon these distraught "relatives". A lot of people learned a lot of lessons that day.

Later that week, I was writing up the "lessons learned" from the exercises, and finding it hard going using the new desk computer. It may be difficult for readers to understand, but at that time PC's had only just arrived. We still had a large typing pool, but each of us received a PC. Most of them were put on a table in the corner of the office, for use in due course. At a meeting one day I actually heard a very senior officer say "If I see an officer playing with one of those things, I'll know he's not working". Times change. Very quickly. It was 1992, and I was only working on my "Word Perfect" computer programme because my boss (who was in advance of his time) threatened to do things to me if I didn't put it on my desk and start using it. So I had put it on my desk, switched it on, and then thought "OK - what am I going to do?" Eventually, I learned that I could write reports on it, so that is what I was doing. I could have done it five times faster in longhand, but I didn't want "things doing to me". I kept having to call on help from the office clerk, who always helped after saying "Don't you know how to do that?" which of course was not really helpful. But it got the job done. At lunchtime, one and a half paragraphs in, I took a break, and then I thought "Hang on, I could practise by writing a letter to my son's pen friend's parents"; our son was due to go out there in a few weeks' time. So I laboriously set off in my best schoolboy French.........."*Cher Monsieur et Madame Barré, notre jeune fils serait avec vous en Juin, et nous esperons que ...."* I was just looking for a word, when I became aware of our Clerk looking over my shoulder in amazement. "That's French, isn't it?" he said. "How do you do that?" I took a deep breath, let out a great sigh, and said "Really, Clerk! Don't you know how to do that? It's Control A, alt f7, Lima Xray Foxtrot. Caps F, f7 again, INT/French/all." And he left, still perplexed but unwilling to ask any more questions. I happened to be Duty that day, so had to stay on until 23.00 to ensure all was locked up, and as I completed my "rounds" I noticed there was a glimmer of light from under the Clerk's door. I entered quietly, to find him trying to make his computer write French for him. I left, knowing that he was responsible enough to lock the door behind him - whenever that would be.

Around this time, I had another "Call-out". My office 'phone rang one day, and the Appointer in MoD said "Alan, we want you to go to HMS DRYAD (the naval shore establishment on the hill overlooking Portsmouth harbour, from where Montgomery and Eisenhower planned and ran D-Day, and which still has all the old charts and maps and battle orders on the walls) to take part in a conference on "Post Gulf War Reconstruction". Monday next. Best uniform. Details coming by letter."

This worried me. I had only two attributes different from most other naval officers: firstly, I was an expert on non-public funds - clubs and associations and messes' private funds and the accounting therefor; and secondly, of course, I was an in-date Russian interpreter. The first I discarded as being too unlikely. The second made me think "If they want me to go and read labels on unexploded Russian bombs on Arabian beaches then I may have to find some excuse - I'm too close to pension for that, and the childrens' education still has to be paid for".

But I poled up at DRYAD as required, on the Monday. It was certainly an impressive gathering. It opened in the vast, circular auditorium which was the operations planning conference room. Well over a hundred people there, of whom I was by far the junior. I took a seat at the back and kept quiet. On to the floor was projected a map of the Persian Gulf and Iran and Iraq. The presenter introduced himself, then each speaker in turn: there were Generals and Brigadiers and Air Marshals, and the occasional Admiral, senior civil servants of unknown rank or knowledge, politicians, senior officers of other nationalities and specialists from various disciplines called in to give expert advice, all speaking about what we should do when the conflict was over. I sat there, quiet and perplexed

Then it was lunch. What a superb meal! No expense had been spared because the whole thing was funded by the Foreign Office. A huge spread of cold meats and seafoods with beautiful salads and all the trimmings, and the best of wines. Something told me to eschew the wines altogether, although it went against the grain, for I had to have my wits about me for the afternoon. One of the best decisions I've ever made.

At about sleepy-afternoon time, the presenter suddenly said "And now, we need to know greater detail about the oceanographic and meteorological situations in the Persian Gulf, so I would like to ask Lieutenant Commander Pearce, Royal Navy, to come down." I was shocked out of my shell, but the one thing I knew was that what I couldn't do was nothing. So I stepped on to the floor. The presenter repeated his request, and I had to take the bull by the proverbials (the horns, that is) and say "I'm sorry, Sir, but I don't know anything about the oceanographic and meteorological situation in the Persian Gulf." To say that there was a stunned silence would be an understatement - the only thing that moved was the presenter's digits as he thumbed through his programme notes. And then he said "You *are* Lieutenant Commander Alistair Pearce from the RN Hydrographic Office at Taunton, aren't you?" and I had no option but to say "No, Sir, I'm Lieutenant Commander Alan Pearce of the logistics staff at Portsmouth". He called for help, postponed that part of the presentation, and bade me farewell. I departed. These things happen.

I went back to work. All work and no play makes Jack a dull boy. Thus it was that in my first year at Portsmouth I had decided to organise an annual Exped. An "Exped" in the RN consisted of anything that got you out and about doing a physical activity, and which if properly organised would bring about other benefits, too. The closest civilian equivalent would be an "outdoor bonding exercise". Ours was to last a week at a time. Members of the RN privately owned between them a canal narrowboat called "Andrew". It was run as a charity and was available to all members of the RN and their families, rented out on a break even basis. She was a seventy foot, nine berth craft, based in the midlands. We gathered an all-ranks crew each year, and set ourselves a challenge - usually a tour of the midlands, of necessity circular so as to return to base for the next crew. The "Midlands Ring" is a circuit of canals of over one hundred miles with over one hundred locks, which would necessitate setting sail before 07.00 daily and going all day. Some would stay on board and drive the boat; others would walk or run on ahead to prepare locks to go through speedily; double, treble or more locks would require a double lock-working crew, alternately opening and closing, and going on to the next lock. Everybody got lots of exercise, so it was a "Good Thing" and a "Useful Exped". It also meant that we were on duty, not on holiday.

Under weigh and making way

The actuality was that we also had enormous fun. As the professional Logistics Officer, I became the cook/caterer. The others had specific duties and shared general duties. The preparations started months before sailing. The "Navigator" worked out the itinerary. The "Engineer" worked out water points and sanitary points. The "Caterer" set a menu and worked out what victuals would be needed. The "Training Officer" worked out who would walk where (because it was a circular route, people could leave the boat at one place, hike miles overland and rejoin at a later place).

The 1994 narrowboat 'Andrew' crew

My task was victualling. Because we were on duty, we were allowed £2.50 per head per day to pay for our food. Even then, this was not much. But I had contacts. I used to go to the naval barracks, where three thousand people were fed daily, and talk to the Chief Caterer. With my list, I asked first for a 2½lb joint of beef. The answer was that since they were feeding so many people they didn't have a 2½lb joint, so would I mind taking an 6lb joint - because it wasn't worth the effort of cutting it up, or of accounting for a fraction of the joint. The same with potatoes, where we ended up with a full sack, and also other meats, vegetables, butter, oil, cheese and so on. Each year we sailed with enough victuals for a small warship. The challenge was keeping them fresh and safe, with no freezer and just a tiny fridge. The answer was to use the chicken on Day 1, the pork on Day 2 and so on. And to marinade the lamb in wine, and to submerge the beef in vinegar so that it could be used in a vindaloo towards the end of the trip. It worked.

The very first year we sailed this plethora of comestibles came to an astonishing and endearing use quite early on in the trip. We were going through the centre of a town and decided to stop for a while. Next to a typical "hump back" canal bridge there was a mooring place, with a bench. On the bench was a quite old woman, who sat quite still, but every so often heaved her shoulders and returned to her face-down position. We tied up. Someone went over to her and said "What's up, love?" There was a heaving sigh and then a flood of tears. Eventually she said "I've just collected my pension from the Post Office. I put it in my purse and then put my purse down while I bought a stamp. When I left, I forgot my purse. When I went back it was gone. I've got no money and no food for the week" and she broke down in tears again. "Don't worry, love," somebody said, "The Royal Navy is here and we can help you". And so we went on board the narrowboat and bagged up a pound of sausages and half a pound of bacon and half a pound of cheese, a piece cut off the beef joint, several pounds of potatoes and carrots and a swede and a pack of butter and a bag of sugar and a loaf of bread and a lot of teabags and presented it to her and then carried it all back to her house because it was so heavy. To say that she was overwhelmed would be an understatement. What a lovely start to the week.

We always had a splendid crew. A word about the crew. The core group was me, my friend Roy Pearce an electronics boffin (no relation), Jim Brady a MoD civil servant specialist in accountancy, Bill McNeill a MoD civil servant specialist in graphics, and Johnny King a stores expert, and then a crew variously drawn from other RN people (including our wonderful Chief Steward "Buster" Brown), a medical man, and Wren officers and ratings. The only requirement was the ability to get on with each other - or in one case, to make it outwardly seem so. Each had different qualities, of course, but it always worked well. It didn't stop us taking the piss out of each other. It was a bit of a lottery who would fall in the canal first. No-one did, but someone was nearly chucked.

On shore for a quick blaw

Each year we had a splendid time, rising early, retiring late, and eating well. The weather didn't deter us. Being late September each year, the elderberry trees overhanging the canals were heavily berried and we had a routine worked out: into the bank, stop, six people with forks stripping the ripe berries into twenty-five litre tubs. From which, each year, I made twenty or so litres of elderberry wine. My target each year was to give each member of the crew a bottle of clear, rich ruby wine in time for Christmas. One year, I lost a bottle at the back of the garage and found it only when I reorganised the garage some years later - by then it was like vintage port.

Quality tells. On one trip Jim Brady was complaining that while the food was exceptional we didn't get enough fresh greens during the day - only at the evening meal. So one day, when we were going through a lock Bill McNeill nipped ashore and swept an armful of greenery from under the hedge - dock, daisy, dandelion, and a host of other weeds which had presumably grown so well because passing dogs had fertilised them well - and made Jim a weed sandwich. He declared it the nicest thing he had ever eaten, and we heard no more complaints. It was 2 p.m. and I think his judgement might have been a bit clouded; Worcestershire cider is quite strong. Not that any of us was unguilty of untoward behaviour - but it was all in the very best of taste.

One year, we took a detour and went to Stratford upon Avon. In the centre of the town there is a large lock basin - but nowhere near large enough for all the canal boats to moor alongside, so they were all doubled or trebled up. We tried to go outside a beautiful residential narrowboat and said "Is it all right if we tie up alongside you?" Usually it is. However, the owner looked at us, and said "The Andrew? No - she's hit me three times already this year. Go away."

Nonetheless, each year we succeeded in circuiting Birmingham, including going on the canal under a tower block - where - incidentally, I saw the only example I have ever seen of graffiti in a golden frame - somebody had a sense of humour. Each evening, we had a pint or two in a canalside pub. They must be the most English things in the whole world. Such was our determination to get there that on one occasion when it was raining so heavily that nobody sane would venture out we cut holes in black bin liners and masking-taped it round our necks to get there - on that occasion we succeeded in keeping dry, and in the crowded pub we played the game of "Ibble Dibble". This is a highly recommended game which involves a lot of chanting and singing, burning the end of a cork and marking the foreheads and cheeks of miscreants - I'll leave the rest to your imagination; suffice to say that by the end of the evening participants, onlookers and staff could hardly contain themselves laughing as we were, bought a lot of beer and we got free rounds from a happy landlord.

Then back to work again. I like to think that we did a lot of good for a lot of people. Contrary to what some today will suggest is "appropriate", the RN treated drug abuse and alcohol abuse as entirely different matters. Many apologists will say they are the same, I suspect, to excuse their own drug misuse ("only the same as drinking, really") while the RN treated illegal drug abuse as a crime and treated problems with alcohol as a medical and social matter. For some reason my job carried with it the oversight of the Alcohol Education Team. I just let them get on with it. I carried on with the routine paperwork, and the routine inspections of paperwork.

Then one day out of the blue came another Russian call-away. You will recall from an earlier chapter how political ice is melted and suspicion lessened and international relations improved by ship visits to foreign ports. Signifying a "thaw". We had received an invitation for one of our major (albeit rather old) warships to pay a port visit to Sebastopol. Sebastopol? Sebastopol! Erudite readers will realise the enormous significance of this: Sebastopol was a "closed port and area" in the Crimea and under the Soviet regime, and even Russians and Ukranians could not get in or out without a passport. (A passport? Yes, under the Soviet regime it was almost impossible to get a passport to travel abroad, but in certain areas it was also completely impossible to get an internal passport to go anywhere else in the Soviet Union. The official line was "why would you want to go abroad? Why would you want to go anywhere else in the Soviet Union?" Why would you not want to answer my questions? I shall find out.)

Thus began a quite short but very intensive chapter in my life, with some astonishing revelations and outcomes. Along with ten or twelve other RN and RNR Interpreters I flew to Naples to join HMS FEARLESS, a large landing ship with helicopter deck. We sailed almost as soon as we had joined, and went round through the Aegean towards the Dardanelles, the Sea of Marmara and Istanbul. Nothing unusual so far. Then we sailed into the Black Sea and crossed towards Sebastopol, and I encountered something I have never experienced before or since. Because the Black Sea is an enclosed expanse of water, because it heats up quite a lot throughout the summer, and because at the time we were visiting - autumn - the air had become quite cold, the effect was the same as putting a tray of hot water outside your back door on a freezing cold day - steam. And lots of it. I had sailed in fog before, of course, but the unique thing about this was that it formed a carpet over the whole sea, about fifty feet high. But of course HMS FEARLESS is much taller than that, so one was able to go onto the top deck and look out in crystal clear air over an expanse of boiling, heaving carpet cloud in which those navigating the ship down below were surrounded - and blinded. On the upper deck, it was exactly like flying an aeroplane above a cloud, and for much the same reason. But not only had we to navigate into the port, we had also to launch our helicopter. The Russians sent out a pilot boat to help us which, together with our radars, was enough to get us in safely. But the helicopter took off, disappeared into the cloud (which helicopters always avoid if they can) and landed safely at the naval airfield where it had been allocated a slot. The Russians were mightily impressed by our skill, both on the sea and in the air. We were not going to be late - at almost any price!

Once alongside, we embarked a large cohort of British journalists who had come to record and report upon this momentous visit. They were all accommodated on board, and given the Gunroom to operate from. We interpreters consulted the ship's officers about what they wanted, but since they themselves had no idea we made a roster of those who would stand on the gangway, those who would engage with visitors, and one or two who would keep themselves in reserve for emergencies. I chose, as senior guy present, to be one of the latter (I know "latter" is the last of two, but you know what I mean.)

First of all, we had the usual ceremonies. The ship safely alongside, there was a delightful display of dancing on the jetty and then our senior officers were called down to accept the Russian greeting of bread and salt. Very moving. Followed on our part by a Royal Marines bugle salute. Then the Russian officials came on board to talk and have coffee etc with the Captain. And invitations were issued for many of us to go and eat and sup in Russian official venues. All the formal stuff.

The author on the bridge of HMS FEARLESS in the Bosphorus en route to Sebastopol, 1994.

The author at Sebastopol Naval College
who's that in the pink?

It wasn't long before I was called upon. There was an urgent message from the gangway to say that a Russian Admiral had arrived completely unannounced and unexpectedly and could someone please look after him? I leapt up there, collected him, and showed him around for a bit. He was supremely uninterested. Then, having arrived at 11.50 (just as RN Padres always do) he asked if he might visit the Wardroom (just as RN Padres always do) and perhaps have a talk (i.e. a drink) with some of the officers (just as RN padres always do). Now, the problem was this. He had his dog with him. It came up the gangway with him, followed us around, and eventually came into the Wardroom with us. It was a manky dog, moth eared, scruffy and a bit smelly - but you can't offend a visitor, can you? Especially not at such a sensitive time. So the Russian uninvited Admiral downed many gin and tonics and then moved to leave when the bar closed. Our Commander took me to one side, and said "Could you tactfully explain that we are not equipped to deal with dogs and would be grateful if they could be left behind, or some such, whatever you think is appropriate". I started to speak to the Russian Admiral, but before I had got half a dozen words out he said "My dog? I thought it was your dog."

The key to this is that while British dockyards are infested with feral cats, Russian dockyards are infested with feral dogs, and this was one of them. It had just followed him up the gangway. A real chancer. And a lucky one, at that. You live and learn.

At the end of the first day our Royal Marine band performed the Beat Retreat and Sunset ceremony in front of a huge crowd of Russian dignitaries, and very effective it was in showing off the best of British. Unfortunately the next morning I was invited to translate the whole of the drill book on Beating Retreat and Sunset Ceremony into Russian for the admiring hosts. No trying to explain, this time, that I was an interpreter not a translator - it had to be done. So I retired to the peace of the Gunroom to do it. The members of the press corps were all filing their copy, so I did have a bit of peace. But then one of them turned to me and said "Alan, what's the Russian name of this jetty we're tied up to?" and I didn't know exactly so I said "I thought you were a member of the press? A journalist? So what does fact matter? Make something up". And they all ragged me. But we became great buddies. I managed to string together some orders for guard and band to perform "Sunset" but I wasn't professionally happy with the result. Fortunately, the Russians were, and I got a great accolade.

Then it was that a junior government minister came out from UK "to add sincerity to the event" - actually to get his photograph in the press, of course. He was a bit wet, but very self-important. He had to address a huge conference, and I was to be his interpreter. He wouldn't admit that he hadn't used a consecutive interpreter before but I could tell that he hadn't a clue. So I said "Please speak in chunks of about twelve to twenty words, then pause for me to say it in Russian. No need to say "tell them that....", just say what you want to say. And please don't suddenly tell a joke - because the vast majority of jokes depend upon either linguistic word play or national quirks or prejudices, and are therefore simply not funny or even slightly humorous in the other language".

Off we went to the conference. About a thousand people in a huge hall. Big microphones, good reproduction. All was going swimmingly - until he decided to add a bit of humour and tell a joke. Now, I knew it wasn't going to work. Any interpreter now has a problem. If a Principal (speaker) does tell a joke which you fully know won't be funny in the receiving language then you have three courses of action open to you: if you are a wimp, you just interpret it and let it fall flat; if you are a good interpreter and know a lot of foreign jokes you pick one which is similar and tell that; and if you're unable to do either you do what I had to do. (Interpreters have to think on their feet - they can't consult dictionaries and grammar books as can translators). Knowing that he could not understand Russian and that the majority of the audience could not understand English I said into the microphone (in Russian) "Ladies and gentlemen.... the speaker has just told a joke. An English joke. It is very funny in English but translated it doesn't mean a thing and sounds rather stupid. But for the sake of my career and for the sake of relations between our two countries please would you all laugh heartily, together, NOW". The place erupted! There were lots of people jumping up and down and cheering and stamping their feet until the minister finally ended his speech.

Good result? Not necessarily. In the car on the way back he said "Alan, my joke went down rather well, I think I'll use that one again tomorrow". At least this time I was able to work something out in advance.

On board, I got less of an accolade from the helicopter pilot when I was showing people around. For some reason we had an army helicopter on board, not a naval one, and its pilot was also an army officer. I rather think he had transferred to the Army Air Corps from a Guards regiment - just as army officers transfer into the Pay Corps or other corps either because their horse hasn't got a sufficient pedigree or because their own lineage has a discovered flaw in it, or something. Whatever, he was still a Superior Pongo at heart - and let you know it. I was interpreting for Russian officers as this SP was giving them the details. As I struggled with the technical terms, he produced more and more of them, eulogising over his "helo dihedral collective" and his "autonomous blade presentation" and enjoying his audience's rapture and my discomfiture; he really turned the screw. I was glad when it was all over. But just as you mustn't upset a Hydrographer, you also upset an interpreter at your peril. Later that evening, SP and another young officer were entertaining a couple of Russian bimbos in the Wardroom and trying to impress them. Cynic that I am (or realist, on this occasion) I recognised the women for exactly what they were, and for a while just observed. Then these two officers asked me if I would interpret for them, because they wanted to take the two ladies out for dinner. "Tell them," said SP, "that we would be honoured if they would come to dinner with us tonight at a good restaurant ashore where we can entertain them with true aplomb and due English panache." How on earth they thought they were going to do this without taking me along with them I do not know, but I strongly suspected that the two Russian "ladies" could probably speak as good English as they could. So I said (in Russian, of course) "These two Englishmen would like to take you out to a restaurant but unfortunately they have no money so they would be grateful if instead you could take their laundry away with you and bring it back when it is washed and dried." The two Russian "ladies" shook their heads slowly, smiled politely, and left. They knew that I knew who they were. SP and his pal were left wondering what the hell had happened. Tick in the interpreter's box. Don't muck about with Interpreters. But I do think I may have saved them from something or another.

I went to bed exhausted at the end of the second day. The

third day of the visit brought another host of inconsequential events, but then as evening approached there was a cri de coeur from the Russians. Now, British sailors are very adept at going to hostelries and downing several pints of beer. This takes some time. If there is no beer, only vodka, they will (and did) down several vodkas. This does not take any time at all. So they bought more. And so on. Two of them had particularly gone over the top and had been thrown into cells by the civilian police. Not wanting an incident, both sides had agreed that I should go and get them out again. Without fuss. From a Russian minion self-important Plod in his Russian minion Plodhouse. I went in full uniform. I was shown into the police station by the said minion Plod who, full of his own importance, showed me to the cells. This was a Dostoyevskian setting: a classic cell, not small, and with an enormously high ceiling, tiny window at the top, unfurnished and whitewashed throughout, and a Marmeladov character to go with it. In it were two sailors in uniform. I went in without saying a word. I stood in front of them and they stood up and looked up at me, recognising the naval officer's uniform with its gold stripes and pleading with their eyes for me to get them out of there. This had to be done without loss of face on either side. So I said to them "Do you know who I am?" They looked up and their eyes gradually focused on what they knew to be an RN officer. They stood up and tried to salute.

"Yes, Sir".

"Right," I said, "You've made a bit of a cock up of this and you could be in a Russian jail forever unless you do what I say. Will you do exactly what I say?"

"Yes, Sir."

I said "Say something in English. Football teams, weather, what you had for breakfast, anything you like. It doesn't matter. Then I will say something in Russian and you will say something more. I will tell the officer that I am interpreting."

This happened, and they ostensibly said, word by word "We are not used to your beautiful Russian vodka and we have been stupid and drunk too much of it and we very sorry for any inconvenience we may have caused and we beg you to forgive us and release us into the custody of this British officer who will take us back on board our ship to face the severe consequences there". The policeman didn't want more trouble, so he let us go. I got the two sailors to thank him, in Russian sounds, and that was that. They even bowed to him, of their own accord. We went back on board. I don't know why, but I felt a bit like an unfulfilled Raskolnikov. There were no other incidents of note.

After what was universally recognised both by military and political authorities to have been a successful visit, it was time to go. HMS FEARLESS had to go on to other duties, so we interpreters and all of the press corps left before she sailed. Our departure heralded one of the most astonishing events of all - our departure from Simferopol airport and our trip to Moscow.

Simferopol is the airport for Sebastopol. It is about 100 kilometres away, by fairly ordinary country roads. We had been accorded official vehicles, big black things, and the journey was highly redolent of the Soviet era. We got into these big black cars in a motorcade and they set off at a huge pace, defying all other road users. When we were outside the city on what you or I would call an "A" Road the eight vehicles fanned out into an arrowhead echelon and speeded up to what could only be described as breakneck speed. Without regard for anything. We watched as tractors and peasants with carts and householders simply jumped off the road out of the way as we sped by. It was exhilarating but, I thought, somewhat demeaning and desultory for the others involved. And quite uncomfortable in the ditch. But we arrived at the airport in one piece.

Much as one would do at any other airport, albeit it was in rather tatty surroundings, we relaxed in the departure lounge.

And then we were told that the aeroplane on which we were scheduled to go to Moscow was either withdrawn or didn't exist in the first place. Or was late. Or was undergoing repairs. Or whatever. It didn't really matter. They didn't care.

Fortunately, one of our number had served in the Soviet Union for some years and knew the drill. He marched up to the airport manager's office, barged in, and said "There are thirty of us to go to Moscow. We have paid hard currency, Western money. If you do not provide the service we have paid for in Western money this will have to be reported to the authorities and you will be held personally responsible."

To say that the result of this was immediate and precipitate would be an understatement. There was a huge Soviet/Russian Tupolev or something aircraft on the apron outside the departure lounge, about fifty or sixty metres away, and we had watched as it had filled up with hundreds and hundreds of people. Now an airport police vehicle screamed up to it, uniformed men rushed on board, and passengers started getting off again at a very fast rate, almost falling over themselves in haste. It was nothing less than a debacle. They got off and they scattered. We never saw them again - perhaps - goodness knows where they had gone to. Then, before too long, the airport manager himself came down to us, wringing his hands; he said "I'm sorry there has been a minor delay, but your aircraft for Moscow is now ready for you. Please board when you are ready." It was, of course, the same aircraft.

But no passenger bus. No walkway. No trolleys. We had to carry our suitcases across the tarmac to this monster of an aeroplane where, fortunately, there was someone to load them into its vast belly. Then we went on board. We were aware that many, many other people milling around in the departure lounge also wanted to go to Moscow, and they were not going to miss this opportunity. So we were closely followed the whole way. The guy who had been to see the airport manager and knew the ropes told us "Get on board. Sit in a seat. Do not get out of the seat for any reason until the aircraft has taken off, not even to look in the luggage rack. Just sit there and refuse to move for anybody". This turned out to be excellent advice as the aircraft filled up. I sat down. After a while, I felt under my seat, as one does, for the lifejacket which we would undoubtedly be shown how to wear, in due course. No lifejacket. Just a bald head. There was somebody under my seat! I sat still, as advised. More and more people got on, some of whom just faded away as they squeezed under other seats. The air hostesses moved up and down the aisles, but didn't proffer anything, and eventually retired to the back. They were all very big girls. They weren't there to serve us, we discovered, as humanity began to settle down; they very efficiently moved from back to front throwing people (literally) off the aircraft when they could. But they obviously had orders not to overdo it, because about half an hour later we took off with about thirty people standing and goodness knows how many people hiding under seats. Now, you may not believe this; if you do not, please read an article in "Style and Travel" magazine dated 5 September 1993 by Matthew Roche of Business Traveller magazine in which he quotes: "passengers stuffed into the cockpit, the lavatories, and the luggage hold.....Russian "Trud" newspaper early in 1993 reported one aircraft taking off with ninety eight extra passengers". Ours was nothing even approaching a record.

In the meanwhile, however, we had an intermission sketch of frightening implications: the pilot came on board last, when peace had been restored, with what was clearly a vodka bottle in his pocket, and strode to the cockpit where he couldn't open the stiff door, because it had clearly jammed. Eventually, he gave it a huge kick and smashed the lock off, thereby ensuring that the door flapped open and closed throughout the rest of the journey. I think he must have been an ex-fighter pilot or a frustrated failed bomber pilot because he wove and swerved left and right and up and down all the way to Moscow, even though it was quite clearly not necessary. En route, the Sumo air hostesses served us with a glass of warm orange squash each. I politely said "No thank you" but it didn't make the slightest difference; I got one. I just tasted it; it was disgusting. So I poured it on the floor, because others were doing the same, and it seemed to be de rigeur.

Eventually, the pilot announced that we were approaching Moscow where the temperature was something quite minus and the precipitation quite severe. We landed safely, to my surprise, and taxied over to our slot. Then more problems began. The first was that the pilot announced that the external doors to the baggage hold had seized shut and they couldn't get the baggage out on to the trucks - so they would open up the trap doors in the passenger floor and we could all go down, collect our own luggage, and come up again, and then get off. Of course, the first few people who went down into the baggage hold wanted to come up again just as other people were trying to go down the same ladder into the baggage hold, so there was an almighty fight at both the bottom and the top of the ladder. Those who managed to get their gear were ready to disembark, but the doors didn't open. There was an announcement that the airport couldn't provide a staircase thing so we would have to go down the aircraft's own flimsy aluminium ladder - which unfortunately didn't quite reach the ground. Which meant jumping the last couple of feet on to an ice-covered tarmac causeway. Needless to say, there were casualties. But eventually the whole thing sorted itself out and we got to Arrivals. Next problem: aircraft not scheduled, so no-one there. We all sat down on whatever we could and waited. It was then that one of the journalists, Iain Ballantyne of the Western Morning News and later a national paper, came over to me and handed me a folder of paper with what was clearly a news article on the top: "Alan," he said, "would you mind reading this and signing this with your official title and the date?" It was a record of our departure from Sebastopol and our just-ended flight. "Why do you want me to sign it?" I asked. "Because," he said, "when I file it with our editor he just isn't going to believe it. Nobody would." So I did, and he was happy. He has since become a renowned author, and his book on HMS CONQUEROR is highly recommended reading. And somewhat alarming.

And then, mercifully, on to a British Airways aircraft, and back to UK. It was all over. It was all over for me, too.

CHAPTER 18
Goodbye to all that

This is the shortest Chapter of the book.

On 24th April 1996 at the end of my contracted period of some 38 years of service and total commitment I reported to the Royal Naval Barracks at Portsmouth, handed in my gasmask and my Identity Card, and walked out of the gate. No ceremony. No photograph. No handshake. No clock. No certificate. No medal. Nothing.

I had put on a blue suit, experienced the drills, thrills and spills, japes, scrapes and escapes along the 'appy roads of this world, and I had then taken off the blue suit. And enjoyed (almost) every day of it.

So mote it be.

The author today - still on the water

Ave atque Vale

Nothing in life has been made by man for man's using

But it was shown long since to man in ages lost

As the name of the maker of it

Who received oppression and shame for his wages -

Hate, avoidance, and scorn in his daily dealings -

Until he perished, wholly confounded.

More to be pitied than he are the wise

Souls which foresaw the evil of loosing

Knowledge or Art before time, and aborted

Noble devices and deep-wrought healings

Lest offence should arise.

Heaven delivers on earth the Hour that cannot be thwarted,

Neither advanced, at the price of a world nor a soul, and its
Prophet

Comes through the blood of the vanguards who dreamed - too
soon - it had sounded.

"Untimely" by Rudyard Kipling

Mors janua vitae

Printed in Great Britain
by Amazon

26218383R00205